State and Society in Soviet Thought

Ernest Gellner

Basil Blackwell

First published 1988

Basil Blackwell Ltd
108 Cowley Road, Oxford OX4 1JF, UK

Basil Blackwell Inc.
432 Park Avenue South, Suite 1503,
New York, NY 10016, USA

British Library Cataloguing in Publication Data
Gellner, Ernest
State and society in Soviet thought.
– (Explorations in social structures).
1. Soviet Union – Intellectual life
– 1970–
I. Title   II. Series
947.085′4   DK276
ISBN 0-631-15787-5

Library of Congress Cataloging in Publication Data
Gellner, Ernest.
State and society in Soviet thought/Ernest Gellner.
p. cm. – (Explorations in social structures)
Bibliography: p.
Includes index.
ISBN 0-631-15787-5
1. State. The – Origin.   2. Political anthropology – Soviet Union.
3. Marxian school of sociology – Soviet Union.   4. Political culture –
Soviet Union.   I. Title.   II. Series.
GN492.6.G45 1988
306′.2′0947 – dc19

Typeset by Joshua Associates Ltd, Oxford
Printed in Great Britain by T. J. Press Ltd, Padstow

State and Society in Soviet Thought

Explorations in Social Structures

General Editors: Patricia Crone and John A. Hall

State and Society in Soviet Thought
Ernest Gellner

Creating Capitalism: The State and Small Business since 1945
Linda Weiss

By the same author

Nations and Nationalism
Words and Things
Thought and Change
Saints of the Atlas
Contemporary Thought and Politics
The Devil in Modern Philosophy
Legitimation of Belief
Spectacles and Predicaments
Muslim Society
The Psychoanalytic Movement
Relativism and the Social Sciences
Soviet and Western Anthropology (ed.)
The Concept of Kinship and Other Essays
Culture, Identity and Politics
Plough, Sword and Book

Communist society ... makes it possible for me ... to hunt in the morning, fish in the afternoon, rear cattle in the evening, criticize after dinner ... without ever becoming hunter, fisherman, shepherd, or after-dinner critic.

KARL MARX AND FRIEDRICH ENGELS

Every illiterate nomadic Kazakh, like all nomads of the world, was in the fifteenth to the eighteenth centuries simultaneously a shepherd and a soldier, an orator and a historian, poet, and singer.

S. E. TOLYBEKOV

Contents

Preface

The studies contained in this volume are the fruit of a sustained interest in Soviet intellectual life, stretching back over several decades. They are based not merely on available published writings, but also on numerous conversations with Soviet scholars, mainly inside the Soviet Union. The ideas investigated are looked at both for their inherent merit and for the light they throw on Soviet society.

The 'fieldwork' aspect of this research was not easy at first. The six weeks I spent in the Soviet Union, when I began to work on this topic systematically, must have been some of the loneliest of my life. I only saw the inside of one single Soviet home, and had to fill my evenings by going to the theatre. My solitary evenings were devoted to a caviar sandwich, a glass of Soviet champagne, and a play in Russian. So, in the beginning, I learnt more about the Soviet theatre than I did about Soviet thought.

I saw *The Mousetrap* in Russian, which gave me a good idea of the Russian image of a home counties hotel. I noted that the King of Bohemia in *The Winter's Tale* was actually made to look like some Slavonic *voevoda*, at any rate as portrayed in romantic history, complete with droopy moustaches, and sandal laces snaking up his calf. Russian actors are superb, and when they impersonate nineteenth-century peasants, they carry absolute conviction: they really *become* Russian peasants. Russian actresses, on the other hand, I found less impressive, because they seemed unable to resist the temptation to prettify themselves implausibly, even when impersonating peasant women. When I made enquiries about why this should be so, one intriguing explanation I was offered was this: the parasitic drone existence of pre-revolutionary upper-class women was such that the Revolution con-stituted a real break in feminine professional life. The same was not true of men. I have no idea whether this explanation is sound, or indeed whether the problem itself would survive a more thorough investigation.

But that's by the way. After this very sticky start, I received a great deal of very genuine help and touching kindness from many scholars. I found their warm generosity all the more moving in as far as they had no illusions at all about my views, which could hardly have made me an ideal guest. I should especially mention Yulian and Natalya Bromley, S. Arutiunov, S. Vainstein, R. Blum, V. Basilov, N. Drobizheva, M. Chlenov, N. Girenko, A. Gurevich, P. Jarve, V. Kabo, J. Kahk, I. Kon, I. Krupnik, V. Kozlov, E. Loone, D. Olderogge, A. I. Pershitz, A. Pork, Yu. Semenov, L. N. Stolovich, S. Vainstein, N. Zhukovskaya. The list is a good deal less than complete, and I apologize for omissions.

Amongst scholars resident in the West, I am deeply indebted for bibliographical and/or editorial help to Rod Aya, Tamara Dragadze, Mark Elvin, John Hall, Caroline Humphrey, Ian Jarvie, Tolya Khazanov, A. Pyatigorsky, Teodor Shanin and Peter Skalnik.

These studies began when I was still at the London School of Economics, and I received invaluable secretarial help from Gay Woolven and Sue Burrett. In Cambridge, the continuation of the work was made possible by most generous direct or indirect assistance and support from Mary MacGinley, Janet Hall, Anne Farmer, and Margaret Story. I am most grateful to Sue Vice for her painstaking work on the manuscript.

Trips to the Soviet Union were made possible by a scheme operated by the British Academy and the Soviet Academy of Sciences, and I am most grateful for the support received. I am also indebted to the Economic and Social Research Council and its Chairman Sir Douglas Hague and its Secretary Mrs Suzanne Reeve for a generous research grant, which made it possible not to worry about financial aspects of the work (though in the event, this research involved very little expense).

The essays have been individually published previously, some of them more than once. Some have been modified since first publication in the light of further evidence. But the first essay has been left strictly unchanged (with the exception of the footnotes), notwithstanding the fact that I might well formulate its ideas differently, were I writing it now. The reason is that it represents my first reaction to an immersion into the Soviet intellectual atmosphere. It may be of interest as the immediate record of culture shock, unmodified by subsequent hindsight.

It is conventional (though none the less true) to say that only I bear the responsibility for the views expressed. In the present context, it should of course be particularly clear that my views may not be attributed to anyone else.

ERNEST GELLNER

Long live slave-owning society – the glorious future of all mankind!
(drawing by C. Humphrey)

1

The Soviet and the Savage

The teaching of Marx and Engels about the evolution of society was based on the best available science of the past century. . . . But in the treatment of specific issues, life inevitably brought refinements and changes. The time at which Marxism was formulated and the present are separated from each other by a whole historic epoch, in which colossal changes took place in the fate of the world. Mankind faces many new problems which did not face the founders of Marxist theory and for which, naturally, one cannot seek solutions in their work. . . . The scale and vigour of current discussions is largely explained by the fact that for a long time, concrete research was limited by the five-term scheme (primitive society, slave society, feudalism, capitalism, communism) . . . this scheme . . . arises from the historical experience of Europe . . . data drawn from the history of other continents makes clear the limitations of an approach to world history as an unilineal process.

These remarks are drawn from 'Problems under Discussion in the Theory of Pre-Capitalist Society' by L. V. Danilova, in *Problems of the History of Pre-Capitalist Societies* a collection of essays published in Moscow in 1968 and edited by a five-person committee of whom L. V. Danilova herself was the 'responsible editor'. All quotations in the present article are from this essay, which summarizes in brilliant form the state of play in Soviet social anthropology.[1]

Terms, definitions, and boundaries of subjects are not the same in the Soviet Union as in Britain. Here a 'social anthropologist' is, roughly speaking, a man who uses the methods and ideas of the tradition of Malinowski and Radcliffe-Brown to study any society to which he

---

1 L. V. Danilova, 'Diskussionye problemy teorii dokapitalisticheskikh obshchestv' ('Problems under Discussion in the Theory of Pre-Capitalist Societies') in Danilova et al. (eds). *Problemy istorii dokapitalisticheskikh obshchestv (Problems of the History of Pre-Capitalist Societies)* (Moscow, 1968). This essay appears in translation as 'Controversial Problems of the Theory of Precapitalist Societies', *Soviet Anthropology and Archaeology*, vol. 9, 1970. All subsequent quotations are from this essay.

thinks those ideas and methods can be applied. This usually, but by no means always, means 'primitive' societies.

By contrast, a Soviet 'ethnographer' (the term used in Russian instead of 'anthropologist') is, also roughly speaking, a student of pre-capitalist social structures. The consequent overlap is great, but far from complete. The most important difference perhaps is not in the exclusions implied by either definition, but in the fact that the Soviet ethnographer is not separated, either in his ideas or his subject-matter, from the archaeologist or the historian.

Someone trained in the British tradition of social anthropology who enters the world of Soviet anthropology undergoes a drastic, and no doubt salutary, culture shock. What precisely is the message that reverberates through one's being as one suddenly immerses oneself, say for six weeks, in the atmosphere and assumptions of Soviet anthropologists?

They constitute a different world, and in many ways an impressive one, a world which stands in sharp contrast to at least British, if not to all Western, anthropology. Briefly and crudely, it is the contrast between the evolutionist-historical and the functionalist-static visions of man and society. Less crudely, it is the contrast between two traditions, each struggling with the inadequacies of its own ideas. Admittedly, the anthropological community in Britain has no loyalty oath to functionalism. On the contrary, its members tend to have a joking relationship with the past of their own discipline. No arguments are settled by appeal to Malinowski's writings. Hence, it would seem, to say that the British or Britain-based tradition is Malinowskian functionalist might be out of date. But one must visit Russia, and expose oneself to the shock of rival assumptions, to perceive just how deep and pervasive certain local assumptions still are.

Among these half-forgotten, taken-for-granted and no-longer-exciting conventions of British anthropological discourse, which recover their salience and their flavour, and their problematical status, when one talks to people who have *never* taken them for granted, the most important is the synchronic perspective. Of course, the days of deliberate ahistorism among British anthropologists are long past. Where evidence permits it, every monograph contains a careful section on the history of the social group under investigation. But one *still* has the impression that each society trails its own past behind it, as a comet trails its tail. The tail is studied as *this comet's* tail, its interest is a function of the interest of the comet, not the other way around. Above all, these shining, even brilliant, tails do not meld and fuse into some world history; such an aspiration is barely thinkable. They tend to live their own lives, and on the whole they remain insulated from each other in time and space.

It is here that the contrast with the instinctive thought-style of a Soviet anthropologist is most marked. One might say that for the Soviet scholar the interest of a comet, generally speaking, is a function of the interest of its tail, and that all such tails fuse, at least in principle, in an all-embracing history of mankind. The idea of an 'ethnographic present', not so long ago an acceptable convention for British anthropologists (it meant roughly the tribe minus the new road and the DO and other change-inducing intrusions), with its tacit bias towards a stability assumption, is barely thinkable in Russia. A Soviet anthropologist is still a man primarily interested in the history of mankind and the evolution of human society. He furthers this end by a temporary concentration on some segment of that history, delimited in space and time only in order to make it manageable. Once, long ago, this was the inspiration of all anthropology; the extent to which this guiding idea has been dropped, for better or worse, in British anthropology, can only be sensed fully by experiencing a milieu where it is still vigorously operative.

To fly from London to Moscow, from anthropological discussions at one end to similar discussions at the other, is to shift from one climate and atmosphere to another: it is to move very suddenly from a kind of vacuum to a kind of plenum. British anthropologists discuss various specific societies, with or without their historical tails, as they move – or stand – in some kind of intersteller social space; comparisons are possible, and indeed are attempted at times. But interaction, though it cannot always be ignored, is still somehow an untypical concern, and incorporation in an overall scheme of historical development is virtually unknown.

This is the central contrast. The other two conspicuous differences – the primarily *social* orientation of British anthropology, and the different attitude to 'fieldwork' – are in part related to this boundary. The separation of British anthropology from archaeology (where links exist, they tend to be vestigial–institutional rather than real), from history, physical geography, etc., and the ritualization and institutionalization of fieldwork, are each of them connected with the Malinowskian revolution, and neither is duplicated in the Soviet Union. The lesser stress on or opportunity for fieldwork is of course also related to other aspects of Soviet life, extraneous to anthropology – the regrettable difficulties encountered by Soviet scholars wishing to work or study outside the borders of the country, and the relative lack of funds (perhaps genuine, perhaps invoked to justify the first impediment).

A society is invariably seen by a Russian anthropologist as firmly *set*, located, embedded in overall human history (whereas such a setting tends to be an irrelevance in Britain); and, of course, it is also subsumed under the concepts, terms, and ideas of Marxism. But what *kind* of Marxism? Here, once again, the visitor from the West is liable to get a surprise – an agreeable one as far as the present visitor was concerned. Contemporary Russian Marxism is *intelligible*. To anyone who has the misfortune of acquaintance with Western high-brow Marxist fashions, this comes as a shock indeed. Here in the West, neo-Hegelian, existentialist, phenomenological, 'structuraliste', etc. interpretations of Marx have completed in recent decades the transition characterized (I think by Raymond Aron) as the move from dogmatic to imaginary (and unintelligible) Marxisms.

Not so in Russia. Russian Marxism is short-haired, not long-haired. The Marxism of Soviet anthropologists is entirely and refreshingly clear, and it is about real things, namely societies and their organization, and not about cloud-cuckooland. After the mumbo-jumbo of Western *Salon-Marxismus*, this is refreshing. What it says about society and societies is intelligible, and it is centred on the five-plus typology of social forms, from primitive communism via patriarchal clans, slave society, feudalism, and capitalism to socialism and communism.

Within the ideas of Soviet anthropologists, one can discern a kind of spectrum from the abstract to the specific: at one end, there is a kind of overall evolutionism, which was once universal and self-evident in all anthropology, and which instinctively places any society in the context of history and of other societies; more specifically there is the classical Marxist typology of human societies, including the once politically septic idea of the Asiatic Mode of Production, now very freely discussed; and more specifically still, there are the ideas of Engels, largely based on Morgan and enshrined in the scriptural *The Origin of the Family, Private Property and the State*.

Concerning these last, it would be idle to pretend that the Western visitor can feel anything but embarrassment. Of course, as Meyer Fortes has shown so brilliantly, it is possible and proper to admire Morgan. The problem here is not internal to anthropology, but concerns the difficulties which arise if anthropological ideas are by some accident incorporated in the official belief system of a centralized society. Marx read Morgan in the last year of his life, was quite properly impressed, and instructed Engels to write about him. Engels duly did so.

If only Engels had predeceased Marx, or at any rate not written *The Origin of the Family*, various issues might be that much less sensitive, or not sensitive at all, for Marxist anthropologists. One may suppose that some Soviet anthropologists at least share my own embarrassment at this point; and one should add that the fundamentalists who try to defend the true doctrine here are not necessarily insincere, but give the impression of honest good faith.

One's impression of Soviet anthropologists is that the Russian soul now, as in the nineteenth century, is torn between the glamour of the

West and the simple verities of the *muzhik*. Only the identity of those home truths has changed: they are no longer those of the Orthodox Church. It is the Marxists who are now the *narodniki* (populists) or vice versa, and it is the sophisticated slickers who stray from the simple and wholesome faith of the *muzhik* in Old Marxism.

There is no homogeneity of view within Soviet anthropology. There are rival trends and groups, which, however, it is agreeable to note, contribute reciprocally critical articles to the same volumes and exchange arguments in letters to the anthropological journal. It is characteristic of the present ambiguous situation that a work such as the one I have quoted can or could be published; but it seems equally characteristic that its proposed and completed sequel, Volume Two, is *not* appearing. One should not assume that those who chafe at these doctrinal restraints are necessarily either dissidents or non-Marxists, at some more fundamental level. On the contrary: their aspiration may be to be recognized as a 'loyal opposition', as men who freely question details of dated nineteenth-century doctrine, but do so within the framework of an accepted wider consensus. Whether they will succeed in having such a situation recognized seems at present uncertain. The loyal opposition is not suppressed; nor, on the other hand, can it speak as clearly as it may perhaps wish.

But let us consider the more fundamental and more abstract aspects of Marxism, in terms of the spectrum outlined earlier. It would be a miracle if all those very specific anthropological doctrines, incorporated in Marxism by a historical accident nearly a century ago, proved to be right; and for this reason, debates about these *specific* aspects of the Morgan–Engels heritage are somewhat painful and comic. The situation is quite different when we come to the more abstract aspects of Marxist doctrine which are of relevance for anthropology: the Marxist typology of societies, and the overall evolutionist approach to social explanation.

Here it is *not* obvious at all that there is nothing to learn from Marxism, or that no plausible anthropology can be erected within the framework of these doctrines. Indeed, the Marxist five-stage typology seems to me rather comparable, in logical status, to functionalism (which could be considered as an extreme case of a typology, operating with one type only). As Claude Lévi-Strauss has somewhere observed, to say that everything functions is an absurdity and to say that some institutions function, a truism. Everyone knows that the truth lies at some unidentified point along the scale between truism and absurdity. The importance of 'functionalism' lay not in its doctrine, which was quite unspecific in its failure to locate that mysterious mid-point, but in summarizing and conveying a certain state of mind and research strategy

– *look for* the way in which institutions reinforce each other and favour stability.

Precisely this kind of defence can also be put up for the Marxist typology of societies. As it contains five or more types, and as the individual types within it are more specific and have a greater theoretical content, on average, than the all-purpose single type used by functionalism, it might even be said that Marxism is richer, more scientific, more exposed to risk, more suggestive of new problems and discoveries, than functionalism. And note that Western comparative anthropology or sociology possess no superior typology, or indeed any typology at all; they do possess types, some of which overlap with the Marxist ones (e.g. 'feudalism'). But these are used in a *most* loose and untidy way ('feudalism' again), as Jack Goody recently pointed out, and apart from being uncodified and chaotic they do not fuse into any overall theory.[2] They are not generated by any principle, even a bad principle, whereas of course the Marxist ones are produced by a possibly dated vision of the general evolution of mankind.

I have offered a tentative defence of the Marxist typology – it gives a coherent theoretical approach, where the rival vision has none. It is somewhat more specific, elaborate and exposed to fact; and it possesses an overall logical status rather similar to 'functionalism'. Generally speaking, I am more struck by the looseness of the approach – in which it resembles functionalism, whether this be a merit or a weakness – than by its specificity. It is an outlook, an approach, a language, a classification, more than a theory. It need not be, and in the hands of contemporary Soviet anthropologists frequently is not, dogmatic. I have defended the Marxist typology by saying, in effect, that it is at any rate no worse than functionalism, and possibly at some points a bit better, and that in any case it resembles functionalism in logical status, which is unimpressive in either case. Soviet anthropologists, of course, do not need to defend the typology in order to use it – it is their starting-point – and, if they did so, would hardly wish to use so lukewarm a defence. To say that an idea is at any rate no worse than the general vision of Malinowski does not, I think, constitute much of a defence of it in the Soviet Union.

What Soviet anthropologists *are* in fact characteristically engaged in is the elaboration, refinement, loosening up, general improvement of the typology, and its applications to concrete historical, archaeological, and ethnographic material. Perhaps they would rise to its defence if only they had more extensive opportunities for genuine debate with Western anthropologists, than, alas, they are granted at present; but in their

2 J. Goody, *Technology, Tradition and the State in Africa* (London, 1971).

current work and preoccupations they seem engaged in the *problems*, rather than with the defence, of this typology.

It is not at all difficult to think of a host of problems which haunt the typology. Its types are logically disparate: 'feudalism' or 'Asiatic society' are good ideal types, each containing a valuable theory of how a given social structure works: 'primitive society', on the other hand, is a residual rag-bag. The idea of a reliable, regular sequence, valid for all or most societies would seem in conflict with history. The echo of the heritage of Marxism from the Old Testament or from Rousseau – the idea that 'primitive communism' is somehow free of exploitation, which only arises from the emergence of classes – is embarrassing. The whole Marxist idea of a sequence of inherently unstable stages, ever propelled by inner strains into new forms, leads to a kind of terribly foreshortened vision of human history, which grossly underestimates the stabilities, circularities, repetitions of actual historical processes.

But there is absolutely no need to *tell* the Russians about these problems inherent in the vision. They are aware of them with perceptiveness and lucidity; they can and do articulate them, both in the abstract and in relation to well-explored, imaginatively interpreted concrete material. As one cannot in an article follow out the rich and subtle arguments of those who work in specific fields, it is perhaps best to look at the abstract and general formulation of these issues, such as is found in the article by Danilova which I cited initially.

A number of deep shifts of vision have taken place in Western social sciences in this century – some, but, of course, by no means all of them, reflected in the revolution in anthropology associated with Malinowski. It is interesting to see parallel shifts in the idiom and context of Soviet science. The Western rejection of evolutionism had at least two aspects, even if in practice these tended to be conflated: the notion of the 'evolution' of institutions has very feeble explanatory power; and the just-so story of 'social evolution' is also empirically inadequate and misleading in the face of the complexity, polymorphousness, multi-linearity, long stagnations, and the frequently circular movements of real history. It offered an over-simple, foreshortened and very Europe-centred view of human history.

It is interesting to see these perceptions articulated within another tradition:

It became manifest that within the overall regularity of the movement of mankind from pre-class society via antagonistic formations of communism, the concrete paths vary. . . .

Above all the proposition concerning the universality of slave-owning society is abandoned. This fact alone – and it now seems to be generally acknowledged in science – basically changes the vision of social evolution. Remember that according to the previously accepted scheme, feudalism ... arises from the disintegration of slave-owning society. But if the latter is not found generally ... the subsequent development must also have been different ... pre-capitalist structures of European nations differ markedly from the corresponding structures of nations, whose spontaneous development did not lead to capitalism. Feudalism ... as known in Europe ... is seldom found outside it.

[The older view] allowed ... deviations from the main line of global history ... but deviations and exceptions turned out to be more common than the cases falling under the rule and secondly – this is the most important point – the operative regularities turned out to be so specific that they could not be explained by the influence of the historic environment alone. ...

Already in the 30s ... certain concepts were proposed, such as that of early-slave-owning-society ... semi-patriarchal–semi-feudal. ... But early slave-society ... was marked by an extraordinary stability ... it stretched over millennia and showed no signs of being a transition to a higher form. ...

The idea of semi-patriarchal–semi-feudal was also aimed at making the scheme more supple. ... A concrete characterization of such societies contradicts the thesis of their transitional character. Moreover, *the simple introduction of the concept 'transitional stage' has not solved any problem*. (Italics mine)

Here we see the intertwining of the empirical and logical inadequacy of 'evolutionist' explanations. The evolutionist is like a man who habitually uses a lift in a fairly small building, say with five floors, and who is not at all demanding when it comes to explaining the movements of lifts. He tends to take lifts for granted, or be satisfied with a most schematic simple theory of how lifts work. When asked why a lift is stuck between the third and fourth floors, he is quite happy with the answer – it has passed the third floor, and it will reach the fourth. (In some ways, it is already at the fourth: the passengers' heads are there, while their feet are still at the third.) Evolutionism, in its justified insistence that lifts *did* indeed move, was no doubt an advance on Aristotle or the Book of Genesis, on the immutability of species and its equivalent in history; but, as Noam Chomsky brutally observed, to insist on evolution (of language, for instance) is to say virtually nothing, other than that *some* (quite unspecified) naturalistic explanation of origins is available. We know that lifts do move: to say so explains nothing.

Once one takes the availability of naturalistic accounts of origins for granted and is no longer excited by it, evolutionism loses its charm. And the perception of its explanatory impotence is heightened by the awareness of facts such as the remarkable stability of some pre-industrial societies. The evolutionist tendency to see ever-present germs of change, or left-overs of past change everywhere, was a piece of European parochialism. The reasons for noticing its inadequacy seem similar in the Soviet Union to those in the West: 'the revival of the discussion received stimulus from the practical need to understand the social structure of underdeveloped countries ... but its fundamental cause lies in the inner logic of historical science itself.'

The parallels in the rejection of the simple-minded, parochial, quick-growing acorn-oak vision of society and history (this is what social evolutionism was) are fascinating. Yet the differences are as important. In Western social sciences, this rejection took place in dramatic and loudly heralded form only in anthropology; elsewhere it was more gradual, and less well analysed or self-conscious.

But at the time the revolution occurred, anthropologists were interested primarily or almost exclusively in 'primitive' societies. Hence they articulated the new vision for simple societies only, and the vision, known as 'functionalism', can be parodied as a theory with one type only. (Its subtypologies, though they exist, are not at all well worked out.) By contrast the Soviet modification of the facile old diachronic approach, and their revival of sensitivity to synchronic problems, to stability, stagnations, or circular and many-directional developments, is not articulated against the background of such a restricted area. On the contrary: it is worked out against the backcloth of data drawn from *all* pre-industrial societies, and starts out from a typology which, whatever other faults it might have, does not suggest that all societies exemplify *one* model. Or rather, in so far as it does commit such an error, it does it in quite another way: not by urging the investigator to look for stability-engendering equilibrium (on the contrary, it was far too ready to see those supposedly pervasive seeds of change), but by its erstwhile over-concentration on the 'mode of production'.

Here, once again, the article under discussion is fascinating: 'Does the ownership of the means of production ... constitute the determining element in all societies? ... is the role of the economy the same in pre-capitalist structures as under capitalism? Is it correct to extend ... the primacy of productive relations to all stages of human history?'

The article answers this question in the negative: 'Contrary to the viewpoint widely diffused in Soviet science, the relations of domination–subjection, conditioned by the development of the division of labour, are themselves by no means relations of production.' And, even more explicitly: 'The dominant relationships in all pre-capitalist structures were non-economic ones.' Admittedly, this attribution of primacy to power (or to kin relations) is qualified by assertions to the effect that these relations are conditioned by the level of economic development and by the type of division of labour. But this conditioning, whatever it amounts to, does not seem to be of a rigid, single-cause kind: 'However, the prevalence of this or that kind of political organization, i.e. of this or that kind of domination–subjection relation, always appears to be the result of the simultaneous operation of a whole totality of factors.'

In other words, it is not produced by the economy alone. The author extracts from Marxism an interesting three-stage overall typology of societies: primitive societies, in which the dominant relations are 'natural' (kin) ones; a second genus, within which they are political (territorial-administrative); and a third type in which alone economic relations, types of ownership, are decisive. Grave difficulties would no doubt arise if these were not allowed to overlap. In her eagerness to assert the primacy of the political in the second stage, Danilova in fact commits herself to a remarkably strong and daring generalization: 'Historical sources show irrefutably that it was not the big landowner, separating out from the top level of the community, who became the feudal seigneur, but on the contrary, the politically dominant groups which in time usurped the land possessions of their subjects'.

Whether or not in pre-capitalist societies the path really was *always* from power to wealth and never the reverse, there can be no doubt that this was very often so, and that, in this sense, the relations of production were not dominant. One might put this in a simple way by saying that the means of coercion were often more important than the means of production.

This is a theme which, in the West, is mirrored not so much in anthropology as in sociology. The most influential theorist in the West at present is presumably Max Weber. It is not unusual to sum up his work as follows: he complemented Marx's concern with economic structures by an account of the types of political domination. The vogue of Weber coincided with the same factors as Danilova invokes to explain the Soviet debates: the extension of horizons to non-European societies, a growing sense of the uniqueness of capitalism, and of the difficulties of 'development' in the Third World, as opposed to the earlier expectation of parallel indigenous developments, powered by supposed internal impulsions.

Whether this partial shift of stress away from the relations of production, even if qualified, is compatible with true Marxism is something I shall leave to Marx specialists. I have no wish to take part in theological discussions. Danilova certainly makes out a powerful case that it is incompatible only with a crude and distorted Marxism. The revisionist devil can cite scripture for his purpose. And in this case with great brilliance:

Marx showed the dominant forms of social relations in primitive society are natural ones of kinship, and in pre-capitalist class societies, they are political ones of domination and subjection. . . .
   Speaking of feudalism, Marx states: 'Rent, not profit, is the form in which unrewarded surplus labour expresses itself.' Characterizing rent as the specific

form of extraction ... Marx underscored that the rent relationship ... is not itself a relation of production. Quite the reverse.

But even if compatible with true scholarly Marxism, this view is incompatible with earlier orthodoxy in Soviet science, about which Danilova has much of interest to say:

These questions are not new ... active discussions began at the very start of Soviet economic science. ... The result of the discussions was the prevalence of the viewpoint maintaining not only the decisive, but the exclusive role of relations of production in all pre-socialist formations. Such an outcome ... was quite natural. In the conditions of struggle, conducted by young Marxist historiography with bourgeois conceptions ... the main task ... was the strengthening of the materialist conception ... stressing the decisive role of the economy. Given the insufficient theoretical training of the learned cadres ... this led to the absolutization of the economic factor, which in good time became an obstacle in the solving of serious theoretical problems, *notably the problem of socialist and pre-capitalist societies*. (Italics mine)

Thus there seem also to be practical implications in this error. The absolutization of the economic factor is applicable to the capitalist period only. *Elsewhere, before and since, we must look to relations of domination—subjection*.

The discussion revealed with great clarity the inadequacy of the logical apparatus ... used for ... the theoretical analysis of pre-capitalist societies. This apparatus was constructed on the basis of the political economy of capitalism ...

The stumbling-block to the solution of many problems of pre-capitalist societies was the direct projection on to these formations of the mechanisms applying to the processes of bourgeois society.

So we must refrain from projecting the primacy of the economic, and remember the significance of the relations of domination (except perhaps for 'primitive' society, in which these are replaced by kin relations). The final moral of such a reinterpretation for socialist as well as pre-capitalist societies is interesting: 'the discussion concerning primitive and early class societies is connected with contemporary discussions of economists, arising from the need of elaborating a political economy serving the practical requirements of socialist society.'

In plain terms: to understand both pre- and post-capitalist societies, we must look at the relationships of power. Economic relations do not uniquely determine these, nor provide automatic solutions for their problems.

There is a certain irony in the rediscovery of the importance of power by Soviet thought, carried out at the risk of a charge of 'revisionism', at the very time when many Western anthropologists, free of such pressures, yet indulge in a facile and power-ignoring Idealism, born of a mixture of wishful thinking and logical confusion. I can think of various recent Western intellectual trends which, starting from the premiss that human actions and institutions are concept-saturated, end up with the absurd conclusion that therefore conceptual constraints are somehow more important than physical ones. Such cheap Idealism, sometimes implicit but often openly avowed, such fantasies of the *Allmacht des Begriffes*, are not a Soviet temptation: men who need to work so hard to secure the admission of the importance of *Herrschaft* as well as *Wirtschaft*, will not wish to conjure away either of them by verbal hocus-pocus.

The recommendation to look at power, at 'political relations', is however, made for pre-capitalist societies, but not for *primitive* ones, which are defined in terms of the predominance of natural or kin relations. This brings me to another interesting, distinctive, but less convincing, trait of Soviet anthropology. To my knowledge, Western theory operates without any serious definition of 'primitive' society; and feels no need of one; the very term is used with a kind of audible shrug, with an implicit disclaimer, not merely of any evaluation, but also of any theoretical content. It means small, intimate, non-urban, and generally pre-literate societies, either self-contained or only very partially in-corporated in wider civilizations; it is simply a category, and it is not intended to contain any theory. 'Functionalism' is only a theory in a very loose sense, of a formal rather than a substantive paradigm; and in any case in so far as it is claimed to be a theory at all it was not even specifically restricted to some limited class of the 'primitive'.

All this is quite different in Soviet anthropology, and anyone who fails to note this will altogether misunderstand Russian anthropological discussions. In Soviet language 'primitive society' is an important, restricted, and above all heavily theory-loaded term, and the theory or theories it embodies are one of the focal points of discussion. A book dedicated to these topics, under the editorship of A. I. Pershits and others, is approaching publication, and will, I expect, constitute an outstandingly important contribution.[3] Soviet 'ethnography' is not defined, even approximately, as the study of 'primitive' society: 'primitive society' is one type among others, within the class of social types (all pre-capitalist ones) studied by ethnography. The theory which the term 'primitive' incorporates it largely owes, of course, to its place within the old Marxist five-term schema of social development. In terms of this

---

3 This has since appeared: A. I. Pershits (ed.), *P'ervobytnoe obshchestvo* (*Primordial Community*) (Moscow, 1975). Cf. ch. 2 below.

schema, primitive societies are the ones which precede class societies (these being slave society, Asiatic, feudal, capitalist). They are not merely classless, but also stateless, for in terms of the old orthodoxy the state only emerges with antagonistic classes.

This is where theoretical problems begin to arise. Whatever the theory which may be incorporated in the term, the intuitive coverage of the notion 'primitive society' for a Soviet anthropologist is nevertheless not so very different from that which it has for his Western colleague. The term will cover *tribes*, the type of community which is the classical object of investigation for Western anthropology. This denotation is in any case imposed on the Soviet thinker by the old theory itself, for the *residue* of human societies left after subtraction of Asiatic despotisms, feudal and slave-based societies, and capitalism, in any case corresponds roughly to the anthropological domain in Western science.

But here trouble arises, as Danilova's article stresses, from the wealth of ethnographic material which is now available. In the rich and very varied world of tribal societies, one finds stateless societies and centralized ones, stratified and egalitarian ones, and a profusion of quite different kinds of social utilization of kinship. In brief, the 'primitive', in this sense, is an enormously wide and diversified category, and a residual one at that, and ought not to be treated as a theoretical, explanatory concept at all.

Nu, chto delat'? (Well, what is to be done?) A number of conceptual devices are available if one wishes to save the theoretical status of the notion of the 'primitive', and other aspects of the scheme, and some of these devices receive comment in Danilova's article. It is possible to loosen the rigidity of *sequences* in the scheme. It all becomes more like a game of snakes and ladders. It is also possible to loosen the definitions of the individual *stages* within the scheme. For instance, one Soviet anthropologist told me that he preferred to work with a definition of 'feudalism' which equates it with any system of exploitation based on force (as opposed to economic constraint). This of course ensures a very wide diffusion for feudalism, though it would then also seem to absorb some other categories previously co-ordinate with it in the Marxist scheme.

It is furthermore possible to save the theory by redefinition of *characteristic* with which the stages are credited: one scholar told me that I misunderstood 'the state' if I equated it with political centralization. The state *really* is the kind of centralization provoked by the emergence of classes and their antagonism. This obviously saves the theory. Or again, one can propel many of those tribal societies which have puzzling characteristics into the realm of class societies by treating them as *embryonic* slave, Asiatic, or feudal societies, which, however, rather awkwardly separates them from their less troublesome fellow tribes. 'Early feudal' or 'early slave', etc. then means a kind of apologetic disclaimer: feudal, but not quite. . . . The difficulties of this particular device are eloquently expounded by Danilova.

Or again, one can adjust the delimitation, not of the stages or of their traits, but of *societies* themselves. As everyone knows who has ever thought about the problems of the comparative method, there is a great difficulty about defining one's units: is a given community a culture of its own, or a marginal member of a wider culture? Few tribes are islands unto themselves, and theoretical issues can be prejudged by the manner in which one draws boundaries. The perfectly legitimate device of redrawing boundaries does give one some theoretical leeway. Some Soviet anthropologists are very interested in the use of the notions of the social *centre* and *periphery*. One does indeed often come across relationships between political centres and tribal peripheries, and neither can be properly understood without the other. Tribesmen who seem 'patriarchal' when artificially seen in isolation, may yet be part of a kind of feudal system when seen in relation to the centre; nomads lacking developed political structures internally may yet constitute a class and even a state, when seen in relation to sedentary populations whom they dominate. And so on.

The concrete work carried out by Soviet anthropologists applying these notions often seems to me of the highest order. Take, for instance, D. A. Olderogge or L. E. Kubbel on the states of West Africa, or indeed the brilliant polymath Olderogge's contributions to a whole range of Africanist problems, or A. M. Khazanov on nomadism, or Yu. V. Maretin on Indonesia, or M. V. Kriukov on Chinese and comparative kinship, or many others.[4] But concerning the general issue, it seems to me that whereas otherwise Soviet anthropologists have an advantage over their Western colleagues in starting from a definite typology of societies where the Westerners have none, when it comes to using the concept of the 'primitive', the theoretical ballast carried becomes a burden rather than a help.

One should add that in the approach to these problems and the deployment of these devices, there is a great diversity of views among

4 D. A. Olderogge, in *Epigamia* (Moscow, 1983); and see Yu. V. Bromley et al., *Osnovnye problemy Afrikanistiki* (*Basic Problems of African Studies*), presented to D. A. Olderogge on his seventieth birthday (Moscow, 1973); L. E. Kubbel, *Songaiskaya derzhava* (*Songhai Empire*) (Moscow, 1974), cf. ch. 4 below; A. M. Khazanov, *Sotsial'naya istoriya Skifov* (*The Social History of the Scythians*) (Moscow, 1975) and *Nomads and the Outside World* (Cambridge, 1984), cf. ch. 5 below; Yu. V. Maretin, 'Obshchina i ee tipy v Indonesii' ('The Community and its types in Indonesia'), *Proceedings of the 7th International Congress of Anthropology and Ethnography* (Moscow, 1964); M. V. Kriukov, *Sistema rodstva kitaitsev* (*The Chinese Kinship System*) (Moscow, 1972).

Soviet anthropologists. There are those who defend and those who repudiate the notion of the Asiatic mode of production, and those who endeavour to refine it. There are those who extend feudalism to make it cover all exploitation based on force, and those who would deny its existence outside medieval Europe and Japan. One anthropologist told me that while the polarity between the communalism of the primitive and the ruthless individualism of capitalism should be maintained, the actual paths of development between these poles were endlessly various.

Will this vigorous discussion end in some new consensus? My own guess – and it cannot be more than that – is that it cannot. Suppose that some Soviet Malinowski, let us call him Ivanov, crystallized a new typological paradigm. His own status would, alas, either be too high or too low within the wider society. A sanctified political leader is not likely nowadays to meddle in the day-to-day contents of science, and to set up as epoch-maker. So we need not expect the descent of a new Marxism-Leninism-Ivanovism from above. But suppose that Ivanov is not a political personage, but a mere humble member of the Academy of Sciences. If he has indeed elaborated a new and convincing improvement of the old typology then, at least in anthropology, one ought in all logic henceforth properly to speak of the new Marxism-Leninism-Ivanovism. But one can hardly conceive such an apotheosis of a mere Academician, which would endow him with an authority out of all proportion to his position. So, either way, no real authority will be conferred on the new scheme.

For these reasons, the ironic fact is that whereas at least British anthropology for long periods exemplified a shared dominant paradigm (and a very fruitful one it was), Soviet science is likely, in these fields at least and within set limits, to exemplify a pluralistic rivalry of diverse viewpoints.

One should add that the notion of the 'primitive' generates theoretical problems and discussion at both ends, so to speak: one end is its relation to *post*-primitive class societies, discussed above, and the other concerns the questions of the early history of mankind, and the role of kinship in early human society. Despite the revival of ethnology in the West or Lévi-Strauss's *en passant* speculations about early kinship, this debate does not seem to have a Western equivalent, just as there is no Western equivalent to the Russian interest in *ethnogenesis*.

There are fields, of course, where the remaining difference between the Western tendency to synchronism and Marxist diachronism make a big difference to the kind of question that is asked. The reconstruction of early history is moreover a field which continues to be haunted by Morgan and Engels. But in this area too there is now an open and vigorous debate, on topics such as the relationship of *rod* and *obshchina* (clan and community, roughly), a problem whose logic I do not fully understand, but which is carried on at a high level, by men who seem to wish to revise the old scheme, such as V. P. Kabo, V. M. Bakhta, and N. A. Butinov, and by its defenders, such as Yu. I. Semenov.[5] (Semonov incidentally is the author of an excellent commentary on western debates on the relationship of anthropology and economics.[6])

It would be a simplification, however, to say that all Soviet work in anthropology falls into this pattern, i.e. the interaction between the old typology and new historical and ethnographic data. There is, for instance, excellent ethnography of Soviet Muslim peoples by men such as V. N. Basilov, G. P. Snesarev, S. M. Abramzon, and others, inspired by the idea (paralleled in the West) that Muslim social life must be studied from below, on the ground rather than through the social self-images of Muslim clerics.[7] Sometimes anthropologists are presented with tasks from above, and employ sociological, statistical methods: there is a major comparative research in progress on social mobility among five different ethnic groups in the Soviet Union. The findings on one of them, the Volga Tatars, are already published. Those of us in the West who interpret nationalism in terms of the tendency of modern industrial society to create culturally homogeneous human pools (thanks to its inherent occupational mobility and universal literacy, which jointly erode minor cultural discontinuities), and who see politically active nationalism as a consequence of inequalities of opportunity between such pools, when they are not separated by political boundaries, will find interesting confirmation in the logic of this research. Apparently the early findings are encouraging: social mobility among the Tatars is now catching up on that among the Russians. The theoretician of this research is Yu. V. Bromley, in *Ethnos and Ethnography*; the first data are to be found in *Contemporary Ethnic Processes in the USSR*.[8]

    5 e.g. V. P. Kabo, 'Pervobytnaya obshchina okhotnikov i sobiratelei (po avstraliiskim materialam') ('The Primitive Community of Hunters and Gatherers (based on Australian data')' in Danilova et al. (eds), *Problems of the History of Pre-Capitalist Societies*, cit. n. 1 above; V. M. Bakhta, 'Papuasy Novoi Gvinei: proizvodstvo i obshchestvo' ('Papuans of New Guinea: Production and Society'), ibid.; N. A. Butinov, 'Pervobytnoobshchinnyi stroi' ('Primordial Structure'), ibid.; Yu. I. Semenov, *Kak vozniklo chelovechestvo (The Emergence of Mankind)* (Moscow, 1966).

    6 Now published as Yu. I. Semenov, 'Theoretical Problems of "Economic Anthropology"', *Philosophy of the Social Sciences*, vol. 6, 1974.

    7 V. N. Basilov, *Kul't svyatykh v Islame (The Cult of Saints in Islam)* (Moscow, 1970); G. P. Snesarev and V. N. Basilov (eds), *Domusul'manskie verovaniya i obryady v srednei Azii (Pre-Muslim Beliefs and Rituals in Central Asia)* (Moscow, 1975); S. M. Abramzon, *Kirgizy i ikh etnogeticheskie i istoriko-kul'turnye svyazi (The Kirgiz and their Ethnogenetic and Historic-Cultural Relations)* (Leningrad, 1971).

    8 Yu. V. Bromley, *Etnos i etnografiya (Ethnos and Ethnography)* (Moscow, 1973); *Sovremennye etnicheskie protsessy v SSSR (Contemporary Ethnic Processes in the USSR)* (Moscow, 1975).

But these complications apart, an overall picture and an interesting contrast do emerge. Both Soviet and Western anthropologists have reacted to the empirical simple-mindedness and logical feebleness of the old evolutionary schemata: the Malinowskian ones reacted by temporarily rejecting evolutionism altogether, and the Soviet ones by struggling with the categories within their version of it. The price paid in the West is the virtual absence of *any* systematic scheme for the comparison of structures or for their location of historical context. The Soviets, by contrast, do have a scheme, which occasionally (as in the notion of *the* primitive) may seriously get in the way of thought, but which, at other points, can be a valuable stimulus. There seems to me no doubt that *a* systematic typology of social structures is desirable; its possession, though not its dogmatic imposition, is an advantage.

At the most abstract level, there is the question of whether or not such a typology should be inspired by the overall direction of human progress – whether, in other words, it should ultimately be evolutionist in kind. If the answer is Yes, then the typology will at the same time also constitute a rough periodicization of human history: for an evolutionist, social types and historic epochs are correlative notions. It is altogether characteristic of the Soviet climate that Danilova's article makes easy and automatic transitions from the question of social types to the question of historic epochs. It is natural to assume that the two go together. In discussions with Soviet anthropologists, this point came up most frequently. Surely, they said, if you admit the desirability of an orderly typology, you must also admit that this typology will be related to the overall direction of social change?

It seems to me an open question. I doubt whether they will convert me on this point. For one thing, within LSE sociology (unlike anthropology), a vacuous, toothless, and sterile evolutionism survived far too long, and its after-taste quite spoils one's palate for evolutionist ideas. More important, it seems to me more fruitful not to seek overall patterns of social evolution, but to concentrate instead of the specificity of the neolithic and industrial revolutions and on the intervening stagnations and circularities – an idea not absent among the Soviets either. But the ultimate truth on this most important matter, on the relationship between the genesis and the structure of human societies, is clearly an open one. One can only hope for far greater opportunities for more genuine and protracted discussions on this and other topics between members of the two anthropological traditions than exist at present.

2

How did Mankind Acquire its Essence?
or
The Palaeolithic October
or
The Marxist Book of Genesis

Marxism predates Darwinism proper by about a decade and a half. A small matter, this, on the scale of world history. None the less, an error seems to have crept into the world-historical timetable. It would have been altogether more neat and proper, had Darwinism preceded rather than followed Marxism. Darwinism does not need Marxism for its logical completeness, but Marxism does need Darwinism. Without it, some most awkward loose ends remain, as Marx himself noted when Darwinism appeared. Materialism requires that man be part of nature: he cannot pretend to be above it, as theology would have it. But if he is part of nature, how did he emerge from it? And why should the laws of social change be anything other than special applications of biological ones?

From the beginning the founding fathers of Marxism were committed not merely to naturalism, but also to evolutionism, in a broad and rather unbiological sense. Their thought is deeply Heraclitean, and imbued with the feeling that change is the law of all things and, moreover, with the idea that a cumulative overall direction pervades the global pattern of change. Within such a vision, it is inevitable that questions be asked about the emergence of humanity. Although Heinz Lubasz has argued convincingly that Aristotle was a living influence, rather than a dead text, for Marx,[1] one doctrine which the founding fathers of Marxism nevertheless could hardly endorse was the immutability of species. Without any shadow of doubt, had Darwinism and an anthropological

1 H. Lubasz, 'The Aristotelian Dimension in Marx', in the *Times Higher Education Supplement*, 1 Jan. 1977; cf. Scott Meikle, *Essentialism in the Thought of Karl Marx* (La Salle, Ill., 1985).

theory of early man been available in the 1840s, the original formulation of Marxism would have taken it into account, and established the required connection.

But the authors of *The Communist Manifesto* did not initially make the connection. Evidently, their mind was on history, and not on biology or anthropology. All that changed later when, in the fullness of time, Morgan partly displaced Hegel as an important inspiration.[2] The *Manifesto* very significantly proclaims that all history is the history of class struggle. In an edition dating from after Marx's death, Engels introduces a most important qualification to this: he adds, 'that is, all recorded history'.

In other words, *unrecorded* history, history of the periods antedating the use of writing, also includes societies that are free of classes and hence of class struggle and its inevitable accompaniments, coercion and the state. What Engels has in mind here is the proper recognition of 'primitive communism' as the first and also non-antagonistic, class-free stage of human history. In Soviet Marxism, since the interwar period, the term *p'ervobytnoe obshchestvo* has come into widespread use to denote this stage, and the expression is, I think, best translated as 'primordial community'. Soviet anthropologists themselves prefer the translation to read 'primitive society'. To my mind this is much too suggestive of a residual negative category – all societies devoid of certain attributes such as centralization, literacy, powerful technology, irrespective of their positive attributes – and it fails to bring out the fact that *p'ervobytnoe obshchestvo* is a theory-loaded sociological category, with an important content: it implies a society which runs itself without coercion, property or classes. Unlike 'primitive communism', which sounds like a theory, 'primordial community' correctly conveys that we are dealing with a *condition*, not a doctrine. It also avoids any inappropriate negative suggestiveness of 'primitive'.

The notion of 'primitive communism', or rather of 'primordial communalism', is not an irrelevant, functionless accretion of Marxism. 'Primordial communalism' is the baseline of human history. Marxist theory of history and society could hardly function without it. The baseline is there not merely in a temporal sense, but also, much more significantly, in a moral and explanatory one. It provides not merely a beginning, but also a norm. In our beginning is our essence. In our essence lies our fulfilment. It not only highlights what requires *explanation*, but also what requires *rectification*. It makes possible the distinctively Marxist way of moral validation, based as it is not on the

2 See V. N. Nikiforov, *Vostok i vsemirnaya Istoriya* (*The Orient and World History*) (Moscow, 1975) cf. ch. 3.

execution of an extraneously imposed obligation, but on the fulfilment of deep basic human potentiality, temporarily thwarted by a pathological social order.[3]

The primitive communism which characterized the primordial community reveals to us and highlights the 'species essence' of man. It demonstrates what human society can be like, and indeed what it was like originally: devoid of unsymmetrical relationships to the means of production, and hence also devoid of classes and of domination. What historically followed it was a terrible distortion of our true human essence, an alienation from ourselves; its eventual elimination will likewise make it possible for our veritable essence to reappear, and to reassert itself. Sir Karl Popper has popularized an interpretation of Marx,[4] according to which externally imposed ethical obligation is avoided by deducing social legitimacy from the inevitability of a certain future condition, thus turning moral reasoning into a species of historical prediction, and thereby also making it vulnerable to any demonstration of the illegitimacy of prophecy: this, however, is a simplification. The prediction also depended on a retrodiction, on the inevitability in pre-history of a social situation which demonstrated the availability, and in a way also the authority, of a classless, free, and harmonious condition.

It is in this way, and this way only, that communist social relations can be shown to be valid and normative for humanity. There is no question of any 'ought', any obligation, anything *imposed*: for Marxism, moral compulsion is as abhorrent as political coercion, of which in any case it is but an ally and an expression. The *Sein/Sollen* distinction is something that mankind will overcome when it emerges from pre-history, just as indeed it had once lived without it, at the very start of history. Kant thought such a transcendence of obligation, the identity of 'is' and 'ought', was given only to angels; but Marxism credits it to man on earth, though only before *and* after the period of class-pervaded history, or rather, morally speaking, of pre-history. True history will begin when our estrangement from ourselves ceases.

Yulian Bromley, A. I. Pershits, and Yuri Semenov, the authors of *History of Primitive Society*,[5] are quite clear about the importance of the notion of primordial communalism in the confrontation of Marxist and non-Marxist scholarship. They add that the concept is also of practical

3 Steven Lukes, *Marxism and Morality* (Oxford, 1985).

4 K. Popper, *The Open Society and its Enemies*, 3rd edn (London, 1957); *The Poverty of Historicism* (London, 1957).

5 *Istoriya pervobytnogo obshchestva: obshchie voprosy. Problemy antroposotsiogenezisa* (*History of Primitive Society: General Questions. Problems of Anthropogenesis*), ed. Yu. V. Bromley, A. I. Pershits, Yu. Semenov (Moscow, 1983).

importance, in as far as many ethnic groups still find themselves, or quite recently found themselves, in diverse stages of the disintegration of primordial communalism. Hence the concept is frequently deployed in analyses of concrete historical situations.[6] Our end is in our beginning, and our beginnings are not yet very distant. They are still discernible on the horizon, and make their contribution to current or recent social structures.

But the most important point is this: the historic reality of primitive communism, of the primordial community, is necessary as a demonstration of the *feasibility* of communist social relations, of the simultaneous absence of classes and of the state. If this social form had always been absent, had it never existed, that would create a grave difficulty for the Marxist anticipation and recommendation of its re-emergence at a higher level, both for its possibility and its moral authority. Had no such thing ever been found on earth, the commendation of communism as a form of social organization would inevitably have the awkward form of a merely abstract moral injunction, imposed on humanity on the authority of – what exactly? If one is to commend communism as the release, the fulfilment of the human 'species-essence', one does, however, need some support for such a claim, some evidence of its possibility. The role of primordial communalism is that it provides such evidence. It shows that the Fall is redeemable. No wonder that its reality is firmly upheld by Soviet anthropological theory.

So this affirmation is not a mere empty formality. The idea that there is a generic contrast between later class-endowed and early classless societies – as the authors of this volume observe, primordial communalism and pre-class society are synonymous expressions – and that the emergence of classes is a relatively definite and virtually datable event in the history of human societies, deeply pervades the thinking of Soviet anthropologists, including some on whose shoulders Marxism otherwise does not weigh too heavily. This view is in marked contrast to the normal Western assumption that inequality might well have been always present, and that it was perhaps only increased and formalized by developments such as political centralization, but that it may never have constituted a definitive innovation in human history, and that hominid and human nastiness are *continuous*. The Marxist view, on the contrary, is that exploitation and aggression did constitute an innovation. There

---

6 Cf. A. I. Pershits (ed.), *Primordial Community*, cit. ch. 1, n. 3 above; A. I. Pershits (ed.), *Stanovlenie klassov i gosudarstva* (*Formation of Classes and Government* (Moscow, 1976); A. I. Pershits and A. M. Khazanov (eds), *P'ervobytnaya periferiya klassovykh obshchestv* (*Primordial Periphery of Class Societies*) (Moscow, 1978); Yu. V. Bromley (ed.), *Etnos v doklossavom i ranneklassovom obshchestve* (*Ethnicity in Pre-Class and Early-Class Society*) (Moscow, 1982).

was indeed a definite expulsion from the Garden of Eden, and it is this innovation, the asymmetrical relation to the means of production, which explains state formation, rather than vice versa.

But there are problems, and some of them are connected precisely to the fact that Marxism was initially formulated *prior* to the arrival of Darwinism. As a result of Darwinism, we automatically think in terms of some kind of continuity between primate and human societies. We know a certain amount about primate societies, and though we may be willing to concede that they are quite free of anything that we would call a state, we are not at all inclined to expect them to be models of equality and community. We have no inclination to see them as any kind of moral baseline for ourselves. In some negative and formal sense, they may indeed be free of property and, much more questionably, of social stratification; but, within the limits imposed on them by the exiguity of their resources, are they free of inequality and of violence? Few of us are tempted by such an idea. We see no reason for supposing that these defects were absent in early human societies, about whose condition, admittedly, we do not possess adequate or conclusive information. But there is nothing that would incline us to imagine them as particularly idyllic.

The general issue can be put very simply. There are only two possibilities: the first one is that the normative human essence (if such a notion be allowed at all), which is allegedly revealed in primordial communalism, is something inherited by man from his pre-human ancestors and shared by them.

Note that this option is not a wholly absurd position. Pragmatism, perhaps the most important philosophy to emerge from Darwinism, does indeed teach something of the kind. It holds that the normatively correct cognitive comportment of mankind is exemplified and practised, albeit in simpler form, *by all life*. The amoeba and Einstein share the same research strategy. But for various reasons, of which the fact that it postdates Darwinism is only one, and not the most important, Marxism does not, and cannot, adopt the pragmatist option and concentrate on what we share with all living beings.

Pragmatism, being predominantly American, concentrated on innovation and discovery and cognition, taking the social order which permits them for granted; and consequently it had little difficulty in crediting the same basic cognitive principles both to our pre-human and even pre-primate ancestors and to ourselves. Adaptation, trial and error, flexibility, characterize their comportment as much as it does ours. The cognitive customary law of mankind is of a truly immemorial antiquity, being the custom and guiding principle of all life, without distinction.

But it would indeed be hard to claim that *all life* also exemplifies communist social organization: and some forms of life (e.g. social insects) which do exemplify it, do not inspire our admiration. What pragmatism attributes to all life – roughly, adaptation and piecemeal improvement by trial and error – is unspecific enough to be ascribable so widely, without excessive implausibility. *Communism* is concerned primarily with the form of social organization and it constitutes a more discriminating and sharply defined principle: it cannot be so easily projected onto all life. And even if it were, it would hardly enhance its appeal; most of us are willing to share our cognitive principles with the beasts, especially if these are reducible to no more than trial and error – but we are somewhat more discriminating and fastidious about our moral ones. (Those of us who endorse the market *because* it revives the jungle are in a minority.) We should, on this view, also be left with the bizarre problem of why something which inheres in all life, should suddenly and mysteriously absent itself for some ten millennia or so of human history. The Fall would become even more of a mystery.

If we reject the biological universality of communism, we are brought to the second option. It affirms that something definite had to happen, which endowed humanity with its particular species-essence, thereby distinguishing it from previous forms of life; and that this occurred as part of the very process of the emergence of humanity. It clearly must have been an event or process of the very first importance. Unfortunately, the founders of Marxism, presumably because they were preoccupied with history rather than biology, because they took humanity for granted, and because their minds simply did not focus on this problem in that pre-Darwinian decade of the 1840s, left us with no theory of the nature of this absolutely fundamental process or development. But in consequence, there is a gaping void where the Marxist Book of Genesis should be.

What is to be done? The *History of Primitive Society* attempts to do it. It offers an account of what must have taken place during the emergence of humanity, an account which does have its inherent plausibility, and which does very properly take account of the Darwinian backcloth. It enables us to retain the theory of the appropriate primordial community, without at the same time, implausibly, also crediting pre-human hominids with a social order that would be exemplary for *us*. If humanity did exemplify a certain norm, albeit at a low technological level, from its very beginnings, then this could not conceivably be a bequest from its pre-human ancestors. The very process of 'anthropogenesis', of the emergence of humanity proper, must itself also have engendered those normative and distinctively human features. Early Marxism failed to contain any theory of the very emergence of mankind, and in particular of the kind of humanity which Marxist eschatology requires, and this is now being made good.

It is all rather as if by some accident the Old Testament had only reached medieval Europe in a mutilated form, without the Book of Genesis. Would not the Vatican have appointed a commission, headed by a respected cardinal, charged with plugging this gap? The Institute of Ethnography of the Soviet Academy of Sciences, by assigning a high-powered team to the production of three volumes on primordial communalism, of which this is the first, is in effect doing something similar. Or perhaps – and this is what in fact appears to have happened – a respected cardinal, eager to employ the talent available in his secretariat and to advance its renown, proposed the scheme. The Book of Genesis must be written!

The principal author responsible for the relevant chapter is Yuri Semenov (not to be confused with other Semenovs whose names appear in Soviet bibliographies).[7] Semenov is one of the most erudite of historians of anthropological and social ideas, possessed of a very thorough and accurate knowledge of Western thought, and a remarkable capacity for fair and succinct presentation. He has to his credit, for instance, an excellent summary of the Western debate between formalists and substantivists in economic anthropology.[8] But he is far more than a mere historian of ideas. He is a creative, ingenious, and original theoretician, whose commitment to Marxism leads him both to perceive the problems which pervade its existing theoretical structure and to propose interesting solutions to them.

For instance, he is the author of an intriguing attempt to square the Marxist theory of social formations, and in particular the theory of their historic sequence, with the well-known objection that most, or perhaps indeed all, concrete individual societies fail to pass through the required canonical stages.[9] Western anthropologists might feel that he exemplifies exactly the kind of speculative historical reconstruction, which some of them pride themselves on having left behind. Similar criticisms, *nur mit ein bisschen anderen Worten*, are also liable to be, at least informally, directed at him by scholars from within the Soviet Union.[10]

This is not the place to settle the relative roles of theory and observation in anthropology: suffice it to say that theories may and must be formulated in advance of data, and that what matters is whether they

7 All subsequent quotations, unless otherwise indicated, are from this chapter.
8 'Theoretical Problems of "Economic Anthropology"', cit. ch. 1, n. 6 above.
9 'The theory of socio-economic formations and world history' in E. Gellner (ed.), *Soviet and Western Anthropology* (London–New York, 1970); cf. ch. 7 below.
10 Vladimir Plotkin and Joran Howe, 'The Unknown Traditions: Continuity and Innovation in Soviet Ethnography', *Dialectical Anthropology* 1985, p. 259.

inspire questions which eventually lead us to locate new and relevant data. Semenov would not (I think) deny that the theory he puts forward is as yet speculative, and that it has not yet been properly established. But it certainly deserves consideration, both on merit and for the interesting role it plays within the overall conceptual structure of Soviet Marxist anthropology.

Semenov begins by denying the theory which invokes hunting as the principal factor in the emergence of mankind. The hunt for large and dangerous animals presupposes co-operation, and this could, on that theory, explain the collectivism of early man. He might have added that the emergence of language and of a high intelligence can also be explained in this way. But Semenov rejects this view, noting that the *explanans* is something very well diffused in the biological world, and yet fails in other cases to produce the required effect. What really marks off early humanity from pre-humans, he affirms, is *productive activity*. One would indeed expect a Marxist theory to focus on man the tool-maker rather than man the hunter as the progenitor of the human essence.

The specification of the manner in which tool production engenders the required properties, leads Semenov into a discussion of natural selection and its forms. He distinguishes between individual and 'gregarious' selection. He is particularly concerned with the kind of selection which operates on collectivities rather than on their individual members. A crucial point in his argument is: the production of tools (including weapons) does not in itself constitute any kind of adaptation to the environment. It is only the deployment of those tools in the procuring of nourishment that constitutes adaptation. Hence individuals who were morphologically well suited for tool production, do not thereby automatically acquire any advantage in comparison with individuals morphologically less well suited to such production. A disposition to produce tools on its own does not as yet confer an evolutionary advantage on its carriers or on communities which harbour them: the advantage emerges only under certain additional conditions.

Semenov also insists that whilst hominids can transmit information non-genetically, by emulation, they lack culture in the proper sense of the term: amongst them, there is no mechanism for freezing, fixing (he actually uses the term *fiksirovanie*) the past experience of the species. The only non-genetic mode of inter-generational transmission amongst them was, he affirms, the tools themselves. If so, it follows that, in a certain sense, materialism was more applicable to them than it is to humanity proper. With them, tools *were* the only form of culture (of non-genetic transmission), whereas with men, though tools may determine it, non-material culture and semantic transmission also unquestionably exist, and in fact often are a condition of the redevelopment of tools.

Here we are faced with an interesting, challenging, precisely formulated, and, at least in principle, testable materialist and anti-culturalist anthropological theory: on the way to the process of the formation of humanity, there was no cultural or symbolic transmission, and the only non-genetic carrier of information from generation to generation was the concrete tools themselves. There was no non-genetic transmission other than that which was embodied in tools; any emulation that was not underwritten by, or incorporated in, material equipment, was evanescent. The interesting thesis is: inter-generational transmission of traits by means of tangible material equipment preceded any such transmission by ephemeral symbolic activity (i.e. by culture).

The crucial step in the argument now approaches. How does a humanity endowed with deeply internalized communistic norms, in other words a humanity exemplifying the essence with which it is now credited, come into being? Note that its emergence is made all the more problematic, in as far as its proto-human ancestors are not believed to possess any of the appropriate communal virtues, even in a rudimentary form. They were evidently *nekul'turnye* (uncultured, uneducated) proto-tool-users. Socially and morally speaking, they were not at all the harbingers, the early trial runs of humanity. On the contrary, they were, as we shall see, deeply antithetical to the values which define humanity. They conspicuously fail to provide us with any model to which we could look up. Quite the reverse: they remind us of that which we most deeply wish to avoid. They exemplify some of the worst traits of recent social forms – greed and domination.

Semenov is quite clear and explicit about these proto-humans and their unpleasant social habits: 'Amongst the proto-human units there *always* existed rather severe systems of domination.' The proto-human bands were marked by hierarchy and domination, and by unequal access to meat. 'Only the severe hierarchy prevalent amongst the herds of late proto-humans endowed the herds with the required firmness and cohesion.' So, emphatically, pre-humans not only lived in inegalitarian and oppressive units, but were positively obliged to do so by the objective necessities of their condition. They had to be horrible so as to survive at all. Survival required cohesion, and cohesion was ensured only by domination.

How then did the required transformation come about? On this account, the greatest moral revolution really took place during the palaeolithic. It was a kind of very early, protracted, and as yet unsung October. Much of the later history of mankind is but a puzzling and, thank God, eventually corrected, Reaction against this very fundamental, early, and deeply moving Revolution.

But how did it come about? It is Natural Selection which provides the main mechanism. Note that if this is correct, it follows that the early Marxism formulated by the founders in the 1840s not only did not, but *could not* supply its own Book of Genesis. Any adequate account of the social beginning of things, would have had to wait – not, admittedly, for very long – for Charles Darwin, or rather, for his decision to publish. 'And here gregarious selection came into play. It saved those herds in which the subordinated members of the herd had a good prospect of access to meat, and destroyed those amongst whom this prospect was small.'

The link between survival of a herd, and equality or near-equality of access to meat of all its members, is the following: there was of course never any correlation between high rank and tool-making talent in a pre-human herd, such rank depending largely on physical strength. Hence, and this is an absolutely crucial step in Semenov's argument, the only way of ensuring the survival and prosperity of the tool-talented was for a herd to be pervaded by an ethos which ensured meat for *all*, weak and strong alike. Such egalitarian sharing protected the tool-makers when they also happened to be weak, which must frequently have been the case. Palaeolithic intellectuals, like those of later ages, had cause to fear the hearties. Apparently there was no mechanism which could *positively* favour the innovative tool-makers; so the only way of allowing tool-use to advance was to do so indirectly, by means of a powerful egalitarianism of consumption, which would at least ensure that the tool-makers, though not faring any better than others, at least fared no worse. And this, according to Semenov, is precisely what happened.

Note that of course this explanation of the emergence of the proper egalitarian and communalistic type of mankind could be charged with biologism, or worse, with social pragmatism or something of the kind. The danger of any kind of racism is avoided by the insistence that the elimination of (insufficiently egalitarian) herds does not necessarily mean the elimination of their members:

The destruction of a herd did not necessarily mean that its members must perish. They could join other herds or form new ones. By preserving some units and destroying others, gregarious selection beat into the heads of productive beings that the deprivation of some individuals by others of access to meat, contained within itself a danger for all members of the units, jointly and severally.

Selection operated on herds and on their ethos, not on individuals and their genetic traits. It favoured those herds which imposed equal distribution of meat on its members. Evidently mankind learnt egalitarianism and communalism the hard way, and it is strange that it later also temporarily unlearnt it. But in any case, the natural selection which engendered humanity *and* communism, operated not on individuals, or on *genetically* transmissible traits, but on *socially* carried types of ethos. Social transmission of culture could have arrived no later than the emergence of a communist ethos, and jointly perhaps they define humanity. The need to *share* could only be imposed through conscious-ness and will, and these jointly constitute a new, *social* form of transmis-sion, of reproduction. But these reflected, transmitted an economic need, which was the prime mover. Thus in a crucial sense, it was communism which almost literally *made* mankind, which engendered a distinctively social, trans-biological realm.

It is amusing to note that on this point, Semenov is in almost total agreement with the arch-prophet of Western economic and other liberalism, F. A. Hayek:

[The] demand for a just distribution . . . is thus strictly an atavism.

[To build] the civilisation on which the members of present mankind depend for their lives . . . [man] had to shed many sentiments that were good for the small band . . . socialism is a result of that revival of primordial instincts . . .[11]

Hayek in effect wholly endorses the conception of primitive commun-ism as an account of our past, though of course he does anything rather than hold it up as a model for us. His account of its roots and function is very similar to Semenov's; but Hayek is eager that we should all unlearn it, and happy that some of us at least did indeed unlearn it, though we are alas vulnerable to its revival; Marxism, by contrast, wishes us to recover the possibility of expressing it fully, of releasing a potentiality which, according to its doctrine, had been so long and so painfully thwarted.

But even if the excesses of biologism are successfully avoided by Semenov, and indeed they are, as we shall see, there does remain the problem that this position appears to assimilate the social to the bio-logical. It invokes a concept – natural selection – not initially available to the Founders, so as to make good an evident major gap in their theory. In so doing, it risks corroding the theory as a whole. Marxism already possesses a theory of social change, and this theory was *not* based on the natural gregarious selection of social units. Such a 'gregarious selection' theory might perhaps have a certain appeal, but it would certainly not constitute a *Marxist* theory. Semenov clearly is aware of this danger, and stresses with emphasis the qualitative discontinuity which obtains between the initial emergence of mankind, which is allowed to be biological, and the processes which subsequently govern further develop-ments. Gregarious selection is only essential for the former, and not the latter.

11 F. A. Hayek, *The Three Sources of Human Values* (London, 1978).

This discontinuity eliminates the danger of assimilating social change to biology. But in the course of his insistence on this discontinuity, another danger appears: that of idealism. The discontinuity between biological and social nature is characterized by Semenov above all in terms of the presence of *consciousness* and *will*. It is these elements that enforce and underwrite the new communal imperative of equal sharing. But if it is these moral and intellectual elements that alone make us human and social, as opposed to remaining proto-human and biological, and if it was consciousness and will that breathed the life of humanity into mere nature, are we not in the presence of some form of idealism?

Semenov is very clearly aware of this peril and takes effective steps to avoid it: 'consciousness and will could not determine productive relations, but on the contrary, were determined by the latter. The system of social relations always acted as the objective source of the consciousness and will of men, as social being, as social matter [*sic*].' In principle, Semenov says, the effective manifestation of a general productive need and necessity required the appearance of a qualitatively new form of reflection of reality, and one which does not exist in the natural world. 'Such a form of reflection of the world is human consciousness, which emerged specially to reflect the unmaterial, intangible, invisible.' What it reflects is the *social*. Consciousness appears to have entered the world to reflect a new reality, namely *social* reality. Consciousness is not required for adaptation to nature, but for recognizing the social and transmitting its requirements. It is an interesting theory of consciousness which has its parallels in the West.[12] Thus the materialistic proprieties are observed. Though consciousness and will are essential to separate us off from the biological, nevertheless they do not constitute prime movers. They are secondary. The economic *need* is primary.

A certain circularity is to be noted, though not necessarily a vicious one, in Semenov's reasoning. It is really imposed on him by his terms of reference. The need to avoid idealism makes it impossible to use consciousness and will as prime movers in the transformation of proto-humans into humans. The role of prime mover is ascribed, in proper and orthodox manner, to objective productive relations and necessities. The trouble is, however: how do these objective necessities impose themselves on social or individual organisms? Here teleology raises its menacing head: just because a thing is 'objectively necessary', does that bring it into being?[13] How does an imperative issued by the productive

12 Cf. N. Humphrey, *The Inner Eye* (London, 1986).
13 Semenov's earlier work was criticized for its 'veiled teleologism' within Soviet scholarship. See S. A. Tokarev, 'Problemy obshchestvennogo soznaniya doklassovoi epokhy' ('Problems of Social Knowledge in the Pre-class Period'), esp. p. 269, in A. M.

infrastructure make itself heard and heeded in the social superstructure? The problem also arises for Marxism in its handling of later steps of history.[14]

However, on this occasion Semenov fastidiously and effectively avoids such teleological explanation. The need does not directly engender its own satisfaction. But he only manages to avoid this by invoking a complex variant of natural selection. This is of course the main role of 'natural selection' in the history of ideas: it enables us to explain design without invoking a Designer or designers. In this particular case, the argument runs: the advantage will go to those bands which impose equal access to meat on their own members, thus liberating the productive talents of tool-makers, who otherwise would not have survived under the pre-social palaeolithic *ancien régime*. Egalitarian communistic bands will benefit from the services of tool-makers in their own midst, and eventually replace domination-prone inegalitarian bands, who snatch the meat from innovative tool-inventors, with eventually fatal consequences for themselves as well as the hapless tool-makers.

Having so used natural selection to eliminate teleology, he is then faced with the double problem of limiting the subsequent role of natural selection, *and* at the same time of explaining the eventual non-persistence of the appropriate ethos amongst the newly successful egalitarian communalists. They might, I suppose, by palaeolithic standards, appropriately be called the *nouveaux riches/nouveaux communistes*. If natural selection alone could make us communists and human, how do we remain human without it? But if it continues to operate, have we really left the biological realm for the social? And how did the egalitarian-communalistic imperative fail to *continue* to operate?

A new, gregarious, and productive necessity had emerged with the late proto-humans, distinguishing them radically from their predecessors. This new imperative insisted on the 'liquidation of domination [*sic*]'. Yet this domination had been the main, or indeed the only, way of ensuring the inner order and external defence of the earlier groups: thus, and only thus, were they able to perpetuate themselves. Had the newly emerging unit remained a merely biological one, then even the weakening, let alone the liquidation [*sic*] of domination would have led to a loss of its unity and stability, and hence viability, and it would have perished.

Reshetov (ed.), *Okhotniki, sobirateli, rybolovy* (*Hunters, Gatherers, Fishermen*) (Leningrad, 1972). The work of Semenov's under criticism is *The Emergence of Mankind* (cit. ch. 1, n. 5 above). See also Plotkin and Howe, 'The Unknown Traditions', cit. n. 10 above.

14 Cf. David Lockwood, 'The Weakest Link in the Chain? Some Comments on the Marxist Theory of Action' in G. and I. Simpson (eds), *The Sociology of Work*, vol. 1 (New York, 1981).

Then, observes Semenov, such a group would have been unable even to achieve immediate adaptation to the environment, let alone advance the emergence of productive activity.

One might put it this way: very early mankind faced a cruel dilemma: in order to develop productive, tool-using and tool-producing activity, it was obliged to eliminate, to 'liquidate' as Semenov graphically puts it, domination. Yet at the same time it desperately needed that very domination and internal hierarchy so as to survive at all, to maintain the essential group cohesion in a cruel and violent world. Perhaps, in order to preserve that crucial social platform, from which alone the truly human enterprise of productive activity could ever be launched, some traces of domination had to be preserved. Were there, one wonders, some who maintained that the new productive order could not be established in a single band, and that all other bands had to be converted to the new order first, before the communalistic practice could become truly feasible in any single one of them? – that there had to be a Permanent Revolution – and others who, on the contrary, bravely maintained that Egalitarian Tool Production in a Single Band *was* possible? The record does not tell us.

It is quite obvious from Semenov's reconstruction that he does not believe that all bands went the same way. Egalitarianism and Tool Production in One Band (or at any rate not in *all* bands) *was* possible. Moreover, the new and the old ways were also in conflict *within* single bands. From this one can hazard the guess that the bands which went over to the new egalitarian ethos, and liquidated domination in their own midst, must nevertheless have retained some traces of domination for a time, if only to maintain cohesion during the transition and defend themselves against the hostility of more reactionary bands, which had retained the principle of domination and hierarchy to the full. Members of such more egalitarian bands were the advance guard of mankind, and they did well, on the one hand, to treasure and preserve their new and distributive egalitarianism and communalism, destined eventually to be shared by all mankind, and yet, on the other hand, not to be too impatiently critical of the surviving elements of domination in their own midst. Once the great transition was achieved and prevailed globally, these would disappear. In the meantime, these survivals helped the progressive bands to protect themselves from reactionary ones.

Semenov's account of the inner development of those bands, which constituted the advance guard of humanity, are written with an elegance and sweep and a kind of passion, and would deserve to stand alongside the great poetic and metaphysical parables of the birth of mankind. His vision is deeply moralistic and full of resonances and echoes of both Rousseau and Durkheim (neither of whom is explicitly mentioned).

Consciousness and *will* are the crucial marks of humanity, the indices of the transcendence of the merely biological, and of the appearance of the social on the cosmic scene. Will in a sense precedes consciousness:

In the earliest stage of its emergence, social consciousness in the narrower sense for all practical purposes appeared almost exclusively as social will, and this social will in its essence was reducible to one single norm – the prohibition, imposed on everyone in the proto-community, of debarring any other member from access to meat. So the emergence of social consciousness in its narrower sense was nothing other than the emergence of this prohibition.

So the root of will and consciousness lies in our need to share. The critical first element of the new ethos was the firm prohibition of special, individual property rights.

The prohibition had the form of a taboo.

. . . taboos appeared as a norm of conduct, which was imposed on society from outside as if by an extraneous force, one which could not be disregarded. The first norms of conduct had to have such a character, emerging as they did as a means of neutralizing the danger which zoological individualism constituted for the emerging community.

Here the echo of Durkheim is unmistakable, particularly so in the first sentence. Men knew not what they did, initially: 'The need for new relationships was initially seen as the danger of the old relationships, as the need to renounce them.'

Semenov does, however, give his Durkheimism a Marxian twist: the objective necessity which speaks to us through our inner compulsions is, in his version, the need for new productive relationships. It is they, rather than simply 'society', which speaks to us in this as yet un-deciphered language, and with an awe-inspiring authority.

We get a Marxian Rousseau as well as a Marxian Durkheim.

In all societies property appears . . . as a relationship of wills. In class society relationships of will are regulated by law and appear as legal. In pre-class societies willed relationships of property are regulated by morality and appear as moral. In this case we are dealing with the emerging willed relationships of property. They are regulated by the emerging will of the proto-community – by proto-morality.

. . . from the very beginning, social will was a phenomenon qualitatively distinct from individual wills and not reducible to their sum.

The heart of the matter lies in the fact that [social will] emerged as the will of the emerging social organism and thereby as the will of all the members of the proto-community, taken jointly.

Though he speaks of the social, rather than the general will, the resonance is obvious: but the will is brought into being by the need for a certain kind of economic relationship – namely, as Semenov repeatedly asserts, the supremely important imperative of equal and unhampered access to meat. Without this, in his view, tool-making society could not have developed properly. This point in the argument makes it materialist (an economic necessity remains the prime mover) and the use of natural selection avoids the danger of the argument being teleological; and the mediation of the social imperative by will, by an inwardly perceived authoritative prohibition, takes us from nature to society, and thus avoids biologism. It is not the inhibition of incest, but of greed, that made us human. It is *will* that avoids biologism; it is biology that evades teleological explanation; and it is the telos, productive need, that avoids the idealism implicit in stress on will and consciousness. The circle is tight, complete, and compact.

Marxism was meant by its founder to be an overcoming of philosophy; man would now fulfil himself in reality and no longer, German fashion, in conceptual fantasy. Notions such as the 'species-essence' of man, visible in man's social beginnings, and due to be liberated again in the Second Fulfilment, were meant to free us of the need to establish our morality, the principles of our social order, by the old and quite deluded method of seeking some outside validation and authority. That was a style of which philosophy was but the latest and perhaps the most absurd exemplar. Man, freed from alienation, was henceforth to be his own authority. But *which* man? That is the question. Post-Darwinian thought is no longer comfortable with the notion of 'species-essence' (which sounds like the immutability of species by another name). So how did we become the *kind* of man that we need to be? How do we explain and recognize the legitimate 'species-essence' of man? Here we are offered an answer to a question which too few have asked clearly, but which cannot properly be evaded.

It is ironic to find, in the work of this learned, ingenious, lucid, and coherent Soviet scholar, the reinvocation of those very themes which Western political philosophy and sociology had made familiar in its attempts to solve the problem of the foundations of social-order, cohesion and obligation. In the course of attempting to answer an insistent question, strangely evaded by other Marxists – just how had primitive communism emerged, what were the roots of its existence and of its normative authority – we find him reinvoking, once again, *nicht einmal mit sehr anderen Worten*, some of the most celebrated ideas of bourgeois thought.

So the member of the primordial communist society is not after all self-generating, he is not the basic moral and, as it were, the given socio-ontological datum – though the notion of 'species-essence' had made it seem that this was so. On the contrary, he too had to be brought into being by some kind of contingent historical process. The elements in that process turn out to be such as bourgeois thought has characteristically invoked in its explanations of its own visions of social order: natural selection, the imposition on individual wills of a general will which is more than the summation of individual wills, and the operation of collective representations which are the means of conveying and imposing social imperatives. Rousseau, Darwin, Durkheim ride again.

It is a truism in anthropology that theories of origins are parables of, and charters for, current problems and their resolution. Semenov's vision, here as elsewhere, notably in his ingenious reinterpretation of the theory of social formations,[15] is an extraordinarily apt echo of the manner in which the social and historical world must now appear to the thinking, but loyal, Soviet citizen. Humanity is at the threshold of a new era, in which scarcity will be overcome by a qualitatively new deployment of tools. The full development of those tools, however, requires a new form of social organization, more egalitarian than that which had prevailed in the past, when survival in a violent world required domination *within* society. The new world will be one which allows the tool-designers' talents to flower to the full, unimpeded by the fact that tool-designers as such may lack the talents required for coming to the fore in a competitive, greedy, domination-addicted society. The new ethos goes against the grain; it is initially felt as an obscure imposition, and may even be a handicap in the vicious inter-group conflicts. Eventually, however, societies which provide these favourable conditions for their creative members will prevail over those which oblige their members to dissipate their energies in internal and external conflict, and whose ethos is directed towards competitive domination rather than egalitarian co-operation. Then, and then only perhaps, they will be able to shed the surviving traces of domination. This prognosis surely has more plausibility by now than the apocalyptic expectation, once fashionable within Marxism, of a self-destructive explosion within capitalism, called forth by its internal contradictions.

This vision also significantly contains an explanation and justification of any seeming temporary deficiencies within the emerging new order. Does that new order contain traces of domination? That is not to be wondered at. Domination had previously been the main and indispensable mechanism of maintaining social cohesion, making possible the very perpetuation of a social group; until such time as the new mechanism, based on a fully internalized identification with social values, is firmly and effectively established, elements of the old social

15 'The theory of socio-economic formations and world history', cit. n. 9 above.

cement may be hard to eradicate completely, and may even be, *faute de mieux*, positively beneficial.

Does the new order feel, for those involved in it, painful and on occasion unintelligible? This is not to be wondered at either. Semenov says explicitly that the new moral order initially appears to the members of the emerging primordial community above all in the form of the need to overcome the earlier inward impulsions. At first, the new morality appears in a negative and painful guise. Does a measure of hierarchy and domination survive in the new order? Once again, no wonder: as long as the progressive carriers of the new ethos need to fight surviving specimens of the old, they may, alas, need to retain some of the bad old habits. Otherwise, they might be at too great a disadvantage in a form of conflict which is thrust upon them, against their will and inclination.

I do not know whether Semenov has deliberately and consciously intended to stress these parallels between the predicaments of early communalistic palaeolithic man and contemporary socialist man. What is unquestionable is that these parallels are conspicuous and resonant. No one taking the argument seriously can fail to sense them. The internal strains of the argument likewise reflect certain stresses inherent in a society living 'under the banner of Marxism'.

As many observers have noted, the Soviet Union is pervasively moralistic, closer in spirit to Victorian, rather than to contemporary Western, society. No doubt there are good sociological reasons why this should be so; but the Soviet Union is also saddled with a materialist ideology, and it is not always clear how a materialist vision of man can be enlisted on behalf of an exigent morality. We have seen that Semenov does in fact square this circle. In his argument, the new social order, the emergent primordial community, whose communism will in the end make it more effective than its internally inegalitarian rivals, operates through the inner compulsion of its members, through their newly emerging social identity. It also needs to combat their old compulsions, and may on occasion find it useful to retain some of them temporarily. But – and this is where materialist proprieties are saved – the inner categorical imperative is but the voice of objectively necessary productive relations, which thus retain ultimate sovereignty. Concrete productive necessity on earth, not a celestial authority, constitutes the foundation of ethics.

To its critics, Marxism seems morally as well as politically utopian. The two elements are of course closely connected. When the true human 'species-essence' is free to manifest itself, uninhibited by the distortions induced by property and the consequent class differentiation, and by its coercive-political protection, then, and then only, will the state, and any form of domination, become redundant and disappear. The same is true of morality, if seen as the imposition of some kind of extraneous command. The contrast 'is' and 'ought', which for Kant was an inherent part of the human condition, and which only angels could escape, was for Marx, along with political oppression, a part of pre-history. With the coming of history proper, obligation and fulfilment would become one and indistinguishable.[16] And here we come to one of the profoundest inner strains of Marxism, highlighted by Semenov's brilliant handling of the problem of the mechanics of the emergence of the primordial community, and hence of the human 'species-essence'.

In one important sense Marx not merely was no essentialist, but was a ferocious destroyer of essentialist illusions. Marxism vigorously denounces and unmasks the manner in which various social formations absolutize their own arrangements and their accompanying conceptualizations. It stresses the manner in which these accommodations merely serve a particular social order and its beneficiaries, and lack the authority and objectivity which they claim to possess. Man is equated with the totality of his social relations, and any firmer and more confirming definition is but an ideological device, intended to justify some particular set of these relations. So far so good; sociology in general has gratefully taken over this Marxist insight. But, as an essential part of the Marxist belief system, behind these spurious and ephemeral absolutizations of this or that social formation, there also seems to be a genuine, universal, inherently binding – or should one rather say, fulfilling and liberating – human essence. S. Avineri has suggested that the two views can be made comparable, by saying that the essence of man lies, precisely, in his multiform volatility.[17]

And how, pray, did this essence emerge? All we know is that it initially manifested itself under primitive communism, was alienated during the age of class-endowed societies, and is due to re-emerge again with non-primitive communism.

Marx and Engels do not seem to have given this matter too much thought, least of all during the early formulations of Marxism. The philosophical problems involved in attributing a generic essence to mankind did not seem to preoccupy them. They were evidently intoxicated with the discovery of the merely ephemeral nature of historically specific value systems, an idea they shared with German romanticism. They were busy with their own unmasking of German ideology, and with their own perception of what lay behind it.

But part of the reason for not being more worried by the essentialist

16 Cf. S. Lukes, *Marxism and Morality*, 1985.
17 S. Avineri, *The Social and Political Thought of Karl Marx* (Cambridge, 1968), p. 85.

character of the human residue, left over when historic diversity of man was understood, must be the fact that Darwinism did not yet exist and had not yet made its impact. At the very least, the non-existence of Darwinism made it incomparably easier to talk about *Gattungswesen*, about the 'species-essence'. The notion was not yet conspicuously suspect. For if there is one thing which Darwinism makes plain, it is this: there is no fixed human 'species-essence'. If species are not immutable, they can have no fixed essences either. In a double sense, Darwinism is a *specific* nominalism. Whatever one may think of essences in general, Darwinism excludes them in the sphere of biological species. These are subject to perpetual change and cannot be endowed with any species-essence. And yet, the notion of a human 'species-essence', manifested in primitive communism, seems indispensable for Marxist eschatology. The primordial community, in which that essence finds expression, is carefully upheld in Soviet anthropology.

Marxism takes great pride in seeing man as the sum total of his social relations, rather than as constrained by some essence ascribed to him by this or that social ideology. Yet behind this unmasking of ideological prescription, there lies the normative authority of a human essence. This is the basic device which endows Marxism with its moral content and authority. But Marxism also wishes to be materialist and naturalist, refusing a dualist picture of the world, and any illusory validation of values by an Other World, which is inevitably but an echo of class interests within this world. There is a deep, and perhaps insuperable, tension between this naturalism–materialism and the authority of the human Essence (revealed in the primordial community).

A Darwinist evolutionism which repudiates the very idea of any fixed species, and obliges all species to be in flux, highlights this tension, which could still perhaps be ignored in the 1840s. Darwinism in one way rounded off Marxism, by providing a new, naturalistic, non-metaphysical basis for its evolutionism. Leszek Kolakowski puts this well in connection with the views of Karl Vorlander: 'Hegel's historic-ism had played an important part in the origin of Marxism, by providing a basis for the evolutionist view of history.'[18] Biology now provided a better and more general major premiss than had previously been supplied by the metaphysics of history. But it was a Greek gift: it also undermined the notion of a *Wesen* of humanity. No wonder Marx was somewhat ambivalent about Darwin.[19] This, in addition to the fact that Darwinism provided a justificatory allegory for the market and the

18 L. Kolakowski, *Main Currents of Marxism*, vol. 2, *The Golden Age* (Oxford, 1986), p. 250.
19 Cf. David McLellan, *Karl Marx. His Life and Thought* (London, 1973), p. 423.

division of labour, made Darwin a suspect ally, even if his naturalism was welcome.

Once it is firmly recognized, under the impact of Darwinism, that species have no fixed essences, but are variable, the problem has to be faced: how did early mankind, or indeed mankind at any stage, acquire this or that 'essence', this or that basic set of traits? The great merit of Semenov's argument in this volume is that he has clearly recognized this problem, and that he faces it with great lucidity and vigour. The precise nature of human identity, of our 'species-essence', may never again simply be taken for granted or assumed to be given. After Darwin, others have sought a new, biological essence of man. Some claimed to find it in aggression, others in territoriality, or in incest-prohibition, others still in loyalty to a gene pool, or in the ever-open bricolage of adaptation. Given such a strong field of contestants, the one true and binding human essence, whatever it may be, will henceforth need to be supported by good arguments and evidence.

Whether his theory is true as well as being lucid and coherent is another question. There is a deep irony about his position. Critics of the Social Contract theory have often ridiculed it in the following terms: what if the scroll containing the original contract were located by some archaeologist, and were found to contain provisions incompatible with our contemporary political constitution – would we immediately withdraw recognition from our current authorities?

Semenov faces a similar problem. In his view the human essence, as revealed in primitive communism, retains its normative authority. But at the same time, in virtue of his own distinguished and penetrating work, that essence, its emergence and nature, have all become parts of a scientific hypothesis, good as far as it goes, but inevitably at the mercy of further archaeological and ethnographic data. I do not think he would dispute the speculative – in the best possible sense – nature of his own position. But what would happen if future data disconfirmed his ingenious theory, and if it were shown that the emergence of man the tool-maker and tool-user had come about through quite a different mechanism, not requiring that early communalistic egalitarianism, expressed and enforced by a compulsive inward commitment to equal shares of meat? Suppose it were shown that the hierarchy and domination, so characteristic of pre-human gangs, were *continuous* with the hierarchy found in class-endowed societies, without ever an interruption by a communistic primordial community? What then? Would such an archaeological demonstration commit us to the prompt dismantling of socialist societies, now deprived of their vindication by a precarious theory of man?

3

The Asiatic Trauma

V. N. Nikiforov, author of *Vostok i vsemirnaya istoriya* (*The Orient and World History*, Moscow, 1975), is a distinguished, erudite, scholarly, pugnacious, fair-minded, and committed *Pyatchik* (from the Russian pyat', meaning five). I have coined the term 'Pyatchik', which is not good or acceptable Russian, to designate adherents of the view that the number five is crucial for the understanding of human society and history, because there are five, and only five, stages of social evolution and hence five basic types of human society. The English word 'Fiver' already has another colloquial meaning and sounds vaguely ironic. 'Quintist' is possible, but does not sound quite right either. Yet we do need the concept, so as to designate a theory that is important thrice over – on merit, for its historic significance, and for its current political role – and to identify those who uphold it. Among them Nikiforov clearly deserves a place of honour.

A number of intertwined yet separable issues are involved. Perhaps the most general among them is the opposition of Pyatism to Trinitarianism. I am myself a convinced Trinitarian and hold that thinkers such as Comte or Frazer or Polanyi were right when they claimed that mankind passes through three, and only three, fundamental stages in its development. Whether or not they correctly identified the stages is another matter. Three versus five is a crucial issue, within Marxism and outside it, and within and outside the Soviet Union. I strongly suspect that Trinitarianism is the pervasive, tacit, but quite uncodified philosophy of history in the West at present; and it is also a very important, partly codified, and self-conscious strand within contemporary Russian thought, whether overt, implicit, or covert. Ironically, it is just because Soviet Trinitarianism needs to define and defend itself *vis-à-vis* the orthodoxy of Pyatism that it is perhaps better, more clearly, and more consciously argued.[1]

1 Western Trinitarianism has the form of foraging–agrarian–industrial. From a

In the West, substantive (as opposed to merely epistemological) philosophy of history, in other words the attempt to specify overall historical patterns, is highly unfashionable and suspect, and this may discourage attempts at defending one specific historical vision against others. The Trinitarianism, which is none the less pervasive, consequently remains implicit in the questions asked, rather than being overtly formulated. Such an under-the-carpet status is probably not conducive to lucid critical examination. One must wonder whether Trinitarianism is better off in the USSR, where it is lucid, but politically suspect, or in the West, where it conflicts with no orthodoxy and remains nebulous in its formulations. Moreover, Western and Eastern Trinitarianism are not quite identical in what they uphold. If a Western Trinitarian sees world history as punctuated above all by the neolithic and industrial revolutions, Soviet scholars agree with this only as regards the latter break: in practice, they do indeed classify capitalist and socialist societies together, thus at least implicitly recognizing the genus 'industrial society'. But they diverge concerning the first great *coupure*, for they are still inclined to think in terms of a primordial communalism that is not necessarily or generally pre-agrarian. Ironically, it is the West that is more materialist in making the material mode of production, rather than the form of social organization, primary in determining historic periodicization.

Pyatism is the doctrine that mankind or individual societies (all, most, or some indifferent formulations), or both, pass through five stages: the primitive-communal, slave-owning, feudal, capitalist, and finally socialist and communist. Pyatism can be attacked from a diversity of viewpoints, substantive and methodological. For instance, it is possible to deny the relevance of the idea of stages on the grounds that the self-perpetuation of every social structure has to be explained on its own terms, whereas its location within a wider evolutionary scheme – the identification of its predecessors and successors – adds nothing whatever to the explanation; or, alternatively, it is possible to deny unilinealism, the view that societies (most or all) pass through the same sequence of stages or social types, irrespective of what these may be.

The distinguished Soviet scholar Yuri Semenov, who has worked out a version of contemporary Russian Marxism significantly different from Nikiforov's, and who is one of the thinkers with whom Nikiforov polemicizes, has stressed with vigour and lucidity that the issues of

Marxist point of view, this is of course offensive in so far as capitalist and socialist societies are lumped together in a single stage. This can be avoided by means of a *quaternary* scheme, as for instance in G. A. Cohen, *Karl Marx's Theory of History: A Defence* (Oxford, 1978), esp. p. 198. But this quaternary scheme becomes a Trinitarian one if its final, quite hypothetical, stage is subtracted.

Pyatism and unilinealism are independent. Pyatchiks must be unilinealists, but unilinealists need not be Pyatchiks. It is, for instance, possible
to hold, as Semenov does, that a pan-global unilinealism, applicable to
mankind as a totality rather than to single societies, is both essential for
Marxism and valid, whilst the precise number of stages along that single
line as well as their correct characterization remains open, and can be
debated within Marxism without affecting its essence.[2]

It is possible to accept both the idea of stages as such *and* unilinealism, but to deny the claim that the five-term scheme within Marxism
correctly identifies the stages and the line of development. Trinitarians
such as myself are, I suppose, both historicists and unilinealists, at a very
abstract level, in that we hold the three stages to be inevitable and
universal, but we part company with Pyatchiks on the matter of both
identification and enumeration of the stages of the global line of
development.

A Spectre is Haunting Marxism

Nikiforov's book is a passionate and richly orchestrated defence of
orthodox Pyatism in general and against all comers; but it concentrates
on one particular attack, namely that based on the alleged existence of
one further stage, which a truly inspired typing error once specified as
the Asiatic Motor Production. The view that there is a distinct Asiatic
Mode of Production (henceforth AMP) can of course be used to
undermine Pyatism in a number of different ways, among which the
mere addition of a sixth stage to the existing five is perhaps by far the
most innocuous.

The idea of the AMP, if pushed further, as can be done most
naturally, breaks up the unity of mankind and of human history. It
suggests that the East or some parts of it are prone to a quite distinctive
mode of social organization, one absent from the West and one that is
particularly tyrannical and inimical to human dignity, liberty, and
progress, and that is specially prone to indefinite self-perpetuation and
stagnation. As Perry Anderson puts it:

Marx's . . . refusal to generalize the feudal mode of production beyond Europe
had its counterpart in his . . . conviction . . . that there was a specific 'Asiatic

---

2 Semenov, 'The theory of socio-economic formations and world history', cit. ch. 2,
n. 9 above; cf. also ch. 7 below. In a more recent work, Semenov reformulates the Asiatic
Mode of Production thesis, but deliberately gives it a new and non-geographic name, and
a very suggestive one – '*politocracy*'. In contrast to Nikiforov, he affirms that Marx never
abandoned the idea, even in the least degree, but merely refrained from using the *term*
when he realized that the social form it designated was also to be found outside Asia. See
Semenov's chapter in *Gosudarstvo i agrarnaya evolyutsiya* (*Government and Agrarian
Evolution*), ed. V. G. Rastrianikov et al. (Moscow, 1980).

mode of production' characteristic of the Orient, which separated it historically and sociologically from the Occident. . . . The political history of the Orient was thus essentially cyclical: it contained no dynamic or cumulative development.[3]

East is East and West is West. The AMP fuses Marx and Kipling – and there was indeed a distinct streak of Kipling in Marx, with his firmly stated view of the beneficial effect of the British drill sergeant on India. It is as if there were one sociological law for the West and another for the East. On one hand, such a view is uncomfortably close to racism, or at best to Western ethnocentric self-congratulation; and at another level, such a view undermines the faith in progress as a universal expectation as of right – as a salvation that may at worst be delayed, but that is present at least as a germ in *every* society.

Nikiforov's book contains two principal theses, which must be sharply distinguished: the negative claim that there is no such thing as a distinctive Asiatic type of society, comparable to, and co-ordinate with, slave-owning society, feudalism and capitalism, as a valid explanatory idea and as a stage of human society and history; and the positive thesis that Pyatism in its classical form is valid and tenable. I do not anticipate seeing many converts to his positive view (I openly avow my own anti-Pyatism and Trinitarianism); but his negative view, his critique of the notion of an Asiatic Mode, seems to me stronger. This argument, to the effect that the Asiatic Mode is incompatible with a coherent Marxism, seems to me entirely cogent. His attempt to demonstrate that the *magistral'naya doroga*, the unique historical highway, does apply, and that slave and feudal societies are regular stages of social development generally, is admirably concrete and empirical (whether or not it is cogent), though it does inspire scepticism about a typology so pliable that it can absorb Indian caste and Chinese bureaucracy in one and the same form, and do the same for Graeco-Roman and ancient Near Eastern 'slave' societies. Nikiforov is fully aware of this diversity and indeed comments on it, yet continues to find the five categories useful. His unilinealist determination to see the development of diverse societies as parallel leads him to see *too few* differences between societies, and *too many* between successive stages of the same society. As a Soviet reviewer, L. B. Alaev, says of Nikiforov's book: '. . . one must conclude: the author has not succeeded in establishing a qualitative difference between the ancient and the medieval Orient.'[4] In other words, the canonical stages do seem to be missing in the East.

---

3 Perry Anderson, *Lineages of the Absolutist State* (London, 1974), pp. 482–3.
4 L. B. Alaev, review of Nikiforov's book, in *Nauchnye Doklady Vysshei Shkoly Filosofskikh Nauk*, vol. 4, 1977, pp. 169–75.

Nikiforov *contra* Wittfogel

The most celebrated and influential book on the AMP is of course Karl Wittfogel's *Oriental Despotism*, and Wittfogel is indeed a prime object of Nikiforov's criticism. Nikiforov generally goes out of his way to maintain a high level of courtesy, insisting that disagreement should not preclude mutual respect, that scholarship progresses above all through debate, and that political interference is to be deplored. Wittfogel is one of the very few about whom he speaks harshly, describing him as a renegade from communism, a reactionary, and one eager to use the hypothesis of the Asiatic Mode for anti-communist ends. Leaving aside the emotive associations of the words used, there is nothing here that Wittfogel himself would wish to deny. Wittfogel's central point is summed up with admirable clarity and fairness: 'The point is that the Asiatic Mode of Production characterized by the absence of private ownership of the means of production – land – provided a basis for despotism in the East, and this cannot fail to suggest the idea of the inevitability of despotism under the socialist mode.' Nikiforov goes on to stress, derisively, that Wittfogel 'failed to produce even a single quotation or fact that would confirm that K. Marx and F. Engels ever perceived implications of the hypothesis of the Asiatic Mode of Production that would prove appalling for socialism'.[5] This is one of the points Nikiforov does score against Wittfogel. The Wittfogelian idea that Marx and Engels were, so to speak, Stalinists-by-anticipation, that they foresaw what was to come, and (before the event) went out of their way to spare Stalin embarrassment, is speculative, implausible, and not altogether consistent internally. Yet there is more to be said.

Consider the points on which Nikiforov seems justified. Wittfogel argues that, given Marx's premises and the data at his disposal, he *had* to endorse the idea of the Asiatic Mode; hence if he failed to do so, some extraneous considerations must have inhibited him.[6] Now the world is absolutely full of people who have eyes but see not, who on the evidence clearly before them ought to reach some sensible conclusions, but who mysteriously and perversely fail to do so. I see no reason to make an exception of Marx, and to insist that if he failed to draw a conclusion that is obvious to Wittfogel, and perhaps obvious in fact, he must therefore have been deliberately hiding or distorting something. It seems unlikely that Marx had a gift of such perspicacious and detailed

5 Nikiforov, *Orient and World History*, p. 131. All translations from the Russian are mine.
6 Karl A. Wittfogel, *Oriental Despotism: A Comparative Study of Total Power* (New Haven, 1957), p. 381.

prophetic vision, or that, mysteriously, he went out of his way to protect those who were, much later, to distort his aspirations. Wittfogel is much more plausible, though questionably consistent, when he accuses Marx and Engels of harbouring 'fanatical superstitions' – precisely as they had criticized the early Utopians.[7] But if, as is eminently plausible, they did have such 'superstitions', could they have attained *at the same time* such incredibly prescient but negative and pessimistic anticipations, and could they also have been fiendish and perverse enough then to take steps to protect those guilty of perpetuating the unwelcome distortions of their own utopian ideals? Could they *both* be utopian *and* anticipate, with dreadful and brutal realism, the coming of Stalinism? And what motives has a man for protecting those who would distort and tarnish his ideal? I do not believe Marx was so clever, or that he had any motive to be so devilish.

But it seems significant to me that while Nikiforov plausibly stresses that there is no evidence that Marx and Engels really were concerned with, or troubled by, the Asiatic or despotic potential of socialism,[8] Nikiforov's interesting list of people who are *unjustly* credited by Wittfogel with this anticipatory cover and cover-up does *not* stretch to include Lenin. Lenin's name is missing from the list, when Nikiforov argues the 'baseless misinterpretation' charge against Wittfogel. Yet, in fact, Wittfogel cites Lenin in the same context as Marx and Engels. And indeed, when we come to Lenin, Wittfogel's 'fiendish foresight' accusation ceases to be speculative, unbased on facts, or in collision with them. On the contrary, it acquires very interesting factual support. Does Nikiforov implicitly concede this charge? Wittfogel quotes a speech of Lenin's in 1921, in which Lenin singles out dangerous contemporary developments in the USSR and, without actually using the expression 'Asiatic', characterizes these undesirable, and then current, trends in terms that correspond exactly to the earlier characterization of oriental despotism: 'small production, and a bureaucracy connected with the dispersed character of the small producers'.[9] Of course, for Lenin in 1921, a sense of this kind of danger no longer presupposed any unusual prophetic powers, with which the *ex ante* cover-up theory has to credit Marx and Engels.

Even more significant than Nikiforov's failure to mention Lenin here is that while he quite plausibly contends that, contrary to Wittfogel, there is no adequate evidence to establish that Marx and Engels saw the danger to Marxist socialism lurking in the idea of the Asiatic Mode of Production, he does not deny that the notion *in fact* contains such

7 Ibid., p. 388.
8 Nikiforov, *Orient and World History*, p. 131.
9 Wittfogel, *Oriental Despotism*, pp. 399–400.

dangerous implications. On the contrary, although he does not say so in this passage, evidence from other parts of the book suggests that the AMP idea does indeed have such an undesirable potential. The general trend of Nikiforov's argument seems to be that the AMP idea is invalid *and* incompatible with Marxism, and that though Marx and Engels commendably saw this, they only perceived it rather late. It is not clear whether they ever saw the full extent of the danger.

Here we come to a paradoxical, but interesting and significant, point: in many ways, Nikiforov's position is very close to Wittfogel's. Leaving aside their politics and values, they agree on points that are by no means trivial in the history of ideas: that the idea of the AMP is incompatible with Marxism; that nevertheless Marx and Engels initially endorsed it; and that they repudiated it only later (wrongly or rightly, according to Wittfogel and Nikiforov's respective viewpoints). This leaves Wittfogel and Nikiforov firmly united against those who say that Marx and Engels never held the AMP idea at all, or that they always persisted in holding it, and that it is an integral part of Marxism. Wittfogel and Nikiforov are at one in seeing Marx's abandonment of the idea of the AMP as a very important development on this issue, though one of them sees it as a (very mysteriously motivated) betrayal, while the other sees it as a laudable advance and victory of truth and reason, without which (though Nikiforov does not say this in so many words) Marxism would have remained sadly defective. They also differ, less significantly, on the precise timing of this development: Wittfogel places what he sees as a betrayal earlier than Nikiforov dates the full self-realization of Marxism through the elimination of the AMP. They also differ, of course, in their speculation about Marx's motivation, and here plausibility would seem to be on Nikiforov's side. They diverge, finally, on the substantial question of whether the AMP actually exists in the real world. This disagreement cuts right across both the East–West and Marxist–non-Marxist oppositions. On this point, Nikiforov has radical opponents in the USSR, just as Wittfogel has radical critics in the West.[10]

10 See, e.g., Edmund R. Leach, 'Hydraulic society in Ceylon', *Past and Present*, vol. 15, 1959; Robert E. Fernea, *Shaykh and Effendi: Changing Patterns of Authority Among the El Shabana of Southern Iraq* (Cambridge, 1970); and Mark Elvin, 'On water control and management during the Ming and Ch'ing periods', *Ch'ing-shih wen-t'i*, vol. 3, 1975. See S. P. Dunn, *The Fall and Rise of the Asiatic Mode of Production* (London, 1982), and Heinz Lubasz, 'Marx's concept of the Asiatic mode of production: a genetic analysis' in *Economy and Society*, vol. 13, 1984, Marian Sawer, 'The Soviet discussion of the Asiatic Mode of Production', *Survey*, vol. 24, 1979 and her *Marxism and the Question of the Asiatic Mode of Production* (The Hague, 1977), A. M. Bailey and J. R. Llobera, *The Asiatic Mode of Production: Science and Politics* (London, 1981), John A. Rapp, The Fate of Marxist Democrats in Leninist Party-states: China's Debate on the Asiatic Mode of Production', *Theory and Society* vol. 16, no. 5, September 1987.

From Hegel to Morgan: or the Exorcism of the AMP

It is interesting to follow Nikiforov's account of Marx's development. In the West there have been diverse studies attempting to locate the precise instant of the incarnation of Marxism. These studies combine the fascination of literary, historical, and hermeneutic detective work with a deep moral significance: tell me just when you think Marxism sprang from the head of Zeus – when the *coupure* took place – and I will tell you what your values are. There is, for instance, Professor Robert Tucker's intriguing demonstration of how Marx, in the spring or early summer of 1844, invented Marxism 'in an outburst of Hegelizing', when he saw in a flash of illumination that Hegelianism was the encoded economic history of mankind.[11] If Nikiforov is right, however, Marxism proper was only completed in an outburst of anthropologizing or Morganizing around 1881.

Nikiforov does not of course say that Marxism did not exist before 1881, but argues that until then, in a profoundly important way, it had been incomplete and seriously flawed. And the flaw was, precisely, the inclusion, before the final completion or purification of the system, of the idea of the AMP. This is not a question of the addition to, or subtraction from, a system of one notion or category more or less; it is a question of the excision of something whose logical implications pervade, infect, and devalue all the rest. If this is so, then in an important sense Marxism was not fully formed until 1881, and its complete elaboration is as indebted to Morgan and Kovalevsky (and through him indirectly even to the Russian populists), just as its earlier elements were indebted to German idealism and British economics. The slogan of this interpretation could well be: from Hegel to Morgan.

In what way is the AMP so noxious for the Marxist system? In a number of ways. It impairs, perhaps destroys, the unity of human history by postulating a sideline of historical development which perhaps leads nowhere and ends in stagnation. This comes dangerously close to having two kinds of humanity, one turbulent and progressive, the other stagnant and despotism-prone. More subtly and significantly, it undermines the univocal economic theory of evil, which makes political domination a consequence of exploitation and class antagonism. Thirdly, it affects our vision of the starting-point of man's calvary. Is it specifically the East, or is it anywhere in the universal primitive community? Does human history begin in the East, as text-obsessed, old-fashioned historiography made us suppose, or does it begin much

---

11 Robert C. Tucker, *Philosophy and Myth in Karl Marx* (Cambridge, 1961).

more symmetrically with primitive bands, as a vision focused on nature rather than on written history would suppose? Hegel or Darwin? These concerns are not unknown in the West:

Perhaps the most puzzling section of *Pre-Capitalist Modes of Production* is its argument that the Asiatic mode of production does not exist – not, mind you, because nothing in Asian social history . . . corresponds [to it]. . . . [T]he Asiatic mode of production cannot exist because its 'concept' entails the self-contradictory notion of a state ruling over a classless society of peasant producers. This is, of course, a contradiction only because Hindess and Hirst hold . . . [that] states . . . exist simply to preserve a pre-existing class society. . . .[12]

This same reviewer quotes some terrible remarks from Hindess and Hirst to the effect that history only exists in terms of the present, and that 'the current situation does not exist independently of the political practices which constitute it as an object.'[13] In other words, current politics roll their own past. . . .

It should be stressed that Nikiforov's book nowhere sinks to the level of such Western private-world Marxism. He sees and stresses with clarity that the AMP is incompatible with a coherent Marxism, but his arguments against the existence of the AMP are properly historical and empirical, and hinge on whether, in fact, the syndrome of the AMP really materialized in history. He may or may not convince one, but the argument is clear, concrete, and devoid of mumbo-jumbo.

Something should be said about the distinctive, morally saturated quality of Soviet Russian discussions of modes of production or social typologies. (This applies equally to 'conservative' versions and to more daringly revisionist or dissident ones.) A Western social scientist who tries to handle the problem of classification of societies is dealing with a theoretical or technical issue, which may of course be in one way or another distantly connected with his moral commitments, his general vision of the human condition. But these connections will tend to be indirect, complex, contentious, and, above all, not something to be pursued in office hours.

The situation is quite different in Soviet and Russian *nauka*, a term closer to the German *Wissenschaft* than to the English 'science'. One has the same feeling that one may well have while looking at some medieval church mosaic, which is only incidentally and unselfconsciously *art*, but whose prime and manifest motive was to convey to those who saw it the pathos, the options, the dangers, and the final aim of human life. *This* is

---

12 Rod Aya, in an admirable review of B. Hindess and P. Q. Hirst, *Pre-Capitalist Modes of Production* (London, 1976), in *Theory and Society*, vol. 3, 1976, p. 626.
13 Ibid., p. 628.

how the sinners will be punished, and see how the torments fit their transgressions; and *that* is how the saints will be blessed; *this* is how they suffered, and behold how they will be rewarded. Yet the sufferings were necessary. If Asia would not budge on her own (an important theoretical question, as we shall see), then, Marx observed, we must approve of what the English did to India, whatever our personal feelings about it.[14] Marx went on to quote Goethe, as Nikiforov reminds us:

> Sollte diese Qual uns quälen,
> Da sie unsure Lust vermehrt,
> Hat nicht Myriaden Seelen
> Timurs Herrschaft aufgezehrt?

Loosely translated: should we torment ourselves with the thought that we have benefited (from history) – that Tamerlane's domination devoured myriads of souls? Both Tamerlane and the English, whatever their sins, are necessary agents in a global morality play.

And so it is with modes of production. These are not, or not merely, cold categories, justified simply by the contribution they make to our classification and understanding of social structures. They are far, far more than that: these are the great stages in man's calvary. To get them wrong is not merely to commit a scholarly error: like a mistake in an inscription on a martyrs' memorial, it verges on mockery of those who have suffered and died. Nikiforov quotes with warm approval Engels's remarks in *The Origin of the Family, Private Property and the State* – for the true vision had prevailed by the time Engels wrote it: 'Slavery is the first form of exploitation, appropriate to the ancient world, and after it follows serfdom in the Middle Ages and wage labour in modern times.' The main message of Nikiforov's book is exhaustiveness of these three stages or modes of exploitation and, to a lesser and qualified extent, their universality. Specifically, what matters is the exclusion of that extra, Asiatic stage. A fourth form of exploitation, distinct from alienation of the person, of the land, and then of tools under 'wage slavery', has never been located by the partisans of the 'Asiatic' hypothesis. That is the essence of Nikiforov's case.[15]

So there is no room for a fourth panel on the triptych of our calvary. The point is repeated where Engels is praised for the significant title of a work he never completed: 'Three basic Forms of Enslavement'.[16] These three forms, and three only, first noted by Saint-Simon and incorporated into the *Communist Manifesto*, cannot be complemented by a distinctive Asiatic Mode of Production.

14 Nikiforov, *Orient and World History*, p. 116.
15 Ibid., p. 30.
16 Ibid., p. 142.

Who's Afraid of the AMP?

So Pyatism is fundamental. Why so? Not, evidently, through any mystical attachment to the number five. On the contrary, Nikiforov objects to the Asiatic Mode, not because it increases the number of historic stages by one, but because of its particular properties. The Asiatic Mode of Production, as Nikiforov stresses, is defined by 'the formula well known to us: primitive community plus government'.[17] This is the heart of the matter. The other traits associated with the notion – despotism, absence of private ownership in land, irrigation, etc. – are indeed connected with these two central features, as either their precondition or their consequence.[18] Another feature which is significantly invoked, the combination of crafts and agriculture within the closed community, is theoretically *necessary* because there is no other place where crafts *could* be located. As Marx observed, there were no real cities – only spin-offs of the royal camp. There is no supra- or extra-communal urban bourgeoisie that could supply craft products to state and peasant. The initial formula excludes it.

The model defined by the formula seems to describe something perfectly conceivable, though I will not pursue the question of whether that something ever existed in historical fact. But Nikiforov seems entirely reasonable to insist that it is incompatible with Marxism – or at any rate with a coherent Marxism that upholds certain tenets. The crucial point is simple: where are the classes and the antagonisms that, according to one of these tenets, are supposed to generate political domination, and alone are capable of doing so? Not within the individual closed communities, since they are as yet undifferentiated. Perhaps between them and the despotic, hydraulic bureaucracy which dominates them? That would seem realistic enough; but just whose interests does this oppressive state machinery represent? Its own? Or that of the peasants who compose the dominated communities? Or both? One of these three answers *has* to be the right one – for *there simply is no one else* in the list of available dramatis personae, with which the formula for this mode has provided us, whose interests could conceivably be considered. No one else is present.

On a commonsensical or 'functionalist' view, the state might indeed be impelled or bound at least in part by concern with the peasants' interest. This is indeed the point at which stress on irrigation agriculture normally enters the argument. In arid lands, no agriculture without

17 Ibid., p. 146.
18 There is an admirably succinct account of the interrelation and intellectual origins of these various traits in P. Anderson, *Lineages of the Absolutist State*, 1974 p. 472.

complex irrigation works; but no edification or maintenance of complex agriculture without central direction and supervision; hence the state is necessary, and without it those communities of peasants could not exist at all, or (at best) their number would have to be drastically reduced. So the state, however despotic, is also functional: without it most of its oppressed subjects would not survive at all. Better red then dead. Better alive under a hydraulic bureaucracy than dead from famine. So the state can afford to be despotic, knowing itself to be indispensable. Perhaps it even needs to be despotic. That is the 'hydraulic' argument.

Alternatively, the state can be explained, not by invoking express or tacit calculation on the part of its subjects about the relative merits of starvation and oppression, but simply by the self-interest of the soldiers and officials who man it. They do very nicely out of it, thank you, and given that they control the necessary means of coercion and persuasion – which may or may not include rational calculation on the part of their subjects – they will keep the system going.

The two explanations – the functionalist and the despotic – can of course be combined. There is no incompatibility between them. In practice most societies that look like candidates for the AMP also possess additional ideological legitimation, which may or may not be of significant help in securing compliance from their subjects. But above all the despotic organization serves either the peasants or itself, or both. *There is no one else*.

But either of these explanations (and *a fortiori* their conjunction) is quite incompatible with the theoretical requirement that the state can only emerge as the consequence or reflection of *pre-existing* class antagonism and exploitation. There is of course an old theory of such an independently existing state, whether conceived as malevolently self-serving, or as above-the-battle-and-neutral and beneficial, or as some combination of these. Peter Nikitich Tkachev, for instance, maintained in the nineteenth century that the Tsarist autocracy did not emanate from Russian society, but 'hung in thin air'. Much to Nikiforov's delight, Friedrich Engels let Tkachev have it straight from the shoulder: 'It is not Russian government, but rather Gospodin Tkachev himself, who hangs in thin air.'[19] Whatever the fate of the levitating Gospodin Tkachev, whom Engels also accused of generating pure hot air, it is most essential for Marxist theory that *governments* at least should not hang in thin air. Their inability to do so would seem to be an essential part of the materialist conception of history. That materialist conception is violated equally, whether these levitating governments are impelled by brutal self-interest, or whether they float benevolently, like a Madonna on a

19 Nikiforov, *Orient and World History*, p. 136.

mural, in the interests of reconciling and furthering the needs and wishes of their subjects, or both. For present purposes, the distinction is immaterial.

Nikiforov's insistence here is, ironically, the same as Wittfogel's: the possibility that government should be either functional (and constitute the genuinely essential precondition of satisfying a shared social need), or evil, but self-sufficient and self-serving (propelled into existence by the availability of means of coercion, and not rooted in any prior social malady), is indeed either way incompatible with an eschatology and theodicy that see domination as the price or consequence of an economic ill – of *prior* exploitation, appropriation, property, and class antagonism. When these go, the derivative evil of domination will also go. This vision is clearly contradicted by either a functional or a self-serving despotism. If such despotism is possible, it also follows that it cannot be exorcised by the canonical methods that orthodoxy specifies.

Apart from the manifest head-on collision of the AMP with Marxist orthodoxy, there is also a set of minor contradictions between them. The stability of Asian despotism, whether in the model or in the real societies that are held to exemplify it, would also seem to undermine the eschatological hope, inspired by ever-present change and conflict: for it is the pervasive and fermenting internal 'contradictions' of societies that would guarantee instability and thus justify hope for progress. Marx himself tended to think of the Orient as stagnant, as when he remarked that the English brought India its only *social* revolution (as opposed to, presumably, mere gyrations of tribes or dynastic merry-go-rounds); and Nikiforov does not hesitate to correct Marx at this point for saying what, in Nikiforov's view, he could not possibly have meant literally.[20]

The notion of the Asiatic Mode thus destroys the crucial Marxist diagnosis of the general ills of mankind (the identification of *the* original sin) by allowing the existence of another and independent sin (namely functional or self-serving political domination), and thereby also undermines the hope of a guaranteed salvation tied to the eradication of that one and only original sin. Perdition then becomes, so to speak, uncontrollable, *freischwebend*, ineliminable. The unity of human history and of the human race itself is thus also impaired: mankind falls apart into two halves, one dynamic and destined for salvation, the other static and either doomed to perpetual damnation or at best only available for salvation through the efforts of others. For this other half, revolutionary salvation will have to be imported. It will be its passive beneficiary,

20 Ibid., p. 117. By contrast, Yuri Semenov willingly invokes Marx's remarks about Oriental stagnation and takes them at full and face value ('The theory of socio-economic formations', pp. 55–6).

receiving it gratefully, as once it was supposed to receive *civilization*. Once again, it is instructive to compare Nikiforov's version of Marxism with Semenov's. Semenov evidently has no such strong aversion to a vision of Orientals open only to a grant-aided, exogenous salvation. If Nikiforov and Semenov were to be used as charters of alternative Soviet policies towards China, then clearly Nikiforov would suit the doves and Semenov the hard-liners.

The difference between these two versions of Soviet Marxism has a curious resemblance to the erstwhile dispute in the West between Lévi-Strauss and Sartre, in which Lévi-Strauss reproached Sartre for ethnocentrically making much of mankind available for salvation only by incorporation in the 'dialectic' of the West.[21] Nikiforov, like Lévi-Strauss, repudiates such unsymmetrical and Western-ethnocentric theories.

In Nikiforov's version, man's calvary does not begin on the Nile or between the Tigris and the Euphrates; it does not begin at any one place or time at all. It begins all over the place in the primitive community, the *p'ervobytnaya obshchina*, which is basically the same everywhere: no property, no classes, no antagonism, no state. It is not only much the same everywhere, at least to the extent of everywhere exemplifying the same social form; it is also much the same at all times; specimens of it even survive into the modern period, as elements within more complex and class-endowed societies. Our beginning remains ever with us, virtually till the present day. Nikiforov comments on how very many class-endowed societies were once but islands in a sea of primitive communities.

How Morgan Saved Marxism

For Nikiforov, the discovery or rediscovery of the 'community' was crucial to that final crystallization or coming to full self-awareness of Marxism, which on his view came so strangely late, in 1881. And one particular anthropologist is the hero of this story, namely, Lewis Henry Morgan. In Nikiforov's version of Marxism, Morgan acquires the status of a key contributor to its theoretical wealth, alongside the more obvious and much earlier names, notwithstanding the late hour at which Marx encountered his work: 'The new achievement of science, which radically changed the conceptions of primitive society, and enabled K. Marx and F. Engels to make a new approach to the problem of pre-capitalist formations, was L. H. Morgan's discovery of tribal social structure'

21 Claude Lévi-Strauss, *The Savage Mind* (London, 1966), ch. 9.

(*otkrytie L. G. Morganom rodovogo stroia*).[22] Engels is quoted as saying that only this provided a solid basis for primitive history, and Nikiforov significantly observes that only thus was it possible to complete the 'harmonious structure' of the Marxist theory of (social) formations, which concludes with 'prevalence – in the distant past and the more or less distant future – of the communal ownership of the means of production'.[23] What is essential is that this line separating the presence and absence of communal ownership should *not* cut across the line between non-oppressive and oppressive (state-endowed) societies: the idea of the AMP does precisely this, by postulating a social order devoid of private property yet highly oppressive. It provides an example of political oppression without an economic root.

Morgan's discovery of the principles of tribal organization links us to our true tribal past. Nikiforov points out that this shift of vision led Engels to add an important new phrase to the 1888 English edition of the *Communist Manifesto*, qualifying the famous statement that all history is the history of class struggles by adding the remark: 'That is, all *written* history.' So, it appears, it was the *un*written sources of archaeology and ethnography that modified this generalization. They were, Engels noted, 'all but unknown' in 1847. Yet without them, Nikiforov argues, Marxism could not be correctly formulated.

So the prehistory of societies and communal organizations was almost wholly unknown in the 1840s, and the real context of property-lessness could not then be understood. But more than that, this discovery seemed to replace the linear philosophy of history, characteristic of Hegelianism, which leads from slavery to freedom, by a new, so to speak, 'detour' soteriology that is distinctively Marxist; from freedom to freedom via alienation – since communal ownership is apparently established by Morgan's findings for *both* the distant past *and* the future.

In our end is our beginning. This semicircular pattern of history, interestingly enough, is linked (as stated) to a more naturalistic and less historicist vision. The semicircular naturalistic picture is this: history begins with any or every internally undifferentiated primordial community; through internal differentiations, it takes a bitter detour through three modes of alienation, and finally returns to an undifferentiated, classless, and stateless condition. By contrast, the earlier, more Hegelian, linear-historicist pattern was: history begins in the despotic East and culminates in the free West. Nikiforov gives the impression that the Founders of Marxism moved from the latter vision to the

22 Nikiforov, *Orient and World History*, p. 144.
23 Ibid., pp. 146, 148.

former, thanks to the empirical discovery of the 'community' in the 1870s.

Morgan was crucial for this development. Engels is quoted as observing that: 'Within the limits of this subject, Morgan independently rediscovered Marx's materialist conception of history.' Government could not occur in primitive society; hence the Asiatic Mode is impossible, for government in it would have to *create itself*, there being no classes within society that could engender it. This then enabled Marx to sneer at the outmoded fantasy of despotism in primitive society, a fable that was 'John Bull's main and favoured doctrine, as he becomes intoxicated with primitive "despotism"'.[24]

As Perry Anderson points out, the first person to blame John Bull for concocting this fable was one Anquetil-Duperron, in 1778, whose sentiments have earned him accolades as an early anti-colonialist. Anderson maliciously shows that Anquetil-Duperron was merely a disappointed rival colonialist, regretting the French defeat in the carve-up of India and campaigning for a French return to the subcontinent.[25] Anquetil-Duperron earned Marx's approval as the first man to deny the Great Mogul's exclusive possession of land under his control. So it was, Nikiforov observes, that Marx finally overcame two centuries of error concerning the socio-economic structure of the East. But Morgan was essential for this final demystification.

From Russia with Love

Morgan did not, however, achieve this alone or without a mediator. Russian developments in the 1870s, Russian thought, and one Russian in particuar, M. M. Kovalevsky, played a crucial part. Morgan was not the only person to discover the community in the 1870s, and the Iroquois were not the only people to have maintained the community into modern or near-modern times. Besides the Iroquois there were the Russian *muzhiki* (peasants); besides Morgan there were the Russian populists.

The closeness, in space and time and moral relevance, of the very beginnings of human society to *us*, for anyone thinking and living within this conceptual framework, is something that ought to be noted here. As indicated, the taxonomy of social forms contained in Pyatism is not just an analytic classification; it is the graphic portrait of man's struggle and suffering, of the successive forms of human bondage. But the first step

24 Ibid., pp. 146, 145.
25 Anderson, *Lineages of the Absolutist State*, pp. 465–6 with footnote.

on this path still remained so close that we could, at any rate in the nineteenth century, literally touch it.

Human history and the social forms it exhibits not only are morally significant, they are also intimate and close; they are part of world history, which is foreshortened, not just chronologically, but also through the paucity in number, the ready intelligibility, the easily available exemplification, and the moral saturation and political relevance of the social forms found in it. Just as love is different in a cold climate, so anthropology is rather special in a populist country. Once again, one feels as if one were seeing some mosaics which graphically sum up the human situation, but their dramatic impact and intelligibility are heightened because there are so *few* of them. Our destiny is dramatic, but its options and stages are few. The story has drama and pathos, but also great simplicity.

It was indeed the moral and political significance of the primitive community that led the Founders of Marxism to it:

In our view, it is particularly in the study by Marx and Engels of Russian materials in the 1870s, that we must search for the point of departure, which prepared the ground for the change of view by the founders of Marxism concerning the historical development of the East. What is at issue is their investigation of problems concerned with rural communities. In effect, the periodic redistribution of land – that significant survival of communal ownership – was incomparably more common [in Russia] than in India. Russia, like Oriental countries, has a despotic government. On the other hand, Russia in the 1870s was an unambiguously European country, with bourgeois and pre-bourgeois forms of private ownership of land. . . .

Russian populists, disregarding one aspect, the growth of capitalism, absolutized and idealized the other, the communal organization.[26]

The tendency of populism to idealize the peasant was the obverse of its tendency to put the blame on governmental oppression and violence, without seeking its class roots. The two errors and their connection are both highly relevant.

Nikiforov stresses that after the failure of the Paris Commune and the termination of the First International, Marx and Engels gave much attention to revolutionary Russia. This involved taking over ideas about the distinctive role of the rural community, in part from Herzen, Bakunin, and Chernyshevsky, and in part directly from the Slavophiles, but without repeating the mistake (which had once been built into the idea of the AMP) of seeing governmental authority as possibly independent of these communities. As Nikiforov rightly observes, by endorsing the class-transcending conception of government and of the creation of

26 Nikiforov, *Orient and World History*, p. 135.

social forms by government, the views of the *narodniki* (populists) coincided with those of the liberal Westernizers, even if the latter viewed the community with contempt as an artificial offspring of central policy. The supposition that human society can be based on violence is but the general form of an error of which the AMP is the most significant single example. No wonder that Plekhanov was tempted by the AMP and even applied it to Russia: 'As is well known', Nikiforov reminds us maliciously, Plekhanov reached Marxism from populism. What can you expect from people like that?

But among these Russians, the one who made the greatest contribution, and at various levels, was M. M. Kovalevsky. In him the two currents whose inclusion of the great river of Marxism was to save it from the previous error of the AMP – the current flowing from the Iroquois and the one flowing from the *muzhik* – merged into one mighty tributary, ready to enter and enrich the mainstream. Kovalevsky is both a *causa essendi* and a *causa cognoscendi* of the final, crucial self-correction of Marxism. He helped bring it about; but also, thanks to him (or, specifically, to Marx's annotations of his book) we *know* about it, or at any rate Nikiforov does. On the one hand, the notes Marx made on Kovalevsky's book about communal land tenure are crucial for Nikiforov's case and for his detective work concerning Marx's illumination on this point. Nikiforov claims that it is Marx's notes on Kovalevsky which justify the conclusion that Marx saw the presence from early times in India of private ownership of land, coexisting with collective communal land (and hence *not* the alleged 'Asiatic' monopolization of land by the state), and that he saw the progress of 'feudalization' in medieval India, and (like Kovalevsky) considered this process to be uncompleted. A critical reader may find some of Nikiforov's reasoning less than fully cogent. For instance, he stresses that while Kovalevsky's book is very hostile to the thesis of exclusive state ownership of land in the Orient, Marx's notes contain not a single objection to this tendency of the work. Marx's failure to comment is treated as assent.[27]

Absence of private property, especially in land, is central to the idea of the AMP. The demonstration of the pervasive existence in Oriental polities of private landownership is thus crucial for Nikiforov's demolition of the idea of the AMP. Private ownership *had* been absent, but *only* in the primordial commune, and *not* in any centralized polity. (Perry Anderson also uses Marx's annotation of Kovalevsky to reach a partially different conclusion.[28]) Kovalevsky was also familiar with North African material, and Marx's annotations make it clear that he saw this. So one

27 Ibid., pp. 138, 137.
28 Anderson, *Lineages of the Absolutist State*, pp. 405–7.

has the feeling that by the late 1870s, tribesmen and peasants from all over the world – Iroquois, Kabyles, *muzhiks*, Indian villagers – were converging on Kentish Town and angrily insisting that the record be put straight. The commune then replaces the Oriental despotism as the one and only place where private landownership really was lacking. The negative fact – the lack of critical comment by Marx in his private notes on Kovalevsky's book – leaps to the eye, Nikiforov says, and it seems to him very weighty, establishing that Marx accepted the presence of private landownership in India, and hence the non-existence of the AMP.

Against this, Nikiforov has to explain away Marx's comment on a book published in 1880 by an English lawyer, Sir John Budd Phear: 'That ass Phear describes the organization of the [Indian] rural community as feudal.'[29] Nikiforov would have us believe that Phear was an ass only for describing the *internal* organization of the Indian commune in this way. Poor Phear seems rescued from oblivion only by being called an ass by Marx in two languages, German and Latin; Marx even describes him, in that Anglo–German mix he used for his jottings, as a 'respectable *Esel* [ass]'. With ironic condescension, Marx also repeatedly refers to Phear as a *Bursch* ('lad').[30] Evidently, in Nikiforov's view Phear could have avoided this fate had he spoken of society *as a whole* as feudal (correct), rather than so describing its constituent communities (wrong). Nikiforov insists that Marx at that time had endorsed the feudalization of Indian society as a whole, even if it was not complete – whatever his view of the quality of Phear's intellectual equipment and maturity.

But, on the other hand, Kovalevsky's role in crystallizing the correct version of Marxism, purged of the AMP, was not merely the passive one of provoking the evidence found in Marx's notes on him. He was also an active agent. Kovalevsky acquired a copy of Morgan's *Ancient Society* on a visit to the United States. In the late 1870s, he was a frequent visitor to Marx's household in London, and even lent his own copy of Morgan's book to Marx. At the same time, he was of course in a good position to put Marx in touch with Russian material. The impact of Morgan's work on Marx is shown in the drafts of his reply to Vera Zasulich's letter, where he alludes directly to Morgan.[31]

29 Karl Marx, *Ethnological Notebooks*, ed. Lawrence Krader (Assen, 1972), p. 256.
30 Ibid., pp. 281, 262, 271.
31 Nikiforov, *Orient and World History*, pp. 110, 144. Marx alludes to Morgan in the second draft of his reply to Vera Zasulich, written in late February or early March 1881 (Karl Marx, 'Drafts of a reply [Feb.–Mar. 1881]: the "first" draft', in *Late Marx and the Russian Road: Marx and 'the Peripheries of Capitalism'*, ed. Teodor Shanin (London, 1983), p. 107). On why the 'first' draft was actually the second, see Haruki Wada, 'Marx and Revolutionary Russia', ibid., pp. 63–9.

According to Nikiforov, these drafts also prove his repudiation of the notion of the AMP, because the term no longer appears; instead, there is reference to the 'archaic formation'. This would not seem conclusive on its own, Nikiforov admits, for it would be compatible with merely renaming the AMP and treating it as the last stage of primitive communal organization (as indeed some have done). Nikiforov replies that the drafts of Marx's answer to Vera Zasulich do not even once mention government – which had always been present in earlier discussions of the AMP, as indeed it should be – but proceed instead to invoke Morgan's general thesis, in which there is no room for the AMP.[32]

I have the feeling that Nikiforov exaggerates the Hegel-to-Morgan transformation of Marx. Nikiforov's young Marx seems to be a kind of Hegelian for whom history begins in the East with despotism; his old Marx is a man enlightened by the facts of Russian, Indian, and other communities, who is liberated from Anglo-French colonialist slanders about the East, and who is committed to a vision of development more Darwinian than Hegelian, in that it is not blinkered by text-bound history, but places man in the context of prehistory and anthropology – and all this thanks to Morgan and his mediator, Kovalevsky. Nikiforov's late Marx thus deprives the Orient of the glory of *initium*, of starting history, but also of the indignity of stagnation and passivity in the face of despotism. Nikiforov himself may feel he is pressing his case too hard and perhaps rushing in where Engels fears to tread, for he remarks apologetically: 'After all, all these facts are not brought forward by us with the aim of denying the indisputable fact that Engels was the sole author of *The Origin of the Family, Private Property and the State*, and responsible for its conception.'[33]

Let us leave the question, which each reader must answer for himself, of whether Nikiforov clinches his case that in, or by, 1881 Marx firmly changed his mind and eliminated the AMP from his scheme. Nikiforov fully persuades me, however, that there is indeed no room for the AMP in a Marxism that requires the state to be endogenously generated by class conflict, nor in one that is to give us faith in the state's eventual disappearance under conditions of classlessness. In other words, the very notion of the AMP contradicts both the story of the Fall *and* the hope of Salvation. On this, Nikiforov and Wittfogel are agreed; on the question of Marx's motivation, Nikiforov's theory seems to me more plausible, though it does rather questionably assume full consistency in the Marxist scheme, and in its formulation in Marx's mind.

32 Actually, Marx's first and second drafts do mention 'a central despotism above the communes' ('Drafts of a reply', pp. 103, 111).
33 Nikiforov, *Orient and World History*, p. 147.

The Primordial Community and its Political Implications

Needless to say, the reformulated Marxist doctrine is full of practical-political implications, which indeed played a crucial part in crystallizing the true picture. Its attainment was a political as much as a scholarly achievement, for it involved seeing the true role of the rural masses, in communities, *in our time* as well as in the distant past. They were potential allies, not inert obstacles or opponents. It all affects the interpretation of, on the one hand, backward societies such as nineteenth-century Russia and, on the other, the erstwhile colonial, now 'Third' World. As Teodor Shanin puts it: '. . . the future of Russia was seen as dominated by the peasantry . . . the majority of the nation. . . . Marxism and Populism . . . formed, together with varying degrees of revolutionary voluntarism, the hard core of Russian revolutionary ideology.'[34]

For instance, the formula rightly held to sum up the essence of the Asiatic Mode, namely primitive community plus government, is still admitted by Nikiforov to have application, and he quotes a letter from Engels to Kautsky of 1884 which makes this perfectly plain: but the AMP is here seen only to arise as a result of the extraneous imposition of government on the primitive communities. The case described in Engels' letter is Java, and the imposition of domination from the outside was carried out by the Dutch. This handling of the matter faces both empirical and theoretical difficulty. A reading of Javanese history that could treat Javanese society simply as primitive-communal prior to colonialism is somewhat implausible, though perhaps the pre-Western state formations could also be credited to other (e.g. Muslim and Hindu) intruders; and at a more fundamental level, there are difficulties for Nikiforov in the whole notion of diffusion, of the explanation of social forms not by the logic of their internal development, but by the transplantation of ideas, institutions, or personnel. In this 'Javanese' passage, Nikiforov seems to be saying, in effect, that what is not possible as a natural endogenous growth (i.e. the AMP) is nevertheless perfectly possible as the result of the impact of one society on another. But, given the frequency with which societies do indeed make an impact on each other, is there not the danger that this qualification might in the end allow too much? So, significantly and interestingly, Nikiforov characterizes diffusionism as an 'idealist' doctrine, which indeed it must be if everything non-materialist is idealist, and if materialism requires the endogenous development of societies.[35] All the

34 Teodor Shanin, *The Awkward Class: Political Sociology of Peasantry in a Developing Society: Russia, 1910—1925* (Oxford, 1972), p. 47.
35 Nikiforov, *Orient and World History*, p. 247.

same, no one can deny that some diffusion has occurred in history. The question is: how much of it can be allowed without submerging the original endogenous view?

So something resembling the recipe for the AMP has in fact existed, but only as a result of extraneous superimposition of a governmental apparatus on primitive communities. But what about correct political strategy in societies where the community still survives in some measure? It is precisely this question that, on Nikiforov's view, led to the final, correct formulation of Marxism. If the material for the correct assessment of prehistory was lacking until 1877, the year of Morgan's crucial work, as Engels asserted, then the situation that inspired the correct *Fragestellung* in the minds of the Founding Fathers existed as of 1871. The failure of the Paris Commune on the one hand, and the emergence of a revolutionary movement in Russia on the other, led them to reassess the role of the rural community. Marx studied Bakunin, Engels polemicized with the levitating Gospodin Tkachev. The outcome, Nikiforov observes, was a fundamental revaluation of the community. In the 1870s, 'they reached the conclusion of the possibility of using the community for a peaceful transition of backward countries to socialism, bypassing developed capitalist society'.[36] The transition can never, however, be direct and unaided. It will only be possible if the community does not disintegrate before there has been a victorious proletarian revolution in Western Europe, which alone will provide the Russian peasant with the preconditions for such a transition. Instead of the White Man's Burden, there would seem to be a kind of *mission civilisatrice du prolétariat*. Moreover, the community will only prove its capacity if (in Engels's words) it is able 'to develop in a manner such that peasants will no longer till the soil separately, but together'. One wonders whether this text or similar ones were not crucial for the establishment of kolkhozy (collective farms).[37]

Nikiforov goes on to observe that the dream of Russian thinkers about a non-capitalist path, which had remained a mere utopia in the hands of Chernyshevsky, only became scientific when Marx and Engels combined it with the idea of a proletarian revolution in the West.[38] Populism is the Pelagian heresy of Marxism. It teaches the possibility of independent, unaided salvation for retarded communities by their own efforts. From a Marxist point of view, it was important to encourage hope and effort, and yet not allow anyone the illusion of the dispensabil-

---

36 Ibid., p. 134.

37 On the interaction of ideological and social constraints in establishing and organizing of collective farms, see Caroline Humphrey, *Karl Marx Collective: Economy, Society and Religion in a Siberian Collective Farm* (Cambridge, 1983).

38 Nikiforov, *Orient and World History*, p. 135.

ity of Grace – for the proletariat still retained the monopoly of Grace. *Extra plebem nulla salus*.

This reassessment seems to have been due to the interaction of diverse elements – the populist 'discovery' of the community, the geographical displacement of revolutionary zeal, and the desire to find theoretical warrant for some measure of optimism on its behalf. Prior to this period, the community, though known to exist, was sadly deficient in great potential for either good or evil, for salvation or damnation. It was also not clear how, or indeed that, it was capable of initiating the historical process and giving birth to class society, from its own resources, so to speak: Engels seemed willing to consider the possibility of the state being set up by the conquest of one tribe by another, without pre-existing class antagonism.[39] On the other hand, if the rural community survived as part of complex class society, it was inert and reactionary. The commune, you might say, was an object, not a subject, of history – contributing from its inner resources little that was essential to the expulsion from Eden, and even less to the eventual redemption.

Perry Anderson derides Marx for simultaneously treating the Indian village community as primordial and as stagnant, thus 'squaring the circle'.[40] Nikiforov himself quotes Marx as speculating whether the English conquest was necessary if India was ever to move. But if this were so, how could history get started? One may suppose that Marx was not so much inconsistent as tacitly relying on a non-endogenous (e.g. conquest) initiation to history. But that leads to more trouble still. Nikiforov seems to me right: if force is ever allowed to be a prime mover in history, and not merely an echo of prior class antagonism, the whole Marxist system becomes faulty. If violence came spontaneously and independently, why should it ever leave us – and why should it not return if expelled? Salvation can only be guaranteed if the source of evil is known and eventually controlled, if the jinn can be put back in the bottle, and if in fact there is only one jinn. If not, evil cannot be eliminated. It is curious that Western Marxists such as Perry Anderson and Maurice Godelier, who avoid these difficulties by including political or other 'superstructural' elements in their definition of social forms, are not worried about this

---

39 Cf. Wittfogel, *Oriental Despotism*, p. 383. It is also hard for Nikiforov's thesis that in 1894–5, Engels returned to a stagnant/cyclical view of the East, though this time echoing the views of Ibn Khaldun – which also seem to have been brought to his notice by the universal cross-fertilizer, Kovalevsky. Cf. Ernest Gellner, *Muslim Society* (Cambridge, 1981), pp. 46–7, and the references cited there, as well as Bryan S. Turner, 'Orientalism, Islam and capitalism', *Social Compass*, vol. 25, 1978.

40 Anderson, *Lineages of the Absolutist State*, p. 490.

problem.[41] Unless it is solved, Marxism has no logical warrant whatever to promise social salvation.

The AMP and the China Lobby

To recapitulate Nikiforov's argument: the political exigencies and opportunities of the 1870s (the failure of the Paris Commune, the emergence of a revolutionary movement in Russia, the populist stress on rural communities) led Marx and Engels to reconsider the inadequacy of the community as an agent, ally, or catalyst of the future: perhaps, if purged of the utopianism that pervaded it in the hands of the populists, there might be something to this idea. Then came Morgan, who showed that the community led *directly* to class societies, from an inner compulsion, not necessarily requiring conquest, and that basically the same mechanisms were to be found among the Iroquois and in the ancient Mediterranean. And when Kovalevsky, who had already done well by history in introducing Marx to Russian material, also lent him his copy of Morgan's book, brought from America, all this flowed together. Before, the AMP had been required at the start of history – to set history proper going, history being the history of class struggle. The primordial community, an Eve without sex appeal, had hardly been capable of triggering it all off. The AMP had also been needed at the end, to explain the stagnant passivity of certain societies. Now it was no longer needed either at the beginning or at the end. Eve herself was seen as capable of arousing passion and action. And the AMP was no longer needed to explain the absence of private property in land in the East. This absence of private landownership, in class- and state-endowed societies, was exposed as a myth. Nikiforov insists that this syndrome has always been located by scholars in whatever Oriental society was at their point of time least well studied and understood. The primordial classless and stateless community, which alone really possessed this negative trait, and occasionally preserved features of it even when incorporated into larger wholes, thus led to the crucial mistake. Nikiforov makes clear that European ethnocentrism, which projected stagnant despotism and absence of private landownership onto the East, and used it to justify its own domination and expropriation there when convenient, had also been willing to do this to Russia. Indeed, some Russians were willing to speak of themselves in this manner. The same mistake had also led to a failure to perceive revolutionary potential anywhere in the East. Wogs begin at Calais, and the Asiatic Mode of Production began on the Niemen.

41 Cf. ibid., pp. 403–4, and Maurice Godelier, 'Infrastructures, society, and history', *Current Anthropology*, vol. 19, 1978.

Thus the central point of Nikiforov's argument is this: the elimination of the idea of the AMP is the obverse of the correct assessment of the historic role of the primordial community. The AMP had been a kind of theoretical cloud of unknowing, obscuring the crucial and dynamic role of the rural community, whether at the start of history or during its later stages, in our own time. Absence of private ownership of land *does* occur, but not in any of the class-endowed stages of man's historical ordeal. (That disastrous error is the very essence of the AMP.) It occurs only at the start and at the end, before and after the ordeal. The harmony (Nikiforov's own word) of the theoretical structure of Marxism is thus recovered.

It is also interesting to consider the implications of Nikiforov's analysis, as noted by himself, for contemporary political issues.[42] As he observes, 'Some authors try to make use of the materials drawn from the discussion of pre-capitalist formations, to explain the causes of recent changes in China. They consider the temporary domination of Maoism a rebirth of the Asiatic Mode of Production or its survival.'[43] Two authors, Yu. Ostrovityanov and A. Sterbalova, are cited as holding this view. But Nikiforov's polemics become even more interesting when he argues with L. V. Stepanov and A. V. Meliksetov. Stepanov apparently coined the term 'statist-peasant' to characterize the Maoist regime in China. Meliksetov seems to have taken the term over and extended it to cover class societies throughout the whole of Chinese history. Meliksetov, as quoted from a symposium on China published in Moscow in 1968, argues as follows: 'Economic, objectified relations, expressed in the circulation of goods, played a big role in the life of traditional Chinese society, but what nevertheless dominated were personal relations, for the general unifying force of small, mutually isolated producers could only be political association, political power, i.e., government'. Nikiforov points out, dismissively, that all this – domination by personal, non-economic relations, by a government divorced from classes – has already been dealt with. Indeed, this is what the AMP debate is all about. But Meliksetov, as Nikiforov reports, takes the argument further and into the present. China in his view had always, in antiquity and the Middle Ages, been characterized by the dominance of state ownership and the suppression of private property. Sun Yat-sen's teaching combined traditional principles with some Western elements and proposed a non-capitalist line of development for China. Chiang

42 Cf. Samuel H. Baron, 'Marx's *Grundrisse* and the Asiatic Mode of Production', *Survey*, vol. 21, 1975, pp. 94–5, and Sawer, 'The Soviet discussion of the Asiatic Mode of Production', p. 108. See also Gilbert Rozman, *A Mirror for Socialism. Soviet Criticisms of China* (London, 1985).
43 Nikiforov, *Orient and World History*, p. 268.

Kai-shek, invoking Sun Yat-sen, also followed this line. Thus only the externals change; the class essence of these various military-bureaucratic dictatorships remains unchanged. But if this were so, Nikiforov asks, how could one explain peasant revolt against landlords under the Guomindang, or the deadly enmity between the Guomindang and the Communist Party?

It is of course perfectly clear what Meliksetov is up to. He is doing unto Maoist China what Wittfogel was endeavouring to do unto Stalinist Russia. Nikiforov, very consistently, rejects such an analysis, and repeats emphatically that the AMP, the ideas of non-economic determining factors, personal relations, etc., are as baseless in contemporary history as they are in the past.[44] If an idea is indefensible in serious analysis, it cannot be used for political denigration either. And though Nikiforov derides political interference with scholarship in Mao's China, including the willingness to treat the Chairman as 'the final court of appeal on issues of ancient history', he does not stoop to attributing such habits to Asian traditions. When he earlier mentions that a mistaken theory was *also* discredited politically, 'compromised . . . by its employment by Trotskyists', he punctiliously separates the scholarly and political issues.[45]

One might put it this way: the obverse of the 'optimistic' discovery of the community in the 1870s, of its progressive potential (though *only* if allied with a proletariat), is the *pessimistic* rediscovery of the AMP. Both concern the consequences of 'progressive' strivings in a backward country. If the formula for the optimistic discovery is the community-proletariat alliance, which saves at least one of the partners from having to pass through the capitalist stage, then the formula for the alternative and pessimistic diagnosis is that the very endeavour to bypass capitalism, in a society whose basic form is the AMP, results in stagnation or even deterioration under a new name and with new equipment of domination. Does this apprehensive view preclude, as Nikiforov suggests by way of refutation, social turbulence or bitter conflict between rivals for control of the new superstructure? If Nikiforov is one kind of Sovietski Wittfogel, in his acute sense of the incompatibility of the AMP with Marxist theodicy, and in his, all in all, similar view of Marx's intellectual development, then Meliksetov resembles Wittfogel in his willingness to extend the consequences of the AMP to the present (even though he applies it to another country) and in his sense of the grave danger of 'noncapitalist paths of development'.

44 Ibid., p. 270.
45 Ibid., pp. 222, 175.

The Importance of Being Materialist

Nikiforov's Marxism has an admirable coherence. It is capable of offering a sociological typology that is consistent with the political eschatology and salvation promise of Marxism. It is also most lucid about the sense in which that theory is 'materialist', which is more than can be said for many Western crypto-idealist neo-Marxisms.

Nikiforov interestingly refers, in so many words, as do other Soviet anthropologists, to the *idealist* theory of violence:

The meaning of the 'theory of violence' [is] the underestimation of the determining role of the economic factor. The protagonists of this viewpoint are naturally attracted by the view that Oriental society consists of stagnant communities, devoid of internal inequalities of wealth; in them, government is unconnected with classes and plays a self-sufficient role; in other words, relationships of pure violence prevail. ... Kautsky ... reached the idealist 'theory of violence'.[46]

And, commenting on Kautsky's *Materialist Conception of History* (1927), Nikiforov observes: 'All [his] conclusions are plainly un-Marxist: instead of government being the product of the irreconcilable nature of class relations, it is class contradictions and exploitation that are the result of the emergence of government.'[47] There are formulations that make 'materialism' sound obvious: people have to eat and survive before they can think. Nikiforov's formulation, brought into such sharp relief by the AMP issue, shows materialism not to be obvious at all but, on the contrary, to constitute a very strong and interesting thesis. What is excluded by it is not just the priority of *thought*, but also equally the priority of *violence*. The phrase about 'production and reproduction' may allow kinship to enter the 'base' and escape the superstructure; but there is *no way* of extending the same courtesy to violence and the means of coercion. Marxism does not of course deny their existence; but they cannot be primary. On its view, they reflect or express pre-existing conflict; they do not initiate and engender it.

This materialism has, as we have seen, another most unobvious and interesting trait: its aversion to, or reserve toward, the notion of diffusion. Once again, Nikiforov puts it bluntly: 'The nations of pre-Columbian America ... did everything to prove the generality of global-historical regularities and the viciousness of the idealist theory of "diffusion".'[48] Diffusion is objectionable in much the same way as

46 Ibid., p. 155.
47 Ibid., p. 154.
48 Ibid., p. 247.

autonomous violence, with which it overlaps: if societies change radically at the behest of their accidental neighbours, by emulation or osmosis or coercion, this destroys the inner necessity both of social sin and of salvation. Moreover, just *how* do they change at the behest of neighbours? Either by sheer mimesis – the demonstration effect – which, by making fundamental changes hinge on conscious emulation, would seem to be blatantly idealist; or by violence, in which case diffusion is open once again to whatever objections may be raised against making violence crucial to social change. (If they trade voluntarily and are thereby influenced, the objection no longer applies – but then they must be *ready* to trade, so the transformation becomes to an important degree endogenous, and thus acceptable to Marxist theory.)

Yet obviously diffusion cannot be denied altogether. Both the facts of history and the works of the Founders of Marxism testify to its reality eloquently, most markedly perhaps in connection with the expansion to capitalism. Nikiforov has no wish to deny its empirical occurrence. He admits, for instance, that many nations, possibly most, including the Teutonic and Slav ones, passed from primordial communalism directly to feudalism, bypassing slave-owning society.[49] Moreover, the perception of the possibility of bypassing capitalism was a crucial element in the plot that led up to the final and correct formulation of Marxism, as Nikiforov himself insists.

Nikiforov allows at least four occasions of diffusion: conquest by one tribe of another, the spread of feudalism to slaveless society, the spread of capitalism, and of course the aid of backward countries by socialist ones. But the condition of diffusion, in each case, is that the diffusing agent, so to speak, has *endogenously* attained the higher form – has attained exploitation or socialism, for example. Diffusion must never be a genuinely innovative agent in history. It may spread both exploitation and liberation when conditions are ripe, but it cannot independently engender either.

Against the conquest/diffusion theory of the origin of the state, Nikiforov observes:

So as to conquer an alien tribe and keep it under their power, the conqueror must have a complete (albeit primitive) government apparatus. The beginnings of an army and officialdom are phenomena unthinkable without the attainment of a definite level of production, a more or less marked accumulation of surplus product; i.e., conquest itself is the fruit of economic development.[50]

In fact, some conquests seem to have been carried out by tribal 'armies' that were virtually coextensive with the adult male population of the

49 Ibid., p. 264.
50 Ibid., p. 154.

tribe. The tribe itself was an army, and its chiefly lineage constituted all the officialdom it needed. Nikiforov's claim here is in conflict with the views of another scholar, A. M. Khazanov, who suggests that tribal nomads could constitute a state *vis-à-vis* conquered populations and yet be, so to speak, stateless when at home. Moreover, Khazanov is evidently willing to consider a 'non-Morganatic' origin of the state: 'Conquest followed by the transformation of inter-ethnic into class contradictions appears to be one of the best-known paths of state formations.'[51]

'But there is more to come,' says Nikiforov. And indeed there is:

The very idea of subjugating an alien tribe with the aim of making it work for the conquerors could not enter the head of a community of equals: the emergence of such ideas testifies to the fact that the members of the community were already familiar with the use of the labour of some for the benefit of others. And that shows that in the given community there already existed exploitation, and thus classes – even if but weakly developed and still masked by primordial forms of social organization.[52]

My intuitions diverge from Nikiforov's on this point. Though the method of imagining what-would-I-do-were-I-primitive-man has been much decried, it is quite irresistible here. Had *I* been primitive man, and had I lived a thousand years, then agriculture, domestication, pottery, weaving, not to mention smelting, would have remained uninvented and awaiting their discovery. That's a fact. My capacity for *bricolage* does not reach that far. But as for appropriating the fruits of the labour of another, I would have stumbled onto that one, provided only that there had been someone stupid or weak enough to let me get away with it. The idea that exploitation needed *inventing*, which is evidently inherent in Marxist anthropology – Nikiforov is not the only Soviet scholar to express it – is profoundly endearing.

But what is significant for understanding the underlying pattern of Nikiforov's argument is this: the primordial community is a kind of moral baseline, from which both exploitation and domination are absent. But it is also a sociological baseline, indicating what requires *explanation*. Of the two elements, only exploitation emerges spontaneously and initially, as the original sin in the global drama. It, but only it, in turn, engenders domination, which is a kind of derivative sin, incapable of independent existence or of an autonomous role in the great collective passion play of history. No domination without (prior) exploitation.

51 Khazanov, *Sotsial'naya istoriya Skifov* (*Social History of the Scythians*, cit. ch. 1, n. 4 above), p. 237.
52 Nikiforov, *Vostok i vsemirnaya istoriya* (*Orient and World History*), p. 154.

The discovery of the primordial community, or rather of its real social potential, solved all at once a problem in both prehistory and modern political strategy. At the same time, this discovery dissipated its own evil shadow, the AMP, which had usurped one of its traits – the absence of private property – and which fused it with the idea of self-sustaining, self-serving violence. *Were* it possible for such domination to exist independently, then sin and salvation would no longer provide the rational pattern of human history: suffering and oppression could enter at *any* point and, worse still, could not be relied on to depart again. Both the understanding and eventual control of history would escape us.

Denouement

But the name for such an autonomous, socially congealed, and in-eradicable domination by violence is, precisely, the Asiatic Mode of Production. So it *may not* exist if history is to be comprehensible and, eventually, if man is really to make his own history, if he is to become fully the subject, not the object, of history, if prehistory is to end. Happily, says Nikiforov, brushing the sweat of temporary fear from his brow, the facts of history firmly established that indeed it does not exist. Private property was ever present under all *political* systems. Only the primordial community lacked it. But these facts have only been properly available since the 1870s, and entered the final and correct formulation of Marxism thanks to Morgan and Kovalevsky. Both the scholarly *and* the political problem situations of the 1870s and early 1880s allowed *and* impelled the truth to emerge, a mere couple of years before Karl Marx's death. The drama of this revelation is a story Nikiforov tells admirably, and it was a cliffhanger indeed. It was just as well, perhaps, for the nerves of the then participants that they did not fully realize how much, how very much, was at stake.

4

Feudalism in Africa

Soviet anthropology differs from its Western counterpart, for better or for worse, by a certain kind of density. It is the social world which is generated by the scholarly activities of the Soviet *uchenyi* (scholar), and which he also inhabits, which has this dense quality. Any social structure or institution which he investigates is held firmly in its place by a wider framework, within which it can be shifted and budged only with difficulty. This framework is of course constituted by a set of ideas and questions and concepts which, in a loose way, one can lump together as 'Marxism'.

These ideas do not, of course, form a whole which *must*, in all circumstances, stay together. In themselves they are separable, and may come as single spies not as battalions. For instance, the overall evolutionism, the sense of a general direction of human history, is quite independent of the characteristically Marxist typology of societies. As outsiders, we can pick and choose amongst these ideas, finding some more useful or stimulating than others. It is only when we look at Soviet anthropology as a school, as a reasonably coherent style, that we must take this clustering as a unity, for it is as unity, more or less, that it fashions the thought-style of Soviet anthropologists. And it is when we look at it in this way that the 'density' strikes us most.

By contrast, societies investigated by Western anthropologists seem to float in a kind of dimensionless thin air, like those figures in Chinese paintings which appear without a background, in isolation. No typological or evolutionary schema seems to exercise constraint on the societies investigated by this tradition, or should one say, on the interpretation of such societies. The expectations or assumptions which do constrain or limit the Western anthropologist's handling of his material are related to the inner organizational possibilities of the society, rather than to its setting in space or history. An attempt to provide such a historical and geographic continuum or setting for West African

societies, for instance, may indeed be one of the traits which make Jack
Goody's *Technology, Tradition and the State in Africa* a remarkable book –
but the point is that the book is, in this respect, atypical, an attempt to go
in a new direction, rather than the following out of an existing custom.

The contextual density or its absence may of course, each of them,
possess both merits and defects. The balance sheet is not simple. In as
far as Marxism is simultaneously an official faith as well as a sociological
theory, the Western observer tends first of all of course to look on it as an
ideological constraint. But clearly that is not the whole story. At the
heart of the liberation of Malinowskian anthropology from the evolutionist vision was, above all, an insistence that social structures are to be
explained in terms of themselves, and not in terms of the demands of
some *welthistorischer* timetable. And so it is. The Durkheimian precept
that the social be explained by the social was complemented by the
requirement that the present explain the present. Malinowski exorcised
survival. Yet there was also a loss, exemplified perhaps in the difficulty
Western anthropology has in getting very far in any kind of comparative
study. The old schemata were not merely timetables for the global
railroad, they also contained some not uninteresting questions which
helped place one society alongside another.

I have previously attempted an overall and abstract sketch of the
Soviet 'dense' or 'contextual' style in anthropology,[1] referring to a Soviet
attempt to sum up the state of play in the subject in the Soviet Union.[2]
Here I wish to examine one specific study by a distinguished and
representative Soviet scholar, namely L. E. Kubbel's work on the
development of the Western Sudan up to the time of the Moroccan
conquest of Timbuktu.[3] The title of this book, *Songhai Empire*, is somewhat misleading, in as far as the author also has a great deal to say about
the two Western Sudanic states which preceded that of the Songhai,
namely ancient Ghana and Mali. His subject-matter is a certain line of
development, rather than either some stable state, or even merely the
terminal condition of a development.

Kubbel himself is an anthropologist of the middle generation. I
believe his work to be of double interest: on the one hand, he exemplifies
a certain tradition; on the other, given the high quality, the logical
tightness, and the empirical richness of his book, his thought is also of
substantive interest as a very significant contribution to West African
studies. And by analysing the argument in a single work, we are able to

---

1　See ch. 1 above.
2　L. V. Danilova, 'Controversial Problems of the Theory of Precapitalist Societies',
cit. ch. 1, n. 1 above.
3　L. E. Kubbel, *Songhai Empire*, cit. ch. 1, n. 4 above.

see complexities and a diversity which were inevitably absent in the previous overall model of the Soviet approach.

Jack Goody has observed: 'Palaeo-Marxists accept a fixed progression, inherited from their nineteenth-century predecessors, from tribalism through feudalism to capitalism.'[4] Kubbel clearly is no palaeo-Marxist, and his book provides interesting evidence of the partial withering away of such rigid adherence to a fixed progression in the Soviet Union. For one thing, the steps of the progression are clearly subject to debate, they are not a norm to which the findings are obliged to conform. The idea that some individual steps on the grand historical ladder may simply be missing in this or that local historical sequence, is clearly treated as admissible.

And yet a good deal of the old evolutionist vision and spirit also survives, for better or for worse. For one thing, it sets the problem: a progression is expected, and its retardations or deviations are precisely what cries out most urgently for explanation. For another thing, some steps in the progression seem more dispensable than others. For instance, the early stage and category of what one may translate, without prejudice, as 'tribal society' seems rather more entrenched than perhaps any other. 'Feudalism' is perhaps somewhat less firmly entrenched, but is still not to be dismissed lightly; it may or may not be significant for the overall intellectual climate in Soviet anthropology that Kubbel does in the end come down on the side of the thesis that feudalism was indeed present in sub-Saharan Africa, though he only does so with a great deal of very thorough discussion of the arguments on the other side. The tone seems strongly to suggest that dissent on this point is well within reasonable limits. The whole omnibus category of 'tribal society' of course differs from the Western notion in that it is used to convey a far more meaty idea – and one whose concreteness, homogeneity, genuine explanatory power and general usefulness are also scrutinized by Kubbel far less severely than is, say, feudalism or slave society.

Kubbel might here claim in his own defence that in as far as he was concerned with a development sequence *moving away from* 'tribal society', in other words in as far as it was not at the centre of his interest, he was justified in using it without at the same time subjecting it to the same critical scrutiny which he clearly did apply to the available classification of African post-tribal *states*. One cannot query everything at once – whilst one questions one thing, may one not accept the locally customary interpretation of surrounding things, for the time being? I am not sure that such a defence would be valid. 'Tribal society' is not just a background, a receding past, a baseline for the phenomena in Kubbel's

---

4 *Technology, Tradition and the State in Africa*, p. 22.

foreground. For one thing, as he himself stresses, tribal communities continued to be parts of more complex West African political formations. For another thing, and this may be more important, the whole argument hinges very greatly on the paired alternative of 'tribal' and 'non-tribal' society. The two are so very complementary logically, that the whole argument is much weakened by a failure to examine either one of the terms sufficiently.

Two further observations are required here. In Kubbel and in Soviet anthropology generally, 'tribal society' is not merely an explanatory, but also a morally significant concept. Its termination indicates, so to speak, the departure point from the Garden of Eden, the traumatic moment when exploitation of the labour of our fellow-humans entered our lives. In other words, what is and what is not a tribal society relates significantly to our thought about the human social predicament. This is quite different, I think, from the Western social anthropologist, who looks at 'tribal societies' not merely as very diverse in their structure and culture, but also as very differentiated in their moral appeal. Some are nasty and some nice, some exploitative and some less so. The idea that they all share a very important moral trait, and that they positively lack the organizational, and apparently even the psychological, tools for human nastiness, or at least for one of its main forms, namely exploitation, sounds eccentric here. In Kubbel's reasoning, this is certainly not treated as axiomatic or self-evident, but it does seem to be a kind of baseline-of-argument, a kind of null hypothesis: evidence would be required against it rather than for it, and its denial would call for far more explanation and support than its affirmation.

The other interesting point to be made here is that attempts are being made within Soviet anthropology to elaborate and refine this notion of 'tribal society', humanity's starting-point. Kubbel refers to the work of Maretin on this point.[5] Maretin's strategy lies in refining the notion of the community, and increasing its explanatory power, by injecting a further, so to speak, mini-evolutionism *into* and *within* the category of (primitive) 'community'. A notion which had apparently begun its career as *a* stage within the famous evolutionist typology of Marxism, is now broken up into a further series of substages, linked to each other once again as steps in an evolutionary ladder. This mini-evolution is however not presented dogmatically. Already in this early paper, presented in 1964, Maretin observes: 'One has to bear in mind that for diverse reasons, the various distinct nationalities (of Indonesia) were not obliged to pass through all the successive stages of the evolution of the

5 Yu. V. Maretin, 'The Community and its Types in Indonesia', cit. ch. 1, n. 4 above.

community, with the exception of one of them, the first one – the kin community.'[6]

This evolution-within-evolution is like a series of receding mirror images. The smaller version reproduces a striking trait of the preceding and larger one: once again, it seems to be the starting-point, the first stage, which is quite specially entrenched. As Maretin observes at the beginning of his article of 1964, 'the community appeared as the basic form of organization of society during the early stages of the evolution of mankind, when it existed as the kin community (*rodovaya obshchina*). The community even survived in class society . . .'[7] He then proceeds to cite slave society, feudalism, and capitalism as social forms within which the 'community' survived, albeit 'in new forms and in part with new functions'.

The survival of the 'community' as part of a wider social order exemplifying other principles is a theme we shall encounter in Kubbel's treatment of the development of West African society. The general strategy of finding subcategories within the 'communal' stage of human history, but persevering in an evolutionary if non-rigid lineal ordering of these stages, has been perpetuated by later and more extensive work on the theme of 'primitive soviety'.[8] More specifically, Kubbel borrows two of Maretin's subclassifications, and believes that, at the time of their first European contacts, most of the Sahelian Sudanic people can be placed as being in transition between those two stages, whose names are the local-clan (*sosedsko-rodovoi*) and the local-extended-family (*sosedsko-bol'she-semeinoi*) variants of communal organization. The whole litera-ture on this problem is, for obvious reasons, extensive. One participant, A. M. Khazanov, whose main work on nomadic societies deals with problems very analogous to Kubbel's, frankly admits: 'The term 'community' (*obshchina*) is, if you please, one of the most poly-semantic terms to be employed in historical science . . .'[9]

There is an account in English of the manner in which this problem arises in the development of Marxism and its relation to anthropology, by Stephen P. Dunn,[10] who observes that his readers (especially those who are non-Marxists) are entitled to ask: So what? This whole

6 Ibid., p. 4.
7 Ibid.
8 See A. I. Pershits (ed.), *Primordial Community*, cit. ch. 1, n. 3 above; and also the same author's comments in *Current Anthropology*, vol. 16, 1975, p. 608.
9 A. M. Khazanov, 'Obshchina v razlagayushchikh obshchestvakh i ee istoricheskie sud'by' ('The community in disintegrating primitive societies and its historical destinies'), in *Vestnik drevnei istorii* (Moscow, 1975), pp. 3–13.
10 S. P. Dunn, 'The position of the primitive-communal social order in the Soviet-Marxist Theory of History'. Paper presented to the 9th International Congress of Anthropological and Ethnographical Sciences (Chicago, 1973).

discussion may seem to them to bear an unmistakably scholastic aspect. Whilst appearing to sympathize with the impatient reader, Dunn insists that we must take the question seriously, because ultimately the identification of the 'motive force for the evolution of society' hinges on it, and to lose interest in the question 'would have philosophical consequences both far reaching and disastrous.' I am not sure whether this is so, and it is possible to be interested in the question simply as one of the crucial normative constraints on Soviet anthropological thought, which sets both problems and the criteria of their solutions, and which helps to illuminate this work.

But the organization of the local community and its development as such is not at the centre of Kubbel's attention, and does not constitute the most intriguing aspect of his argument, even if it makes a contribution towards the central theme. That central theme is constituted by the problem of state formation.

This is an issue which continues to be crucial to Soviet anthropological Marxism. Unilinealism is debatable not merely in the sense that it is debated, but also in the stronger sense that the constraints on possible answers are much relaxed. Evolution occurred, but its paths are, within reason, variable and open to speculation and research. On the other hand, the tie-up of class- and state-formation is more sensitive. This is an equation which is expected to come out right. One has the feeling that this is where the line is drawn, that it is held that you cannot deny this connection and yet continue to claim to be a Marxist.

In the West, this question does not seem to have a correspondingly central position in anthropological theory. Take I. Schapera's *Government and Politics in Tribal Societies*. Schapera begins by complaining that:

Anthropologists have on the whole neglected the comparative study of political organization in primitive societies ... in contrast with what has been written about primitive kinship and marriage, economics, religion, or even law, relatively little attention has been paid to defining or comparing types of political unit in primitive societies, or ... the organization and use of political power ... and the relations between rulers and subjects.[11]

The passage incidentally highlights the difference between Western and Soviet anthropological terminologies. In Soviet anthropology, it would be a contradiction to speak about the relations between subjects and rulers in a primitive society, which is, by definition, a pre-state society. Schapera's and Goody's complaints of inadequate attention to the topic in the West is, incidentally, in marked contrast with Kubbel's praise: 'in the regulation of emerging class contradictions, the role of political

11 I. Schapera, *Government and Politics in Tribal Society* (London, 1956), p. 1.

institutions was crucially serious. This also explains the attention, which has for so long been paid in non-Marxist West European anthropology to the study of the political structures of traditional societies.'[12] He proceeds to invoke C. Monteil, L. Tauxier, and M. J. Herskovits as examples of a 'purely sociological approach to the societies under its investigation'. Kubbel also praises Radcliffe-Brown[13] for that very definition of politics, in the Preface of *African Political Systems*, which Schapera selects for criticism.[14] Whilst there are these interesting differences between the two scholars on points of detail, it is noteworthy – and no doubt will be noted by Soviet scholars – that Schapera's general conclusion,[15] though evidently not inspired by Marx (who figures neither in the bibliography nor in the index of Schapera's book), are at the very least perfectly compatible with Kubbel's:

the following are some of the apparent trends . . . The community tends to become larger and more heterogeneous . . . Kinship recedes in importance as the basis of political attachment . . . With increased diversity of population we tend also to get distinct social classes, in which the chief and his descent group constitute a dominant aristocracy . . . In the heterogeneous communities where the central government is dominated by a hereditary aristocracy, there are likely also to be revolts by subject groups resenting ill-treatment or economic exploitation . . . To counteract such disruptive tendencies, special techniques of control may develop that are not needed in simpler communities.

Nothing in all this should cause any raised eyebrows in Moscow or Leningrad. Admittedly, when Schapera speaks of the apparent trends,[16] it is not wholly clear whether this is to be taken in any historic sense. His evidence is synchronic, rather than based, as is Kubbel's, on historical reconstructions. It is based on 'the contrast between Bushman hunters and collectors and Bantu cultivators and pastoralists'. But this, in Schapera's own words, links these trends to the 'increased efficiency in method of food production' which 'does seem to render possible certain developments that otherwise would not occur'. Thus Schapera's synchronic argument can easily be translated into an at least conditional evolutionist one ('certain developments' are rendered *possible* simply by the addition of the not very contentious premiss that the efficiency of food production does, by and large, increase in the course of human history). Even the careful conditional summary of this argument is eroded a bit if we look in detail at the trends specified by Schapera. Though Schapera carefully talks of size, specialization, and complexity

12 Kubbel, *Songhai Empire*.
13 Ibid., p. 346: 'Radcliffe-Brown was not in error . . .'
14 Schapera, *Government and Politics*, pp. 217–18.
15 Ibid., p. 219.
16 Ibid.

making possible the development of government, yet it is hard to see how these enlarged tasks could generally be performed without it; and if so, the conditional argument would turn into a functional compulsion. Schapera's actual words do not allow one to credit him with this step, but it is a very small one, and the argument does seem to nudge one in this direction.

There does of course remain an important difference: in his specification of the trends, Schapera mentions both the emergence of classes and the fact that 'the functions of government become more numerous and varied',[17] but he never takes the crucial step of saying that the emergence of classes *causes* the emergence of government. He merely says that both in fact appear; if anything, the causal connection seems to be in the opposite direction, in as far as the new governmental class creates the stratification: 'the chief and his kin-group *constitute* a dominant aristocracy'.[18] In other words, they *are* the ruling class; they are not its agents, tools, representatives or shadows.

So Schapera does not satisfy Marxism at this point. But as we shall see, it is by no means obvious that Kubbel does so either. Or perhaps this thesis was wrongly credited to Marxism in the first place?

Thus it is through the intellectually strategic position, so to speak, of this very issue, that Kubbel's treatment of the first link in the West African chain is so specially interesting. Kubbel is dealing with an historic sequence, a continuous and in some measure self-contained development, which is what in his view gives his subject its importance:

The concrete-historical situation in the relevant region constituted itself in such a manner, that it made possible the sufficiently long independent existence of several governmental formations, which replaced each other, and which on the one hand did not enter into any direct military-political contacts with their northern neighbours, and on the other, failed to attract to themselves the disrupting effect of the European slave trade in the more modern period. Thus Songhai society, whose matured class character I endeavoured to show . . . was in considerable measure the result of a prolonged historical evolution of the autochtonous social structures of the peoples, inhabiting the Sudanic-Sahelian zone of West Africa.[19]

It is natural that for a Marxist, the methodological significance of relative insulation (and it is not claimed to be more than partial) is that it makes possible to observe, not stability and equilibrium in a pure state, but a relatively pure example of endogenous *development*. For the functionalist, the problem arises – how do you relate the change, which

17 Ibid., p. 219.
18 Ibid. (italics mine).
19 Kubbel, *Songhai Empire*, p. 337.

indisputably does occur as the result of the *interaction* of diverse societies (however 'functional' internally), to the theories concerning internal functional 'equilibrium'? And, worse still, what do you do with a world in which these interactions are far more prominent, pervasive and important than the 'internal', supposedly functional processes? What indeed.

But here we are not dealing with a functionalist, but with a Marxist. And what is interesting is that a strikingly analogous problem arises for him too. What precisely is the relationship of the theory of endogenous development to the phenomenon of mutual impact, whose existence is not denied (but on the contrary which also plays an important part in the argument)? What happens when the latter kind of phenomenon becomes more prominent than the 'autochtonous' kind? Just what are the limits of variations of autochtonous developments? Is there a clearly formulated *theory* concerning the nature of the interaction type of process? As we shall see, Kubbel invokes propositions which seem to be drawn from such a theory, but which are, individually, questionable.

This individually questionable proposition, which sounds like a fragment of some unspecified theory concerning the mechanisms and effects of diffusion, is put forward in answer to the question – why did no slave society emerge in West Africa? (Kubbel is convinced that this is so, that no such society arose, and invokes the almost total anthropological consensus, inside and outside Marxism, in support.) The reason appears to be

... the period, in which early-class society began to be formed within most West African nations, i.e. basically at the beginning of the second millennium AD, was altogether *too late* to allow the erection of class relations of the kind proper to slave society as a socio-economic formation. If we take into account that peripheral societies generally in greater or lesser degree carry out those forms of socio-economic and political organization, which they see with highly developed neighbours ... one must admit, that the African periphery during the Middle Ages had no model which could have stimulated the emergence of slave-owning class society.[20]

M. Diop[21] is then rebuked for failing to take note of this principle, when he claims to find slave-owning societies on the territory of modern Mali towards the middle of the nineteenth century.

There seems to be a time and place for everything, including slave-owning societies. One wonders how the contention that peripheral societies are restricted in their options by the models offered them by

20 Ibid., p. 360 (italics mine).
21 M. Diop, *Histoire des classes sociales dans l'Afrique de l'Ouest*. I: *Le Mali* (Paris, 1971), cit. in Kubbel, *Songhai Empire*, p. 394.

the centre, fits in with Kubbel's stress on endogeneous development, or indeed how it is supported anyway. What of the American South or the slave-owning Caribbean? This is a theoretical problem with which we must leave him.

The stress on endogenous and autochtonous development is however also rather marked in his argument, providing him even as we have seen with the justification for his very choice of topic. It becomes even more prominent at the very conclusion of his argument.

The independent development of Songhai was interrupted by the Moroccan conquest when the emerging system of serf exploitation was destroyed, and in consequence in the beginning of the seventeenth century the population of these regions found itself in large measure pushed back in its socio-economic development. Now we can only guess what the results would have been without this extraneous disruption. But if we consider the acceleration of social development in each of the three great governments (or pre-governmental political structures) of the Sudanic middle ages . . . I propose, on good grounds, that on such a hypothesis the gap between West Africa on the one hand and North Africa and the Middle East on the other would have been markedly smaller, than in fact it became.[22]

As indirect evidence for this Kubbel counts the speeding up, as it were, of dynastic periods. Ghana lasted from the fourth to the twelfth century; Mali from the middle of the thirteenth until the 1430s; and Songhai lasted from the 1460s until 1591. This 'endogenous acceleration' point is in fact the final observation of the book. One can see the argument: *if*, as Kubbel claims to have shown, each dynasty corresponds to a stage of social development, and if their periods become successively shorter, it does look as if history was speeding up. But did not the 'speed' depend on occasion on external incursions, whether by the Almoravides or later by the Moroccans? And more fundamentally, is there not a danger here that Kubbel allows himself to be swept away by the 'movement' metaphor inherent in the evolutionist picture of human history? If one thinks of historical change as the pattern emitted by a kind of ticker-tape machine, then, naturally, if someone turns the handle faster, developments will come out that much faster. But I doubt whether this is the correct way to think of it, and whether dynastic periods or the wheel of fortune are indeed the turns of the *welthistorischer* organ-grinder. But I would not wish to be dogmatic about this; it is an aspect of one of the methodological questions which arise from Kubbel's approach.

But as indicated, the most intriguing aspect of Kubbel's argument is

22 Kubbel, *Songhai Empire*, p. 372.

connected with the crucially strategic position of *state-formation* in Soviet Marxist theory.

The most important distinctive feature of the West African (transition from the primary to secondary socio-economic formation) was the enormous class-formative role played by the caravan trade with North Africa and Egypt. This manifested itself with special vigour in the formation of the first of the great Western Sudanic political association – ancient Ghana. One has sufficient grounds for claiming that the appearance of this governmental formation (*gosudarstvennogo obrazovaniya*) was called for in greater measure by the requirements of trans-Saharan trade, than by the internal development of Western Sudanic peoples.[23]

Kubbel goes on to observe that this is not exclusively true of West Africa, but is typical of all contacts of 'peripheric' societies with more developed ones, throughout sub-Saharan Africa. He notes that whilst this phenomenon hastened class formation in West Africa, in another way it also acted as a brake. The Near East and the Mediterranean provided a constant and enviably stable [*sic*] demand for above all two items of West African export: gold and slaves. But neither of these products was strictly speaking local: each came from the tropical forest zone further to the South. So, the *near*-peripheric societies of the Sudan acted as mediators in the exploitation by the center of *far*-peripheric societies. (Aksum performed a similar role at the other end of the continent.)

But this very fact has as its consequence the conservation of archaic forms of production and social organization, and effected the growing gap between North and West African development. West African backwardness had several reasons – Kubbel here invokes the analysis by the Polish historian M. Malowist[24] – but the prime mover seems to have been this 'intermediary' role and the way in which it discouraged other, more progressive forms of exploitation.

There seems to be a certain analogy between what Kubbel says about the effect of the early Sahelian trade, and the economically harmful role credited to comprador traders by some theories of economic development. Just as 'enclave capitalism' may hinder the emergence of the real thing, so enclave class formation, so to speak, by slave- and gold-traders,

---

23 Ibid., p. 339.
24 There appears to be much Polish work in this area. See Marian Malowist, *Wielkie Panstwa Sudanu Zachodniego w Poznym Sredniowieku* (*The Big Empires of the Western Sudan in the Late Middle Ages*) (Warsaw, 1964); Tadeusz Lewicki, *Dzieje Afryki od Czasów Najdawniejszych do XIV Wieku* (*A History of Africa from the Earliest Times to the 14th Century*) (Warsaw, 1969); Barbara Stepniewska, *Rozpowszechnianie sie Islamu w Sudanie Zachodnim* (*Diffusion of Islam in the Western Sudan*) (Wroclaw, 1972); Michal Tymowski, *Le Développement et la régression chez les peuples de la boucle du Niger à l'époque précoloniale* (Warsaw, 1974).

may hamper *real* class formation, and thus genuine historical development on a larger scale. Those interested in the manner in which Marxist social typology is used to imply historical value judgements will note that these judgements seem to be squarely on the side of development – never mind that this would have meant class-formation and exploitation. Evidently we must cross this vale of tears before we can return to Eden. There is little if any romantic regret: backwardness, *lack* of class formation, seems to be deplored, and the central society (Mediterranean and Near East) appears to be blamed for causing retardation. These are more ruthless valuations than any to which Western anthropologists are nowadays inclined.

The basic picture of ancient Ghana offered by Kubbel is this: neither slaves nor gold had any real internal significance within the Sudan.[25] Inside the local community and its productive processes, there was no use for slaves. The demand for these two in export goods was conditional on the emergence of class societies proper to the north of the Sahara.

The sources, Kubbel stresses, offer no warrant for speaking of the internal employment of slaves in Ghana. In ancient Ghana, from the ninth to the twelfth century, class formation was still in its very earliest stages. Evidently, says Kubbel, there is no basis for characterizing Ghana even as an 'early-class' society. And yet at the same time, we can learn from Al Bakri about the presence in Ghana of considerable elements of governmental organization, of an indisputable economic inequality, including a privileged material position of the dominant clan. The inhabitants of Ghana were, says Kubbel, fully familiar with the idea of slavery, i.e. the possibility of exploiting the labour of another, even if they did not employ slaves in production. And there we come to the crux. It will be best to quote Kubbel's own words:

And here emerges a most serious theoretical problem: is there not a contradiction in admitting, on the one hand, the existence of some kind of governmental apparatus, and at the same time asserting that Ghana cannot be classified even as an early class society? This problem brings us back to the specificity of class formation in tropical Africa.[26]

There would indeed seem to be a contradiction: if indeed it is class antagonism which (alone) generates the state, how can we have even the rudiments of state organization when there are as yet no classes? We can all see the difficulty, only too plainly.

But Kubbel tells us severely that there is no real contradiction here. For one thing, 'government' and 'elements of governmentality' (*elementy*

25　Kubbel, *Songhai Empire*, p. 344.
26　Ibid., p. 345.

gosudarstvennosti) are by no means identical. A society may possess elements of separate administrative-political institutions, characteristic of emerging government, and yet have no government, i.e. no fully formed apparatus of class domination. Secondly, the emergence of separate administrative elements is immediately linked to the separation of productive and managerial functions, a separation which occurs much sooner than does the formation of antagonistic classes.

All political power, adds Kubbel, must have two aspects: administration and domination. Properly speaking, Kubbel admits, the idea of administration does already contain the potentiality of the idea of domination – as the inevitable form of removing opposition to the administrative acts, whether from those to whom it is to be applied, or from outside forces. Kubbel here seems, perhaps unwittingly, to be echoing the liberal rather than the Marxist definition of the state – as the agent of elimination of hindrances of the good life. Only when domination becomes an independent function of power, may we speak of government in the full sense of that word. It is at this point that Kubbel praises Radcliffe-Brown for the definition which Schapera criticizes. Radcliffe-Brown said: 'The political organisation of society is that aspect of the total organisation which is concerned with the control and regulation of the use of physical force.'[27]

But Kubbel does go on to criticize Radcliffe-Brown for failing to raise a second question, concerning the criteria for or ends of the use of such force. The force may be applied outside society, or to its own members. Only in the latter case may one speak of domination. And it is most natural, adds Kubbel, that the need for the specific emergence of domination only emerges after the need for administration, i.e. only when antagonistic classes have emerged within society.

One can only admire the tightness of Kubbel's reasoning here. Each step in the argument contributes to the final resolution of the seeming paradox of the contradiction with which he began. Indeed: if government is divided into administration and domination (suppression or enforcement), and enforcement is again subdivided into external and internal enforcement, and only internal enforcement counts as government proper, it does follow that there cannot be real government without internal opposition, for there cannot be enforcement where no-one opposes. QED. A critic might object – but must opposition necessarily be *class* opposition? But if a dominant *clan* also counts as a ruling *class*, then evidently any opposed (antagonistic) groups *are* classes. Objection overruled.

27 M. Fortes and E. E. Evans-Pritchard (eds), *African Political Systems* (London, 1940), p. xxiii.

A more persevering critic might object that the whole argument is somewhat scholastic, in the sense that all definitions are so manipulated as to preserve the fundamental equation, the link-up of class- and state-formation. No taxation without class-formation! The critic might go on to mumble that this should be called state-, class- and tautology-formation in West Africa. The critic mighty well be too harsh. For one thing, there is an indisputable elegance and tightness in this system of ideas, which in turn is by no means incompatible with at least some non-Marxist work on the topic. Moreover, the system of ideas does not move in a void: it is most carefully meshed in with the empirical, historical material. The Ghanaian pre-class governmental formation (not govern-ment proper, mind) did not need to exploit its own agricultural population. It left it to its own archaic communal social devices and its backward productive methods. Its perks and benefits were tied to the long-distance trade, to its middle-man role between the tropical forest and the northern shores of the Sahara. For this, it needed force to protect trade, and indeed to secure the trade goods. So the force was applied, at least primarily, *outwards*. The distinction between the internal and external application of force was also used, for instance, by the then Soviet anthropologist A. M. Khazanov, with respect to Eurasian nomads. The consequence of such reasoning can be that these nomads are considered stateless internally, but at the same time constitute a state in relation to the non-nomadic populations whom they exploit and to whom they apply force.

This is a very distinctive picture of one kind of state or, if you prefer, as Kubbel does, a pre-state and pre-class proto-governmental forma-tion. But whilst the picture does fit the argument, it was not simply invented for its benefit. This whole social syndrome has been noted quite independently by many others, who have no need of it whatever for ulterior doctrinal ends. For instance, Jack Goody observes: 'In West Africa I have been impressed with the apparent ease with which small-scale, temporary polities of a centralised kind arose around (or in opposition to) the raiders for slaves and booty during the period immediately prior to the coming of the Europeans.'[28]

Obviously, Goody's 'polities of a centralised kind' would be 'elements of governmentality' in Kubbel's terminology (or rather, in my inelegant English rendering of his Russian). There is a difference between the two hindrances, in that Goody repeatedly stresses the ephemeral nature of these slave-trading states, whereas Kubbel is very impressed by the continuity and cumulativeness of the Sudanic developments. Goody, incidentally, uses this phenomenon in a critique of a diffusionist theory

28 Goody, *Technology, Tradition and the State in Africa*, p. 18.

of the state: 'These investigations suggest that any idea of the diffusion of kingship or chiefship from a single source, Egypt or elsewhere, should be treated with great reserve.'[29]

Kubbel, by contrast, we saw, is a very partial diffusionist, but not on this point. He does not seem to think that those elements of governmentality had to be demonstrated and on display in a socially more advanced source before they could emerge around the Niger bend. It seems to have been enough that administration-plus-external-application-of-force was required by long distance trade, for those elements to be, so to speak, called into being. So, as far as the emergence of pre-governmental political institutions goes, he seems to be a functionalist.

He is, however, a diffusionist, or something like it, on other points: (a) The very need was generated by the presence of slave and gold-consuming class societies *elsewhere*. This is a mechanism of diffusion more sophisticated than sheer mimicry. (b) The presence or absence of models seems nevertheless to be relevant to forms of economic organization, at least negatively. It was in this manner that the absence of slave-owning society in West Africa was, implausibly, explained. (c) He seems to think of the idea of exploitation as an invention, something which needs to be discovered and may not be easy to assimilate psychologically. This must be part of the Marxist vision. To a Westerner, the idea of appropriating the labour of another seems as natural as breathing, and requires no demonstration-effect for its diffusion. It is only its occasional absence which might require explanation. No theories are postulated to explain how, why, or when men began to take things from each other. It came naturally.

There are of course many examples of the kind of state which Kubbel finds in ancient Ghana. For instance, Éric de Dampierre's *Un ancien royaume Bandia du Haut-Oubangui*[30] describes very much this kind of state, with a Spartan, markedly un-Veblenesque ruling class (with little conspicuous consumption other than of women), which in the pre-colonial period used male captives for export, and female captives for prestige, breeding, and the maintenance of internal patronage links. Women not land were allocated by lord to vassal. Given its low demands for other kinds of consumption, such a state would, as Kubbel insists for ancient Ghana, have little incentive for the internal application of force for the exploitation of the *labour* of others. It would reserve its violence for the capture and subsequent export of personnel. Both activities would fit Kubbel's category of the *external* use of domination.

29 Ibid., p. 19.
30 É. de Dampierre, *Un ancien royaume Bandia du Haut-Oubangui* (Paris, 1967).

Kubbel would of course be reluctant to follow Dampierre in calling this a 'state'.

The notion which Kubbel does use he finds warranted in Engels. In ancient Ghana, he observes, class formation commenced through the 'monopolization of social functions', an expression of Engels's, rather than through any internal development of social production, which would make possible the alienation of the surplus product. Kubbel notes however that even such a monopolization of social functions already presupposes some form of alienation of production, as those who thus monopolize social functions cannot personally participate in production.

There is a certain ironic convergence between the assertions of Kubbel and those of Schapera – or perhaps one should say, a convergence in which what they will *not* say. In each case, the data – drawn from West and South Africa respectively – would seem to impel one in the direction of saying that it is the state (concentration of power) which generates social stratification. But *neither* of our authors can bring himself to say this.

In the case of Kubbel, it is of course an overall conceptual system which insists on making 'the state' a consequence of class antagonisms, and which consequently inhibits such an assertion and requires conceptual epicycles such as 'elements of governmentality'. Schapera, on the other hand, does not vouchsafe us his theoretical premises. He is greatly admired as a most firmly down-to-earth anthropologist, with a high regard for accurate elegant ethnography and a shrewd distrust for high-flown theory. If this is the clue, is it a kind of empiricist *pudeur* which scorns to go beyond what the evidence clearly permits? Is this why we cannot find, in his conclusion in the book cited, assertions any stronger than the guarded contention that increased efficiency in food production 'does seem to render possible' certain political developments, or that the existence of larger and more complex political communities 'is possible only where people do not depend for their livelihood solely upon the natural resources'. Empiricist caution (in the English-speaking tradition, empiricism and caution are sometimes equated) seems to have the same effect, at this point, as Marxist theory.

But it is worth following the subsequent stages of the Sudanic story, as presented by Kubbel. To sum it up so far: the emergence of early forms of governance in the Sudanic Sahel was stimulated by trade. Salt was essential, but not locally available in adequate quantity. As class societies proper emerged on the northern shore of the Sahara, salt could be secured by exporting slaves and gold. But there was no real local demand for either of these goods. But the capture of slaves and the ensuring of minimal security for the export trade required an administrative apparatus capable of handling problems more serious than those of mere clan/tribal society. This apparatus inevitably arose prior to the growth of material inequality, which was brought about and accentuated by that very trade which the apparatus endeavoured to protect. In the end, this did lead to the appearance of antagonistic classes. Here Kubbel quotes an interesting observation of Engels, to the effect that the emergence of such central government is a necessary condition of the continued existence of a nation. 'A nation consisting of small communities, whose interests are similar, but for that very reason not general . . . requires centralization if it is to survive.' Engels's view on the limited cohesion potential of segmentary societies and mechanical solidarity here resemble those of Durkheim, and both, it appears, were influenced by North African material.[31]

The base for this administrative superstructure was the old clan elite (*rodovaya verkhushka*) or tribal aristocracy (*rodovaya znat'*), ready for such a transformation through having begun to alienate, in its own favour, the traditional prestations, and thus approaching economic differentiation. The monopolization by this group of social functions, which in Kubbel's words included both economico-administrative and military-organizational ones, emerged earlier in human history than did the right to dispose of some essential part of the means of production, such as land, labour or cattle. The right to administrative-organizational functions preceded property rights. In tribal society, says Kubbel, the right to take decisions is based not on property but on the possession of social functions. But such a division does not yet for Kubbel constitute a state.

The big transition, for Kubbel, is from power based on personal position to that based on property. In his view, this process was not completed anywhere in pre-colonial sub-Saharan Africa, with the exception of Ethiopia.[32] He stresses, however, that during the transitional period what he calls the inverse or contrary (*protivopolozhno*) connection obtains: positions based on non-economic factors are used to acquire an economic position of dominance. In simple terms, power leads to wealth.

The preconditions for the transformation of this elite into a class were already present, Kubbel says, by the eleventh century. It acted as the

31 Cf. P. Lucas and J.-C. Vatin, *L'Algérie des anthropologues* (Paris, 1975), p. 18.

32 This manner of drawing the big dividing line is in interesting contrast with another notable Soviet scholar, L. V. Danilova, in the work cited ch. 1, n. 1, above. She draws the line between capitalism and all previous social formations (except the first?); within capitalism, ownership is decisive, whilst in the other forms, it is power which counts. Kubbel's case for drawing a line in time between earlier and later Sudanic societies, and classifying the later ones as feudal, hinges on the claim that in the later stage, land-ownership *did* become important.

agent of the North African trade, and vast quantities of gold and slaves passed through its hands. But though economically differentiated, its interests were directed outwards. It was not concerned with the agriculturalists and hunters living on 'its' territory, and not exploitative towards them, a view for which Kubbel invokes the authority of Balandier. This stratum was parasitic. (Note the paradoxical use of 'parasitic' here: the stratum was parasitic from the viewpoint of the historic process, not of the people, precisely because it failed to be parasitic enough from the viewpoint of its own population.)

This character of the ruling class was underscored by the arrival of a large Muslim trading class. During the Ghanaian period it was mainly foreign (Arabo-Berber), though Al Idrisi, says Kubbel, already notes the presence of Mande-speaking Vangara traders. But the fusion of tribal aristocracy and of the traders into one feudal class was to take half a millennium: ancient Ghana was, says Kubbel, an enormous foreign-trade-oriented superstructure above society. Inside society, communal organization survived.

In the Mali empire, which succeeded Ghana, Kubbel sees a number of new traits. The centre of gravity moved to the south, further away from the nomads and closer to gold; there was a determined attempt to control all the ports of the Saharan trade – Djenne, Timbuktu, Gao. Production expanded, notably of cotton; the Mande term *birikan* entered medieval French literature, as a testimony to the effectiveness of Sudanic textile exports. But why the expansion? Trade declined in relative importance, Kubbel claims, and proceeds to criticize Suret-Canale for exaggerating its role in the Mali period, and even more so in the subsequent Songhai one. Kubbel invokes with approval the views of the Soviet scholar I. L. Andreev,[33] who holds that expansion is the natural tendency of societies in transition from kin to class society. Is imperialism the last stage of primitive communism, then? More concretely, Kubbel also invokes the need to expand in order to control all the transit points of trade, notably the import of salt.

But even in Mali, there was not yet a great deal of exploitation of the ordinary members of society. 'To raise the rate of exploitation would simply not be advantageous in comparison with the relatively easy appropriation that was necessary ... from weaker southern neighbours.'[34] This was all the more so, as the receipts of gold increased during the thirteenth and fourteenth centuries in consequence of new mines on the territory of modern Ghana.

---

33 I. L. Andreev, *Problemy sotsial'nogo razvitiya* (Problems of Social Development), Studies of the Tiumen Industrial Institute of Philosophy (Tiumen, 1969).
34 Kubbel, *Songhai Empire*.

Nevertheless, Mali did constitute a qualitatively new stage in the development of West Africa. The best way to see this, says Kubbel, is to consider the composition of its ruling elite. Within two decades of the death of the founder of Mali power, Sundyata Keita, sources testify to the presence of a powerful new group, the imperial guard, recruited from slaves. It was they who organized the first Malian palace revolution, replacing one of Sundyata's sons by another kinsman of his. Later, notably during the decline of Mali power in the second half of the fourteenth century, this guard became the decisive force in the land. We find here, says Kubbel, a phenomenon familiar from the history of ancient Mesopotamia or the early khalifate – the replacement of the old aristocracy by the king's men.

Why should this force have arisen? Kubbel observes that he had previously tended to explain this by the need of the central authority to make itself independent of the old aristocracy – but that he no longer holds this view. The main explanation, he maintains, is that the great military expansion required a professional army. Ancient Ghana could make do with a tribal army, based on the Soninke (Sarakole) ethnic group. The much expanded territory of Mali could no longer be controlled in this manner.

This argument will strike any North Africanist or student of Ibn Khaldun as odd; in the Maghreb, it was precisely the largest empires which were also sustained by tribal armies. But whether or not the argument holds, either in general, or in the specific circumstances of the Niger bend region, it is interesting to see the use Kubbel makes of it. Stratification 'proper', the systematic utilization of the labour power of others, began in a sphere other than the productive. Only thus, says Kubbel, may one properly understand the organization of a slave guard by the rulers drawn from the Keita clan. Whilst the end product is the same, as Kubbel carefully stresses – a system of alienation of the surplus product – yet the path towards it here was distinctive, through the monopolization of social functions and the subsequent further strengthening of it through the military-administrative employment of slaves. (Once again, one feels like observing that a simpler way of putting all this would be to say that the state came first, and economic classes emerged subsequently.)

Here the plot thickens. The new social category, the slaves of the guards regiments, had no access to the traditional prestations, which were the preserve of the old aristocracy; nor could they take part in the northward trade, in which that aristocracy was also too well entrenched. So the new slave class (if the term be allowed us) had but one way out, apparently, if it was to find a permanent social base for itself: to strive to set up a new kind of economy. The only possibility of doing this was on the basis of semi-unfree labour. Kubbel himself observes that he is avoiding the words 'slave' or 'slave labour'. 'Real' slaves were utilized in Mali in spheres other than agriculture. In the main productive area, agriculture, this semi-unfree labour continued to be carried out in the context of the labourer's kin group. The new exploitation of entire ethnic groups, subjugated by this central apparatus, flows together with the older forms of mere 'patriarchal' slavery. The process is not unique: analogous developments occurred with the Mossi and the Serer.

We are now approaching the completion of the development which is Kubbel's theme, and indeed the completion of his argument. The process begun in the Mali empire is pushed much further by the Songhai. In Mali, the central administrative-military apparatus was strong enough to expand, and at least one segment of it – the professional slave army – was impelled towards subjecting entire populations in order to provide itself with its own needs. These populations were exploited as communities rather than as individuals; and we also find in Mali, for the first time, the acquisition by the rulers of the right to assign free lands.

In the Songhai empire, the military-administrative and the clerico-commercial parts of the ruling classes melded. At the same time, the peasant population becomes homogeneous in status (if not ethnically), the free and the subjugated groups becoming closer to each other in social position. New kinds of social relations appeared, in which priority was for the first time given to land rather than to its inhabitants. Kubbel admits that this was not general, but only occurred where land, notably irrigable land, was scarce; but he endeavours to turn this fact into a support for this thesis – that Songhai was feudal – by insisting that this shows that these 'feudal' relations appear even in an area such as Africa, where their emergence is badly hampered by the availability of enormous tracts of free land.[35]

Thus, finally, in the Songhai realm, two classes faced each other – an aristocracy, disposing of land (a class which was evidently the result of the fusion of tribal elites, slave soldiers and of traders), and a dependent peasantry. The two classes confronted each other in the manner characteristic of feudal society. This led to a strengthening of the

---

35 The connection between the availability of land and the subjugation of agriculturalists can incidentally be argued both ways. It may be *necessary* to suborn peasants because land is available, to which they could go if free; alternatively, it may be *easy* to suborn them because there is *no* land to which they could go. Kubbel is concerned to counter the argument that one cannot constrain them through control of land when so much land is available.

The fact that shortage of men in relation to plentiful land leads to the imposition of servitude is argued, for instance, by Professor J. D. Fage, in *States and Subjects in Sub-Saharan African History* (Johannesburg, 1974), p. 15.

apparatus of suppression and its organization along territorial and functional, rather than kin, lines. Islam was finally entrenched in the ruling class.

All these traits appeared with special clarity during the reign of Daud I (1549–83), and in particular during its first half. In his period we also find what Kubbel calls the obverse of the flowering of feudal society – the tendency to fragmentation. Others have seen this trait as an integral part of feudalism,[36] and it is not quite clear what status it has in Kubbel's argument in virtue of being declared the 'obverse' of feudalism. Kubbel plausibly explains this tendency as the confluence of two forces: the survival of the old communities within the empire, with their autarchic tendency, and the ambitions of (members of) the new feudal class based on control of land. One wonders how these fissiparous or segmentary strivings in each of the two classes fit in with the contention that two classes now 'faced' each other: they seem not to be so homogeneous, or at least cohesive, after all. But Kubbel claims even these weaknesses as evidence of the feudal character of the Songhai realm, and declares it to be the highest achievement of the peoples of the central and upper Niger basin in the pre-colonial period – both in the socio-economic and in the socio-political spheres. This achievement and the continuation of this development were interrupted and destroyed by the Moroccan conquest, which, as we have seen, Kubbel greatly deplores.

It is thus that Kubbel endeavours to save sub-Saharan Africa for feudalism. This view is of course contentious, not merely in the West but also amongst Soviet Africanists. I find Kubbel's effort to save the Songhai for feudalism interesting, but not as fascinating as his attempt to save the ancient Ghanaians from having a state. He does not deny the absence of very many feudal traits, which indeed he enumerates, and he does not deny that this constitutes a problem. He does not deny the availability of free land, but partly, as we have seen, tries to turn this in favour of his thesis, and partly himself invokes it as the reason why feudalism was so long a-coming.

This argument hinges on making certain traits central to feudalism: stratification as between peasants and rulers, partial unfreedom of the working population,[37] rights defined in terms of land, at least in some regions, an unambiguous state apparatus not articulated in terms of kinship, and indeed the replacement, by an impersonal idiom, of kinship in other spheres of life. (One may reflect that the fact that relations

36 Cf. R. Coulbourn (ed.), *Feudalism in History* (Hamden, Conn., 1965), p. 7.

37 Both Professors Dmitri Olderogge and John Hunwick have pointed out to me that this point hinges in part on documentation which purports to be dated in the sixteenth century, but may be a nineteenth-century forgery. Cf. I. Levtzion, 'A Seventeenth-century chronicle by Ibn al-Mukthàr', *Bull. SOAS*, vol. 34, 1971.

become articulated in terms of things, not persons, is not generally considered a *feudal* trait.[38]) Kubbel invokes both centralization and fragmentation, when either occurs, in favour of his thesis. He is struck by the fissiparousness not merely of the military-administrative aristocracy, but also of the spiritual-commercial part of it, and declares this to be a specific trait of the Muslim clerisy in West Africa. He notes, with evident astonishment, that it never acted as a united force. This is a surprising surprise; if clerisy means the office-holders of the great Muslim orders, its behaviour in West Africa was hardly more disunited than it was anywhere else in the Muslim world – and certainly not more so than in the Maghreb. Muslim religious brotherhoods are at least as much in competition with each other as any tribal segments or feudal barons. Is this a residual case of European ethnocentrism, the anticipation of a united Church?

Kubbel also comments on the diminished relative importance of trade in this later period: this is, amongst other things, a way of helping to eliminate one of the interpretations which is an alternative to the 'feudal' one, namely the allegedly distinctive 'African mode of production', in which a trading or trade-controlling state sits on top of a relatively unexploited peasantry.[39] (We have seen that Kubbel allows something like this for the earlier stages; but this position in the end seems to be that this merely determined the distinctive Sudanic road towards feudalism, but could not prevent its emergence.)

The present author can hardly pretend to contribute towards the solution of these substantive questions, nor could it have been done in such a limited space. What I have endeavoured to do is to highlight both the constraints and the flexibilities of Kubbel's conceptual scheme. Its interdependent use of evolutionist, functionalist, and diffusionist themes, the elegance of its deployment, its overall style, the manner in which it meshes in with the concrete material at his disposal, the symbiosis of sensitivity and metaphysics in it (not unknown in Western anthropological styles), and the way in which it overlaps with or diverges from some Western approaches. One's final reflection must be this: it is curious how, for reasons which I think are quite internal to this system of ideas, rather than imposed on it from outside, its most sensitive point is the relationship between the state and the economic aspects of society, between the forces of production and the forces of coercion (or what Goody in his book calls the means of destruction). Does the possession

38 *Feudalism in History*, p. 5.

39 Argued, e.g., by Coquery-Vidrovitch in 'An African Mode of Production', *Critique of Anthropology*, vols. 4 and 5, 1975, or criticized by Emmanuel Terray, 'Long-Distance Exchange and the Formation of the State: the case of the Abron kingdom of Gyaman', *Economy and Society*, vol. 3, 1974.

of the means of coercion merely reflect, or also produce divisions between diverse socio-economic categories? This is a question full of resonances in modern as well as in traditional societies. It is not only amongst the ancient Ghanaians that the problem is intriguing.

5

The Nomadism Debate

Russian history and consciousness – whether through education or through a genuine folk memory – is pervaded by awareness of the nomad problem, more so presumably than in any other European nation. The Magyars may look back romantically to a nomadic past, and their populist ethnographers may seek the nomad origins of institutions still found in nineteenth-century Hungarian villages; but the Russian connection with nomads is deeper and more persistent. The first Russian state was destroyed by nomads. The Muscovite state began its career as fiscal agent of a nomad empire, and when the balance of power tilted away from the inhabitants of the steppe to those of the forest, this tax-collector state first ceased to pay up, keeping its revenue for itself, and then expanded to become, in turn, an empire eventually incorporating and administering a number of nomad societies, including its own erstwhile rulers. The expropriators were in turn expropriated. If the conquest *by* nomads has left its mark on the Russian soul, mythology, and literature, then the conquest *of* nomads has left behind rich administrative and other records of the functioning of nomad society.

It is not merely the Russian background that is relevant. The specific questions asked spring from the sociology of Marxism, and indeed from the wider tradition which has dominated Russian social thought since the nineteenth century, and of which Marxism is but an element.[1] The central theme in that tradition is the notion of progress or social evolution. This was a natural idea in a nineteenth-century milieu: it was the perception of massive and apparently persistent change that inspired social thought and presented the problem. The meaning, mechanisms, direction of that change, if located, would have constituted its solution.

In Western anthropology and sociology, a rival theory or approach,

1 Cf. Alexander Vucinich, *Social Thought in Tsarist Russia, The Quest for a General Science of Society, 1861–1917* (Chicago–London, 1976).

known as Functionalism, was to be found. This took social cohesion and persistence as the central datum, and strove to explain it. The best-known criticism of that school, so well known as to become a hackneyed and almost a joke phrase, was that it 'failed to account for social change'. The critics of Functionalism sometimes went further and suggested that functionalists had a political motive for ignoring or denying change: perhaps they were paid by the established order to try and stop it, or to discourage anyone from endeavouring to initiate it, by pretending it did not or could not occur, and ought not really to occur; that society was essentially a self-maintaining, self-reproducing system, and that any deviation from this norm was pathological.

Functionalism has often been attacked in this manner. Marxism, much criticized in other ways, has strangely seldom been attacked by means of the mirror-image criticism to which it seems conspicuously open: *can it account for stagnation?* Pastoral nomadism is not the only area in which this question is pertinent. In fact, the most proper way to put the question is in a generic form. Was nineteenth-century thought justified in being so smitten by the fact of change and development as to make it the central trait of social life? Is not change, and in particular sustained cumulative change and really radical, structural change, something quite untypical, which may indeed constitute *our* predicament, but is not normally part of the human condition?

Marxism is not allergic to the *appearance* of stability. In as far as its diagnosis of this illusion is the same as that which functionalism offers of the reality of stability, Marxism has a marked affinity with functionalism. It would be possible to summarize the Marxist position by the assertion that functionalism is 98 per cent correct – but it is the remaining 2 per cent that really count. The Marxist account of the entire social superstructure is entirely functionalist: the elements of the super-structure are there so as to help *perpetuate* the system. They succeed to a very large extent, helping to keep the system going, at least for very considerable periods. Moreover they endow it with a spurious air of permanence and, so as to reinforce it, with an aura of moral absoluteness and legitimacy. The system is permanent, or so its ideology claims, because it is legitimate, and it is legitimate because it reflects the permanent traits and conditions of humanity.

So Marxist theory can tolerate – indeed it insists on – the *approximation* to stability of most societies at most times, and the accompanying illusion of absolute and so to speak normative stability. So Functionalism at least approximates to the truth. The deep-rooted *in*stability which *must* be inherent in all class-ridden societies works but slowly, and only reveals itself in relatively rare cataclysms which usher in a new order. The poison works but slowly; it takes a long time for a sufficient dose of it to accumulate in the social body to bring out the malady into the open. But *then* it is fatal for the old order. But the new order thereafter revives the illusion of stability in another guise, unless of course it is the *last* social form.

But whilst Marxism does have this quasi-functionalist aspect, it is none the less incompatible with a fully, genuinely stable, yet class-endowed, society, one in which the illusion of stable self-perpetuation becomes a reality. So how can it cope with societies, if such are found to exist, which genuinely perpetuate themselves, which are *not* covertly unstable in the long run, in which no seeds of change are at work, or which only undergo cyclical change, such as never leads to radical social innovation?

When Marxism did eventually come to face this problem, it did not happen primarily through the consideration of pastoral nomadism. It was the famous Asiatic Mode of Production which really brought the issue into the open. This form of society, if it exists, contradicts both the sociological theory and the eschatological hopes of Marxism, a number of times over. It is stagnant and self-perpetuating, thus offering no hope to the humanity caught in its toils, unless it be accidental liberation from outside which, however, must then be contingent on the existence of some other and less stagnant society, and on the conquest of the 'Oriental' society by it. It also offers the spectacle of a self-serving political order built upon violence, and serving the members of the state machine itself and no one else – in other words, a machine of oppression set up not in defence of pre-existing class system, but by autonomous violence and coercion, and serving a class brought into being merely by its control of the means of coercion, rather than of production. By allowing coercion to be, in this manner, an independent agent in history, a prime mover, it destroys the optimistic theory that coercion is only a by-product of economic exploitation, and will finally be eliminated when such exploitation ends. It thus encourages what Soviet anthropologists have called the 'idealist theory of violence'. This contradiction between the central doctrines of Marxism and the Asiatic Mode of Production has been invoked both against Marxism and against the very idea of the Asiatic Mode of Production.[2]

Pastoral nomadism presents a problem for Marxism which is just as fundamental, if less immediately conspicuous. The societies of pastoral nomads are not in themselves offensive and repugnant, notwithstanding the way in which they might appear to hapless populations whom they conquer from time to time. On the contrary, they have often exercised a fascination for outside observers, as objects not merely of investigation,

2 See ch. 3 above.

but of admiration. As one Soviet scholar pointed out, here every man was not merely shepherd, but also bard, orator, soldier, historian, senator, and minstrel. Nomadic societies know a certain equality (or at any rate a precariousness of fortune precluding stable and deeply internalized inequality), a wide diffusion of civil, political, and military participation, an encapsulation of almost the entire culture in each individual, and a certain quite conscious aversion for that division of labour, that specialization, which Karl Marx also abhorred and wished to see abolished. They often feel and express a certain repugnance for the specialist, even when they need him, and they relegate him to an inferior and stigmatized status. If his specialism is religious and requires reverence, this reverence is liable nevertheless to be tinged with ambivalence.

Ironically, it is the very attractiveness of nomads which creates a problem. It is not simply that the charm of their society is but one side of the coin, of which the other is their brutality and rapacity as raiders and conquerors – facts of which the Russians retain a well-maintained historical recollection. The problem does not arise from the fact that they are not *altogether* attractive. It is rather that as far as theory goes, they have no business to be attractive *at all*. Their cohesion, egalitarianism, wide social participation, aversion to specialization, and rudimentary political structures, would be all very well, if only pastoral nomads were still at the stage of primitive communism, or if they had but recently left it. Then one could welcome the appealing traits of nomadic society as charming survivals, confirming that piece of sociological reconstruction and its moral authority. The attractions could be credited to the absence, or at any rate to the but recent emergence, of private property.

Unfortunately the facts of the case firmly exclude such an interpretation. The rough formula which seems to be accepted (rightly in my view) amongst Soviet ethnographers for the social organization of nomads is this: communal ownership of pasture, family ownership of herds. Moreover, the focus of the major debate – and it was long, persistent, and fascinating – was land tenure amongst the nomads, not the ownership of animals. The critics of the above formula contend that in fact land was being, or had been, monopolized by one class within nomadic society. The private, non-communal ownership of herds was not disputed, even for the past, as far back as the first millennium BC. If any nomads did genuinely pass, as nomads, through the stage of primitive communism, as some Soviet scholars do claim they did, then this stage had to be short and sweet indeed, short enough to leave no traces in archaeological or any other kind of record.

In reading Soviet authors of studies of nomad societies, there is a certain danger of misunderstanding their terminology, springing as it does from a different conceptual background. For instance, A. M. Khazanov, in his most remarkable *Nomads and the Outside World*[3] speaks of *inequality* amongst nomads. No doubt there may be a genuine empirical disagreement here with those who find that such pastoralism is conducive to a relative equality; and indeed, the degree of inequality amongst nomads varies according to time and place, and the whole issue is subject to legitimate debate. But part of the disagreement at least is terminological and conceptual rather than substantive. Even when not directly concerned with the reconstructed 'stage' of primitive communism, Soviet ethnographic theory is so pervaded by this base-line idea of 'primitive society' – an incomparably more heavily theory-loaded term in Soviet discussions than it is in the West – that it is difficult for a Soviet scholar not to have this notion at the back of his mind, as a kind of backcloth and yardstick, and not to be influenced by it in his choice of language, whether or not he is interested in that alleged historic formation. Where a Western scholar will be struck by the egalitarianism of nomads in comparison with the (to us) repellent extremes of inequality amongst Asiatic sedentary agrarian societies, the Soviet scholar – noting the communalism of nomads, their non-specialization, rudimentary political centralization, and collective control of land – can hardly fail to note that, all things considered, nomads are a bit less equal than might be expected, given the lack amongst them of the preconditions of inequality (class monopoly of the means of production) or indeed of its political reflection (developed state formation). Compared with other real, concretely observed large-scale societies, they do seem rather egalitarian, but when silhouetted against the backcloth of primitive communism – which they evoke by their feeble stratification and centralization, and their rudimentary division of labour – they seem *less* equal than they should be.

Pastoral nomads are a problem for Marxism not merely because of the lack of coherence between their attractive traits and their individualistic or at least family-based economy. As in the case of the Asiatic Mode of Production, it is difficult to explain their political structure in terms of the preconditions or requirements of their economic and class organization. Given their private ownership of the crucial animals, they seem to have too little by way of a state, and also too little class stratification. What state formation and social stratification there is, seems to be ephemeral and unstable and elusive.

On the other hand, from time to time they seem to acquire far too

3 See ch. 1, n. 4 above.

much of it: nomads have founded astonishing empires. Too much or too little, but never just right: the superstructure does not seem to adjust itself to the requirement of the base, as theory requires. Moreover, if the state oscillates between being underdeveloped and overdeveloped, theoretical decency would require that the base keep in step and oscillate similarly (preferably a little ahead in time, as would be fitting, given its causal priority). The available evidence, alas, does not confirm any such expectation. Furthermore, the general nature of that superstructure, the social and political institutions of nomads, seem often to be dictated directly by political-military considerations, by the needs of defence, cohesion, and security, rather than being a reflection of the requirements of the social organization of production.

Closely linked to all these problems, there is the issue of whether nomadic societies *develop*. Marxism is profoundly Heraclitean and requires change to be the law of all things: you ought not to be able to immerse yourself in the same society twice, or indeed once. Development towards new and higher forms, through the eventually uncontrollable tensions of every class-endowed society, is essential both for the sociological mechanics and for the soteriology of Marxism: it guarantees the final deliverance of mankind. This issue is central, for instance, in Khazanov's treatment of nomads, and the issue has a long, complex, and fascinating history of Soviet thought, the landmarks of which can only briefly be indicated here.

Soviet orthodoxy had at one time endeavoured to incorporate pastoral nomads in the general onward march of humanity, and to some extent still continues to do so. The general device employed for this end was the attribution to such pastoralists of their own special nomadic feudalism. There was, as one nomadic member of a primitive communal society might have ruefully observed to another, a distinctively nomadic way towards feudalism. Was there indeed? One of the paradoxes, from a Marxist viewpoint, of Russian ethnography of nomadic peoples under Tzarist rule, was that it was possible to find some who were still semi-patriarchal and not *yet* properly feudal, and others who had entered market relations and were semi-capitalist and no *longer* properly feudal, but there was a marked shortage of nomads who were properly feudal, neither too early nor too late. The two demitones were available in plenty, but the primary colour in between seemed to be missing from the spectrum.

None the less, feudalism was credited to the nomads. The giant amongst the scholars putting forward the thesis of nomadic feudalism was Vladimirtsov (who died in 1931). Academician Vladimirtsov was a scholar with roots in pre-revolutionary Russia. He became interested in the Orient in 1905 as a result of the disastrous Russo–Japanese war, and wanted to study Japanese. The University of St Petersburg, however, was ill provided with Japanese scholars, although well equipped with Mongolian ones; so he became a Mongolist instead. Though he noted the need to study Mongol social structure in his diary as early as 1910, he spent most of his life publishing works on Mongolian language and literature, as well as a biography of Ghengiz Khan, a translation of which by Prince Mirsky appeared in London in 1930. But it was close to the end of his life, in 1930, that he set out to carry out his project, and his crucial book[4] appeared posthumously. Its subtitle – *Mongol Nomadic Feudalism* – conveys its thesis.

Whether or not all his details have stood the test of further research, and whether or not one agrees with its central idea, it is an impressive piece of scholarship. Moreover, it predates the excesses of Stalinism and contains neither sycophancy nor any evidence of political motivation of the main thesis. If one does not accept his conclusions one may, leaving aside details, invoke the following considerations. Vladimirtsov was primarily an Orientalist, and relied on texts above all. Texts tend, however, to stress ideal and legal requirements, rather than concrete social reality. In texts at any rate, Mongols appear subject to complex nuances of unsymmetrical rights and duties between various ranked layers of the population, in a manner which certainly suggests a 'feudal' society. Furthermore, and more significantly, much of the material supporting the feudal interpretation comes from the imperial period of Mongol history, and shows that, at a time when Mongol herdsmen were doubling up as soldiers of the empire, a streamlined military organization was superimposed on the system of clans. The leaders of the decimally organized military units had to be located in prescribed places so that the Emperor could mobilize them, and the ordinary Mongol in turn had to graze his flocks in the area assigned to his superior military officer. This can be made to look like the granting of land in return for military service. In general, the central charge that can be levied against the feudalizing thesis is that it takes its evidence from periods when either the Mongols were conquer*ing*, or when they were conquer*ed* and incorporated in the Manchu empire.

Another volume also appeared in 1934: *Osnovnye problemy genezisa i razvitiya feodal'nogo obshchestva* (*Basic Problems in the Genesis and Develop-*

---

4 B. Ya. Vladimirtsov, *Obshchestvennyi stroi mongolov. Mongol'skii kochevoi feodalizm (Social Order of the Mongols. Mongol nomadic feudalism)* (Leningrad, 1934), translated into French as *Le Régime social des Mongols: le feudalisme nomade*, with preface by René Grousset; translation by Michael Carsaw (Paris, 1948).

One of the early Soviet ethnographic affirmations of the feudalist thesis is to be found in R. Kabo, *Ocherki istorii i ekonomiki Tuvy* (*Sketches of the History and Economy of Tuva*) (Moscow – Leningrad, 1934).

ment of Feudal Society).[5] It contained a contribution by S. F. Tolstov, destined to play a very major role in Soviet social science, entitled 'Genezis feodalisma v kochevykh skotovodcheskikh obshchestvakh' ('The genesis of feudalism in nomadic pastoral societies'). Tolstov's contribution to the general problem of the genesis and development of feudal society, though published the same year as Vladimirtsov's study, but is very far away from it in spirit. For instance, it humbly pleads to the charge of not yet having fully carried out the theoretical task placed before the workers on the theoretical front by Comrade Stalin in his historic speech to Marxist agrarian experts, but ominously adds that these problems are already being solved in the practical struggle. *Solvitur ambulando*, or perhaps *non-ambulando*, may have a special and somewhat sinister application for nomads. Tolstov has an acute sense of the unity of theory and practice:

This problem is by no means of merely academic significance . . . its solution enables us to sharpen our weapon of a correct Marxist understanding . . . it is relevant to the immediate practice of the political struggle, the practice of class war both in the Soviet East and abroad, in the colonial Orient . . . the correctness of the practical work of the socialist reconstruction of the nomadic and semi-nomadic *aul* of the Soviet East depends on the correct theoretical solution of this problem . . .

The political relevance of the correct interpretation of nomadic social structure could hardly be made plainer.

Tolstov's scholarship is impressive, but at the same time he had an acute sense of the political significance of scholarly errors, and of the need to apply both scholarly and political criteria to preferred solutions. In his view political need and truth happily converge. One big error consisted of 'nationalist-populist' tendencies, which underestimate feudal-capitalist elements in feudal and semi-feudal society, and idealize the survivals of a kin-based society. People he described as bourgeois nationalists, specially prominent amongst Kazakhs, it seems, held a view he describes as the congruence of the kin group and socialism, a theory which ignores the fact that amongst nomads the kin group has long ago transformed itself into a class society. But there is also a 'leftists' error which underestimates kin-feudal elements, and attempts to assimilate the nomadic community to the capitalist village. Generally, populist and Trotskyist tendencies are castigated for falsely claiming a scholarly and Marxist status. They converge with rightist

5 S. N. Bykovskii et al. (eds) (OGIZ, 1934). This contained the proceedings of a plenary session of the State Academy of the History of Material Culture, which took place on 20–2 June 1933.

tendencies, the over-estimation of kin relations, and the ignoring of the presence of deep class differentiation in the *aul* (nomadic community). Tolstov also polemicizes with scholars who deny the existence of class differentiation amongst the ancient Scythians,[6] and equally with others, who wish to revise the Marxist-Leninist anarchist conception, by projecting private property, classes, and so forth backwards, onto the kin community, right back, in Tolstov's words, 'to the time of Adam'.[7] Near the end of his article, he sums up the position: 'At present, "tribal survivals" emerge as the most dangerous weapon in the hands of the class enemy, who aims to use them at this new stage of the class war in his struggle against the construction of socialism.'

At the practical level, Tolstov's strictures seem aimed at enemies both on the right and the left. The former would deny the presence or importance of an enemy feudal class, hiding behind the screen of fraternal kin groups; the latter would minimize their importance for the opposite reason, by exaggerating the importance of capitalist elements. (In this connection, he ironizes retrojections of 'finance capital' onto ancient oriental societies, such as would locate it even at the time of Hammurabi, as apparently the Soviet scholar N. M. Nikolskii had done, or in Mecca on the eve of Islam, the latter view having being proposed by Lammens in his work published in 1924 in Beirut.) Right-wing idealization of the clan and left deviations meet in the hope of basing socialism on a surviving kin community. The concrete situation seems however to be that the struggle taking place within the Soviet Union required that there be enemies in the nomadic and semi-nomadic regions, that they be *feudal* enemies, and that they should not be allowed to hide behind a kin façade.

On the theoretical level, Tolstov is concerned with denying two theses: on the one hand, the affirmation of the genuine survival of kin communities amongst nomads (as opposed to the fraudulent use of kin camouflage of feudal relations); and, on the other, the denial that a genuine community, without private property, had *ever* existed. In other words, the importance of the erstwhile existence of a genuine communitarian social form in the Marxist scheme is firmly upheld but, oddly enough, no actually documented nomadic community is credited with exemplifying it. Even the Scythians, who, being extinct, do not

6 E.g. S. A. Semenov-Zuser, 'Rodovaya organizatsiya Skifov Gerodota' ('Kin Organizations of Herodotus' Scythians'), *Izvestia GAIMK*, vol. 9, 1931.

7 Authors he cites are V. Kushner, *Gornaya Kirgiziya* (*sotsiologicheskaya razvedka*) (*Mountain Kirgizia* (*Sociological Reconnaissance*)) (Moscow, 1928); P. F. Preobrazhenskii, 'Razlozhenie rodovogo stroya i feodal'nyi protsess u Turkmen-Tomudov' ('The disintegration of kin structure and feudal process amongst the Tomud Turkmen'), *Etnografia*, 1930.

require or allow the liquidation of any class enemy in their midst, are firmly endowed with a slave-owning social formation.

The canonical quotation which he invokes from the collected works of Marx and Engels affirms that in *all* oriental tribes one can find the existence of a relationship between a sedentarized part of the tribe, and another part which *continues* the nomadic form of life.[8] The passage invoked seems a bit contradictory, in as far as the suggestion that the nomadic segment of a mixed tribe *continues* the old way of life, would seem to imply that previously, tribes has existed which were *fully* nomadic. Tolstov's reliance on material which documents the presence of severaly exploitative relations amongst such mixed, partly sedentarized and partly nomadic social units, is of course compatible with the rival, 'anti-feudal' position. Those who deny the existence of feudal relations amongst nomads do not deny that complex stratified societies do indeed emerge when conquest, either *by* or *of* nomads, engenders larger units with a significant sedentary component.

The other criticism which could be levelled against Tolstov would be that, extending as he does the 'feudal' or at any rate class-endowed interpretation so far back, as opposed to merely finding the feudal enemy where he was required to exist by the contemporary context, he comes very close to conceding one contention central to the rival school: that nomadic societies have not changed and developed much, or at all. On the other hand, his eagerness to find the class enemy even in the distant past might well encourage scepticism about whether the primordial community was ever to be found, anywhere.

It is noteworthy that Tolstov relates this problem to that of the Asiatic Mode of Production, castigating an article written in 1932 by V. I. Ravdonikas (who however is also a fellow contributor to this very volume), in which Ravdonikas declared that Asiatic Mode of Production to be a pre-class society, thereby, says Tolstov aligning himself with Guomindang theoreticians, and generally with nationalist, populist interpretations of Oriental history. Western anthropologists will be interested to note that Malinowski (though his name is misspelt) receives praise from Tolstov for his 'brilliant description' of a pre-class society in *The Argonauts of the Western Pacific*.

Generally speaking, one might say that Tolstov's essay highlights in the most conspicuous manner possible the intimate links between the theoretical issue of nomadic social structure, and the on-the-ground struggle which was at that very time taking place within the nomadic or partly nomadic societies inside the Soviet Union. It was evidently

8 See Tolstov, 'The Genesis of Feudalism', p. 171.

necessary to find a Marxist characterization of those who opposed the construction of socialism and the establishment of Soviet power, just as a Kulak class had to exist to explain resistance to collectivization among sedentary peasants. The link between theory and practice which he brings out so vigorously was destined to remain important or dominant at the very least until the Tashkent conference of 1954, convened to consider the nature of erstwhile social relations amongst the nomadic nations of Central Asia and Kazakhstan. By then, however, it was no longer a matter of *guiding* the conflict on the ground, but rather of explaining and justifying its outcome retrospectively.[9]

Vladimirtsov's relatively un-doctrinal work had not even cited the classics of Marxism; by contrast, in later years even revisionists quote scripture for their purpose. In Tashkent in 1954[9] the feudalists prevailed again, but were not able or allowed to extinguish all opposition. At least one firmly dissenting voice, that of Tolybekov, refused to be silenced. But before we reach this high point in the debate about the feudalizing thesis, one other book, highly relevant to the manner in which Soviet ex-nomads were related both to the national question and to the pattern of human history, should be considered.

In 1947 the Soviet Academy of Sciences once again published a book of great interest for the history of this debate, namely Vyatkin's *Batyr Srym*.[10] The hero of the book is the leader of the Kazakh struggle against Russian Tsarist imperialism in the late eighteenth century. The book is concerned with the issue of nationality and nationalism, and the analysis of Kazakh nomadic society is only introduced indirectly, in so far as a national struggle, for a Marxist, must also be interpreted in class terms. Vyatkin's formulation of the problem is interesting. Stalin had shown, he notes, that the national problem is in its essence the peasant problem. Now that is all very well, but what do you do when you plainly have a national conflict, but you have shepherds and pastoralists where there should have been peasants? What do you do in a situation in which peasants and serfs are in very short supply? That is the question. Is the national question not merely a peasant question but also a shepherd question? There seems to be no canonical authority for saying so. So what's to be done?

Another solution is, however, available. At the Tenth Congress of the

---

9 *Materialy ob'edinennoi nauchnoi sessii, posvyashchennoi istorii srednei Azii i Kazakhstana v dooktiabrskom periode* (*Documents of the Combined Academic Conference devoted to the pre-October history of Central Asia and Kazakhstan*). (Tashkent, 1955). L. P. Potapov reaffirms the feudal thesis, with special reference to Tuva, in his contribution to a publication which appeared as late as 1975, namely *Sotsial'naya istoriya narodov Azii* (*Social History of the Nations of Asia*), ed. A. M. Reshetov and C. M. Taksami (Moscow, 1975).
10 M. P. Vyatkin, *Batyr Srym* (Moscow – Leningrad, 1947).

CPSU(B) in 1921, Comrade Stalin had provided invaluable help towards the solution of this problem, Vyatkin notes, by characterizing the recent condition of the various pastoral nations of the Soviet Union as 'patriarchal-feudal'. Vyatkin here uses an *a fortiori* argument: if they still retained patriarchal elements even at the time of the October Revolution, they can be assumed to have been endowed with them even more plentifully two centuries earlier! This solution, which consists essentially in seeing nomadic society (or rather, in this case, a single nomadic society at a certain time), as possessing a mixture of patriarchal-communal and of feudal traits, was one destined also to be adopted later in the masterly studies of Kazakh society by Tolybekov.

Vyatkin sees and recognizes that under conditions of pastoral nomadism, the maintenance of clan units is essential, and these in turn perpetuate collective ownership of land. So a proper feudalism, in which a class would monopolize land and also deprive ordinary clansmen of their freedom and turn them into serfs, does not develop. Nevertheless, masked by the retention of the ideology of kinship and collectivity, feudal relations *do* emerge. Vyatkin is sympathetic to his hero and sees him as the champion of the oppressed Kazakhs both against Tsarist imperialism and against their own emerging aristocracy, tempted by its own interests into collaboration with the alien conquerors, or at least into dragging its feet in the national struggle. But a proper pastoral equivalent of a *Bauernkrieg* never developed, simply because neither the leader not the followers ever freed themselves from the false consciousness of tribalism, which masked an emergent feudal reality.

A theme which is of interest, and which was subsequently to reappear, is the idea that feudalism amongst pastoral nomads liable to be connected with the imposition of alien domination. It should be added that although Vyatkin wrote and published at the height of Stalinism, and his book does contain the inevitable canonical vindications of central points, it is nevertheless very interesting, and is argued at an extremely high level.

The next important occasion in the debate occurred, as already mentioned, in 1954, after Stalin's death, when an inter-disciplinary conference was convened in Tashkent to discuss the pre-revolutionary history of the nations of Central Asia and Kazakhstan. The proceedings were published the following year.[11] This seems to have been an openly political occasion, and one which confirmed the status of the feudal and development theory of pastoral nomads as the orthodoxy. Its main protagonist was one L. P. Potapov. He castigated[12] the view, prevalent

11 *Documents of the Combined Academic Conference*, cit. n. 9 above.
12 Ibid., p. 17.

before the Revolution and even during the early years following it, that these populations had lived within a tribal structure in which kin relations prevailed and hence there were no classes or class conflict, as a 'theory ... used by bourgeois nationalists, rightists, opportunists and rigid ideologists and *defenders of exploitative classes destined for liquidation amongst these nationalities*' (italics mine).

Potapov's concern is clearly different from Vyatkin's. Vyatkin endeavoured to give a class interpretation to a national conflict which had occurred two centuries earlier. Potapov is, in effect, offering an interpretation of very recent, post-revolutionary conflicts. If he had allowed that these nomadic nations were made up of kin communities, without anything much in the way of class formation, he would have been faced by a problem. One can imagine a Kazakh herdsman in his pastoral collective, scratching his ear with a bit of stubble as his herd grazes peacefully, and wondering: 'Now if we Kazakhs really had no classes to speak of before the Revolution, who exactly was it that we liquidated during the recent decades? A rum business ...'

Potapov's emphatic feudalism provides a clear and unambiguous answer to this conundrum. In his own spine-chilling words, they were 'exploitative classes destined for liquidation'. Nothing could be clearer. At the same time, he rescues nomads for a developmental vision of human history, endowing them with a social growth potential, and ensuring that they, and thus humanity at large, were available for eventual salvation, whether or not they happened to be engulfed by an alien imperialism. On Potapov's account, nomads must have passed through, *as pastoral nomads*, at least three very important and distinct stages – primitive communism, patriarchal society, and feudalism. Potapov asserts in so many words[13] that the earlier nomadic pastoral community had shared ownership not merely of pasture, but also of herds.

His use of the argument from survivals is strange. He admits that the conditions of nomadic pastoralism were unfavourable to collective ownership of herds, that nomadism only began in the first millennium BC, and that by the middle of the millennium, when historical archaeological evidence concerning nomads becomes more plentiful, communalism is no longer to be found. Yet survivals of it are alleged to persist in more or less contemporary ethnography. This seems to imply that a highly unstable social condition, which could barely have lasted a few centuries before it was displaced because of its internal organizational incoherence, nevertheless leaves social marks which then tenaciously perpetuate themselves for two and a half millennia.

13 Ibid., p. 22.

Whatever the merits of his anthropological ideas, it would be difficult to deny that Potapov was capable of eloquence and vigour in political denunciation.[14] The person whom he denounced with specially forceful irony was S. E. Tolybekov. 'It seems to me, Comrade Tolybekov, that the Khans and Sultans, if only they were here, would receive you with a standing ovation . . .' These feudal lords would welcome Tolybekov's views that they were not true feudal lords after all, because they did not own the land and pasture used by their societies. Starting out from such erroneous theoretical premisses, one can reach erroneous political conclusions, and end up objectively as a defender of large feudal property-owners, Potapov notes pointedly. Tovarishch Tolybekov, Potapov adds ominously, finds himself in just such a danger.

The objective dangers of Tolybekov's position (in whichever of the two possible senses one chooses to interpret that phrase) evidently did not intimidate him. Far from it. On the contrary, they seem to have stimulated him into a lifetime of devoted scholarship concerning the social history of the Kazakhs, the theoretical backbone of which is clearly a passionate repudiation of the 'feudal' thesis, and of the charges made against himself in Tashkent in 1954. Manifestly the Tashkent trauma of 1954 guided his subsequent scholarly activity. His two books on this subject, which admittedly repeat each other in some measure, contain superb and extremely rich ethnography, coherently and interestingly organized around his central ideas.[15]

---

14 Ibid., p. 138.

15 S. E. Tolybekov, *Obshchestvenno-ekonomicheskii stroi Kazakhov v XVII—XIX vekakh* (*Socio-economic Structure of the Kazakhov in the 17th—19th centuries*) (Alma-Ata, 1959); and *Kochevoe obshchestvo Kazakhov v XVII — nachale XX veka. Politiko-ekonomicheskii analiz* (*Nomadic Kazakh Society from the 17th to the early 20th century. Politico-Economic Analysis*) (Alma-Ata, 1971).

A year before Tolybekov's first book, a volume appeared dealing specifically with the Kazakhs, and still affirming their feudal status, at any rate during the first half of the nineteenth century. It was S. Z. Zimanov's *Obshchestvennyi stroi Kazakhov pervoi poloviny XIX veka* (*Social Structure of the Kazakhs in the First Half of the 19th Century*) (Alma-Ata, 1958). But Zimanov was obliged to moderate his thesis: 'The monopolistic right of the feudals to pasture was a factual and not a juridicial right' (p. 148). Here again, feudalism is said to be lurking under a communal, tribal guise, preserving earlier legal forms. Zimanov stresses in particular the role played by the subtle rank differentiation within the two principal, 'real' classes (the rulers and the exploited), in inhibiting the development of an effective class-consciousness. The consequence of this was that when genuine social movements did arise – and he is willing to class Srym's rebellion as such – in the end they serve not the people (*narod*), which provides its driving force, but the egoistic interest of this or that substratum of the ruling class, which happened to associate itself with it (pp. 288–9). He admits that the feudalism of the Kazakhs was poorly developed, even in the nineteenth century, but connects this with the absence of urban traders, artisans, etc. amongst them (p. 290). This is a theme which also reappears in the work of S. I. Vainstein (see n. 23 below).

A similar picture of part-feudal, part-patriarchal, and communal society emerges from

One of the most interesting aspects of Tolybekov is his values. He is himself of Kazakh background, and his name is clearly a Russification of Toly Bey. (Amongst the Kazakhs, however, unlike other Turkic groups, *bey* is an honorific term not implying membership of a hereditary aristocracy.) Unlike his predecessor Vyatkin, Tolybekov repudiates Batyr Srym's rising of 1783, which he insists was motivated by nothing better than the pursuit of loot, slave-raiding, and opposition to the unification of the junior Kazakh *zhus* (maximal segment) with Russia. Elsewhere, and more than once, Tolybekov insists that the Kazakhs united with Russia voluntarily. (In fact, fear of renewed aggression by the then ascendant Djungarian Mongols may have had some connection with Kazakh eagerness for Tsarist protection.) His admission that Batyr Srym and his followers *opposed* this unification does not amount to a contradiction, in so far as he explicitly says that the beneficiaries of these raids by Batyr Srym were simply the members of the parastic *batyr* class, such as Srym himself. (On this point he agrees with S. Z. Zimanov, who otherwise takes a kinder view of Srym's movement. See n. 10.) Srym was, as you might say, a feudal bandit, rather than a social bandit.

Tolybekov's warm *ex post facto* endorsement and ratification of the incorporation of the Kazakhs in the Russian world, does not, so to speak, hang in the air in an opportunistic manner, as a piece of mere political sycophancy. Tolybekov's retrospective repudiation of the primary resistance of the Kazakhs to Tsarist imperialism is, on the contrary, rooted in an important, convincing, and persistently re-affirmed sociological theme: nomadic society is stagnant. It does not, and cannot, *as* pastoral nomadic society, develop any further. It constitutes a sociological cul-de-sac, or, to use the expressive Russian word, a *tupik*. The sociological reasoning as to why this is so, and must be so, is complex, subtle, and well documented: it would certainly deserve intensive study and a much more detailed exposition than it is possible to offer here. It also contains some surprising elements, such as the idea that the protracted period of awaiting economic reward amongst pastoralists, which is a consequence of the long gestation period of

---

the major book devoted to the Kirgiz, S. M. Abramzon's *The Kirgiz and their Ethnogenetic and Historic-cultural Relations*, cit. ch. 1, n. 7 above. The author asserts the presence of 'feudal relations' amongst the Kirgiz in the sixteenth and seventeenth centuries, and asserts that these must have emerged no later than the end of the first millennium A D. But he rapidly goes on to qualify this by saying that the low and backward level of productive force found amongst pastoral nomads, ensured that these features remained intertwined with 'pre-feudal, kin-patriarchal, communal relations' (pp. 155 and 146). Such a formulation is certainly congruent with Tolybekov's view. But Abramzon also goes out of his way to polemicize with L. Krader (*Social Organization of the Mongol-Turkic Pastoral Nomads* (Indiana, 1963) for exaggerating the importance of corporate kin groups, and missing out the feudal traits (p. 209).

camels, inhibits the development of productive forces. This is in marked contrast to the Western tendency to see Delayed Return, and the capacity to wait for it, as the prime mark of economic virtue and a crucial factor in innovation – an idea forcefully reintroduced into anthropology by James Woodburn.[16] Tolybekov's repudiation of Kazakh nomadic separatism strictly follows from this theory. On their own, they were debarred from any real development.

More specifically, and with a great wealth of ethnographic and historical documentation, Tolybekov denies the capacity of pastoral nomads in general, and of Kazakhs in particular, to advance anywhere near a ripe and proper feudalism. *No feudalization without sedentarization* might well be his motto. The picture of Kazakh traditional society which emerges from his analysis and documentation contains precisely those traits which have led Western scholars to use terms such as 'segmentary' in connection with pastoral nomads: the weak, elusive, ephemeral nature of political centralization, the wide diffusion of power and political participation, the precarious and relatively mild degree of social differentiation, the prominence of collectives practising mutual aid and self-defence. One may perhaps speak of a ruling stratum and also of a servile one, but both are very small in comparison with the numerically dominant stratum of ordinary free tribesmen. The number of servile families attached to the household of a ruling khan, head of a maximal segment, barely reaches double figures. This suggests the camp of a chieftain, not the court of an oriental monarch.

Tolybekov roundly accuses the feudal school of projecting Western or Russian medieval developments onto the Eurasian steppe. Even as conquerors, the Hun or Mongol rulers did not have the capacity for establishing feudalism which was displayed by Teutonic barbarians, who were already familiar with the use of serf labour. Tolybekov argues in effect that, compared to Central Asia, the West was fortunate in possessing a better class of barbarian, if you know what I mean, endowed with a far greater potential for progress. If anyone had developed a mature feudalism in central Asia, it was the sedentary population of Khorezm, but what it had built up was destroyed by the Tatars. Tolybekov invokes Tolstov[17] who pointed out that it was Khorezm and Kiev that, by their resistance and sacrifice, exhausted the Mongols sufficiently to save Europe from also being overrun by them. It was Khorezmian and Kievan blood that saved Europe for feudalism, and thus allowed it to develop further.

16 J. Woodburn, 'Hunters and Gatherers today and reconstruction of the past', in Gellner (ed.), *Soviet and Western Anthropology*.

17 S. F. Tolstov, *Po sledam drevnekhorezmskoi tsivilizatsii* (*On the Traces of Ancient Khorezmian Civilization*) (Moscow–Leningrad, 1948), pp. 321–2.

Thus Tolybekov unambiguously condemns nomadic pastoral society, when considered from the viewpoint of its contribution to the evolution of human society. It is a dead end. It constitutes a barrier to further development. He firmly denies that it can ever reach even mature feudalism – let alone anything beyond that. He firmly rejects the view of his predecessors that underneath the patriarchal and kin terminology of nomads, a feudal society was hiding, wildly signalling to be liquidated. He rather manages to score against his opponents, who claimed that this underlying feudal reality had succeeded in establishing itself surreptitiously, under the guise of patriarchal and clan ideas, and had used this camouflage to befuddle its potential opponents, such as the hapless Batyr Srym. If this doctrine is taken seriously, it seems to imply that a transition from one social form to another can take place quietly, without the aid of violence as the licensed midwife of history; that, in brief, a peaceful transition to feudalism is possible. Tolybekov evidently obtains a good deal of satisfaction from highlighting this implicit heterodoxy of his opponents.

Tolybekov himself characterizes nomadic society as patriarchal-feudal, as a transitional stage in which some weak feudal traits appear in the pre-feudal social order. His use of the term *perekhodnyi* (transitional) is strange, in so far as it is absolutely central to his much reiterated position that this transition can never be completed by nomads *as* nomads. Is a *transition* that can never be completed a real transition? Can a bridge be a cul-de-sac?

But if Tolybekov roundly condemns the lack of growth-potential of a nomadic society, and welcomes its incorporation in a society which *did* have the seeds of growth, he is far from hostile to nomad culture, and Kazakh culture in particular. His account of its merits is eloquent and moving. 'Every illiterate nomadic Kazakh, like all nomads of the world, was in the fifteenth to the eighteenth century simultaneously a shepherd and a soldier, an orator and a historian, poet, and singer. All national wisdom, assembled by the ages, existed only in oral form.'[18]

Thus, though Tolybekov does not say so, nomads already in some measure exemplify that multiplicity of roles, that overcoming of the division of labour, that rich multi-faceted human personality, which Marx in *The German Ideology* predicted only for the liberated man of the future. Tolybekov also warns the Russian reader against the unimaginative philistinism which might lead him to fail to appreciate the beauty of Kazakh lyrico-epic poetry, in which, for instance, the movements of the great Kazakh beauty, Kyz-Zhibek, a kind of Helen of Troy, are compared to those of a three-year-old ram. The failure to appreciate the

18 Tolybekov, *Socio-economic Structure of the Kazakhs*, p. 426.

beauty of such a simile, Tolybekov sternly warns us, only goes with an inability to realize that aesthetics must vary with the material conditions of life. Certainly, given a pastoral infrastructure, it is entirely fitting to compare a girl with a three-year-old ram. Even without being a pastoral nomad, I find the idea of a girl moving like a three-year-old ram rather exciting. Perhaps, one wonders, the Kazakhs actually preferred a three-year-old ram?

Whatever the truth about these details of Kazakh culture, and whatever the general terminology he employs to describe it, there can be no doubt concerning Tolybekov's characterization of Kazakh society and of pastoral nomadic society in general. Its culture is widely and evenly diffused and encapsulated in its members, full participation extends to most adult males or at least heads of households, stratification is ephemeral and weak, political formations are fragile and elusive, and even if on occasion the social units grow into something bigger, this leads to no permanent, irreversible, structural changes in society. It is this doctrine, and all it implies in terms of the intellectual tradition within which it was articulated, which is central to Tolybekov's work, and to his lifelong struggle with the 'nomadic feudalism' thesis, though he must be valued at least as much for the richness and suggestiveness of his historical and ethnographic material.

The two men who continued Tolybekov's argument against the feudalizing thesis, and for the recognition of the basically stagnant or oscillating nature of pastoral nomadic society, are G. E. Markov and A. M. Khazanov. Khazanov presents his own case in the volume available in English better than anyone else could do on his behalf, and there is no need to summarize his position. But the remarkable work of Markov, the present holder of the Chair of Ethnography at the University of Moscow, does deserve mention in this context.[19]

Markov and Khazanov (Markov is somewhat older) seem to have reached similar conclusions independently. If Tolybekov's central concern is with the Kazakhs (though he does firmly generalize his conclusions), the main concern of Markov's book and of Khazanov's later work is comparative (though this is not quite so much the case for Khazanov's earlier work on Scythians). The background knowledge they bring to this theme is not identical. Markov refers in his book to many years of repeated seasonal field trips to the nomadic, or rather ex-nomadic, parts of the Soviet Union, and in his book he combines this ethnographic background with a very thorough use of the traditional historical documentation concerning the nomads of Asia (those of Africa being excluded from its purview). Khazanov was initially a historian of

---

19 G. E. Markov, *Kochevniki Azii* (*The Nomads of Asia*) (Moscow, 1976).

the Scythians, and his major previous work deals with them. His concern, in that work, with the cyclical pattern of Scythian history, is later broadened into a general theory of pastoral nomadism, expounded in the volume published in English, and is sustained by a remarkable familiarity with modern Western anthropological literature concerning pastoral nomads.

As Markov's excellent study is not available in Western languages, a brief account of some of its points is apposite here. He notes that the origin of pastoral nomadism remains unclear, but that it was preceded by complex non-nomadic agriculture.[20] He locates the emergence of full nomadism at around 1000 BC. He explicitly endorses Tolybekov's assertion that in essential social features, the Huns of the third and second centuries BC, the Mongols of the eleventh and twelfth centuries, and the Kazakhs of the fifteenth to eighteenth centuries, were similar. However, whilst endorsing Tolybekov's critique of the feudalizing school, and castigating the evidently traumatic 1954 discussions as scholastic, Markov does not endorse the terminology – at least – of Tolybekov's positive solution, i.e. his general characterization of pastoral nomadic society as 'transitional patriarchal-feudal'. He shares Tolybekov's view that evidence for feudal land relations amongst nomads is drawn either from what the Tsarist administration had imposed on them, in violation of their own customary law, or (when based for instance on Plano Carpini's reports on the Mongol empire) from temporary devices superimposed by Ghengiz Khan on the Mongol clan organization in the interests of military centralization. He also asserts explicitly that amongst nomads, developed forms of class conflict are absent. 'History knows no rising of nomadic tribes, comparable to peasant risings.'[21]

Inequality amongst nomads is not very great, and when it does emerge, is a consequence of war and trading rather than of the normal functioning of the economy, within which leaders, members of the privileged stratum have no interest in depriving their fellow tribesmen

20 A recent work dealing specifically with this issue is V. A. Shnirelman, *Proiskhozhdenie skotovodstva* (*The Origins of Pastoralism*) (Moscow, 1980). See also n. 24 below.
The latest contribution to the problem of the socio-political organization of nomads seems to be S. A. Plemneva's *Kochevniki srednevekov'ya* (*Medieval Nomads*) (Moscow, 1982). This work combines an attempt at formulating a three-stage theory of nomadic society, with a stress on the impermanence of political formation amongst nomads (a stress specially manifest in a fourfold typology of their political decline and disintegration). This would seem to imply a marked concession to an 'oscillatory', rather than developmental, theory of nomadic political formations.
21 Markov, *Nomads of Asia*, p. 305. The absence of visible or self-conscious stratification in central Asia was, as stated, a practical and political, as well as a theoretical problem for the Soviets. Cf. Gregory J. Massell, *The Surrogate Proletariat* (Princeton, NJ, 1974). The book discusses the attempt to see the feminine sex as a whole as the exploited class, for lack of any other plausible and really satisfactory candidate for this role.

of access to the means of production. (One might say that if capitalism requires a reserve army of unemployed, pastoral nomadic chiefs need a reserve army *sans phrase*; and they can hardly deprive themselves of it, by denying their shepherds-reservists the means of subsistence.) Productive relations had the form of economic cooperation or consent, not of feudal dependency. Markov criticizes even Tolybekov for overconcentrating on the relatively small classes of leaders and servile dependents, to the detriment of the far larger and more typical middle stratum of free tribesmen. It is this stress which enabled Tolybekov to include the feudal element in his 'patriarchal-feudal' formula.

In other ways, Markov is distinguished from Tolybekov by his theoretical caution. Where Tolybekov did use his 'transitional' formula (with a never-to-be-completed transition) for a generic characterization of pastoral nomads. Markov declares the problem of the sociological classification of nomads to be unsolved, and thus refrains from attaching any formal label to their social structure. Where Tolybekov asserts with firmness, and perhaps a touch of bitterness, that nomads *could not* develop further than they did, Markov contents himself with asserting that they *did not*. Further, he insists that in order to understand their social structure, we must look at the position and role of chiefs amongst them. It could be considerable, in temporary military and imperial situations. But the leaders did not form a closed stratum and did not retain their status when they lost their leading position. The kinsmen of Ghengiz Khan did have a few privileges, but it did not amount to much. Members of the White Bone clan amongst Khazaks (supposedly kinsmen of Ghengiz Khan) had no great power, even if they attained chiefly status, and were often called chiefs-faineants (*mnimye nachal'niki*). They collected no rent and, to maintain their position, were obliged to entertain lavishly, which put a great strain on their households.

Markov asserts explicitly that the nomad empires had no economic base. Amongst agrarian populations, government, once it appears, is irreversible, and leads to permanent structural changes; but amongst nomads, centralization, in any case incomplete, is ephemeral, and is followed by a reversal to communal organization. Thus Markov ends with a cyclical or oscillatory account of the socio-political organization of nomads, not unlike that of Ibn Khaldun (who is not invoked by name). But before claiming Markov's conclusions for an Ibn Khaldunian sociology, it is only fair to note certain differences. (These may in fact reflect significantly the differences between the Eurasian steppe on the one hand, and the Arabian peninsula and North Africa on the other.) For Ibn Khaldun, urban life is a permanent necessity, essential for the pastoral economy, and pastoral tribalism is the *only* source of state-formation, the state being the gift of the tribe to the ever-present city. The tribesmen need the city economically, the townsmen need the tribes politically. Neither is ultimately self-sufficient. Markov's account on the other hand does not make urban life quite so essential as a complementary element for the nomads, and sedentary areas are credited with an endogenous and independent capacity to generate political centralization – they do not need to be provided with it by tribal conquest. Unlike Middle Eastern cities, they are independently capable of state formation.

Finally, it is worth noting the extent to which Khazanov's remarkable earlier work on the Scythians[22] already formulates the ideas systematized in a comparative perspective in his later general work. The central idea of continuity in the Eurasian steppe, as opposed to a developmental pattern, is already asserted. In the steppe, Scythians, Sarmatians, Huns, Alans, Khazars, Pechenegs, Turks, Polovtsi, Tatars, the Golden Horde, Kazakhs, and others all followed each other, but without any basic structural change. He criticizes effort by scholars such as Vainshtein,[23] Artamonov, Griaznov, Chernikov, and Smirnov to find a systematic difference between early and late nomads. It is true that the earlier 'houses on wheels' were replaced by *yurts* which can be dismantled, and that nomads of Iranian speech were replaced by others of Turkish/Mongolian speech; but there has been no fundamental social change.

Within Scythian history itself, a certain cyclical pattern had emerged. The Scythians established three successive empires, and only the last of these was accompanied by sedentarization and hence by a real state, as opposed to a merely rudimentary tribute-extracting organization of the first two Scythian formations. During this earlier period, the tensions between urban and sedentary life and the pastoral nomadic style was already apparent, in the form of hostility between Greek and Scythian. The greater their economic and cultural complementarity, the greater also the political conflict. The young Scythians, as Khazanov describes them on an implicit analogy with the Young Turks, were notoriously drawn to Greek music and wine (a taste which was of course ruthlessly exploited by Greek exporters), and they delighted in the flute-playing of

22 Khazanov, *Social History of the Scythians*, cit. ch. 1, n. 4 above.
23 One of these authors is accessible in English: Sevyan I. Vainstein, *Nomads of South Siberia*, ed., with an Introduction by Caroline Humphrey (Cambridge, 1980). This work of Vainstein's however is concerned primarily with the ethnography of the Tuvinians, rather than with questions of theory, though the book does contain a brief summary of Soviet debates on these matters. For a recent discussion by numerous Western scholars of these general problems, see *Pastoral Production and Society*, collectively edited (Cambridge, 1979). A Western anthropologist specifically concerned with the central Asian peoples in the Russian orbit is L. Krader. See his *Peoples of Central Asia* (The Hague, 1963).

a Greek captive. But their *narodnik* (populist) king repudiated these alien innovations, and was heard to observe that he preferred the neighing of his horse to that damned Greek flautist. *Plus ça change...*

The general conclusions of that study of the Scythians could be summed up as follows: there was urban-tribal economic interdependence, combined with political and cultural tension; political development was cyclical; and social stratification and political centralization was weak amongst the nomads except at times when they turned themselves into a dominant, conquering stratum of a wider society. Such conclusions, later generalized, can only give pleasure to the present writer, who is after all a card-carrying Ibn Khaldunian.

Yet in the end, notwithstanding the continuing steady stream of 'feudal' interpretations, opinion, and in particular influential opinion, seems to be swinging in favour of the rival view. In 1986, a book appeared[24] which is in effect the second of three volumes of a work intended to reformulate the theory of early, pre-class society. The editor-in-chief, Academician Yulian Bromley, is Head of the important Institute of Ethnography of the Soviet Academy of Sciences, and occupies a crucial position in the section of the All-Union Academy which encompasses both history and ethnography (i.e. social anthropology). His authority in the world of Soviet anthropology is considerable. The problem of nomadism is discussed in chapter 4 of the book. The author responsible for that particular chapter is V. A. Shnirelman, who had previously written an important book on the origins of pastoralism.

On page 244 we read: 'the development of agriculture and pastoralism opened up fundamentally different possibilities, constituting the conditions for the formation and evolution of class-endowed social organisms.' This sentence in itself is significant, constituting a kind of recognition of the role of the Neolithic Revolution in the emergence of complex, stratified societies. The original formulation of Marxism had preceded the work of Gordon Childe and the theory of the 'neolithic revolution', and the previous stress had been on the growth of the use of the tools, rather than the discovery of agriculture as such. This had the curious consequence that Western archaeology, preoccupied with the neolithic revolution and the implications of agriculture, often has a *more* materialist ring than its Soviet equivalent, which seems to look for the mechanism of the first (and perhaps greatest) social revolution of human history in social, rather than in productive transformations. The

24 *Istoriya pervobytnogo Obshchestva: epokha pervobytnoi rodovoi obshchiny.* (*History of Primitive Society: The Epoch of Primitive Kin Community*), ed. Yu. V. Bromley, A. I. Pershits, V. A. Shnirelman (Moscow, 1986).

sentence may be seen as a kind of implicit ex post incorporation of Gordon Childe amongst the basic texts of Marxism.

But it is the passage that follows on this that is really striking, and most relevant to the present theme:

Here it is important to discuss an exception, connected with nomadic pastoralism. Nomadic pastoralism, though it constitutes one of the varieties of productive society, *none the less does not allow society to rise higher than pre-class relations, or, in rare circumstances, as far as early class relations.* In a historic perspective, the development of highly specialized societies of hunters, fishermen and gatherers, *and of nomadic pastoralists, represent dead-end branches of development.* Only agricultural or complex agricultural-pastoral economy allows society to cross the boundary of class-formation and successfully to evolve further. It is evidently in this sense that one must understand the essence of that revolutionary transformation, which history attained with the transition to productive economy. (Italics mine)

The role of agriculture, rather than tool-use, in setting mankind off on the evolutionary path through the various class formations is recognized, *but with an important exception*, and this exception is of its very essence: nomadic pastoralists are expelled from the dialectic of history. Lévi-Strauss has ridiculed Sartre for excluding unhistorical people from the dialectic of history, and allowing their inclusion only by courtesy of their incorporation in the community of more complex societies.[25] Here we see Soviet Marxism doing the same, and in almost identical terms. Tolybekov had in fact defended the inclusion of his own nation in the Tsarist empire for this very reason: there was no other escape from the nomadic cul-de-sac.

The passage quoted is in fact even more extreme and uncompromising than the contentions found in the works of the anti-feudalist specialists of nomadism, that is to say in Tolybekov, Markov, and Khazanov. Far from being granted a nomadic feudalism of their own, pastoral nomads are allowed only 'in rare circumstances' to attain even *early* class relationships. In the 1980s, the question as to who exactly was liquidated in the steppe between the wars, and why, seems no longer to be pressing.

Neither Tolybekov nor Markov nor Khazanov are actually cited in this authoritative volume. But their conclusion, formulated in an even stronger and more uncompromising form than is found in their own works, seems to be accepted.

25 Lévi-Strauss, *The Savage Mind*.

6

Modern Ethnicity

In recent decades, a minor revolution has taken place within Soviet Anthropology. 'Ethnography' is one of the recognized disciplines in the Soviet academic world, and corresponds roughly to what in the West is called social anthropology. This revolution has as yet been barely noticed by outside observers.[1] Its leader is Yulian Bromley, a very Russian scholar with a very English surname, Director of the Institute of Ethnography of the Soviet Academy of Sciences. The revolution consists of making *ethno*graphy into the studies of *ethnos*-es, or, in current Western academic jargon, into the study of *ethnicity* – in other words the study of the phenomena of national feeling, identity, and interaction. History is about chaps, geography is about maps, and ethnography is about ethnoses. What else? The revolution is supported by arguments weightier than mere verbal suggestiveness; but by way of persuasive consideration, etymology is also invoked.

In our view ... the name of a scholarly discipline should not be in direct contradiction with the name of the object of its inquiries ... In other words, there must be a definite correspondence between the naming of a scholarly discipline and the reality it investigates ... So in our case we have in the term for the science – ethnography (or ethnology) – a direct indication of the delimited area of objective reality ... the ethnos. It follows that our conception of ethnography largely depends on what we denote by the term 'ethnos'.[2]

This revolution is of at least triple interest. It is of concern to anthropologists who may well be intrigued by the developments in a parallel

1 It has been the subject of an article by Stephen P. Dunn, 'New Departures in Soviet Theory and Practice of Ethnicity', *Dialectical Anthropology*, vol. 1, 1975, p. 61, and of another by Tamara Dragadze, in Gellner (ed.), *Soviet and Western Anthropology*.

2 Yu. Bromley, 'Towards the Question of the Subject-matter of Ethnographic Science', paper presented at the Wartenstein conference, July 1976, and published in English in *Ethnography and Related Sciences* (Moscow, 1977). All subsequent quotations, unless otherwise indicated, are from this article.

scholarly tradition. It is of utmost relevance for those preoccupied with nationalism and ethnicity, or specifically with their roles in the Soviet Union; and it is of interest to those concerned with the intellectual life (or what the Russians call 'spiritual culture') of the Soviet Union. The revolution should be seen from each of these viewpoints.

The cluster of questions which is known as social anthropology in British universities faces a number of basic dilemmas. Using the fashionable method of binary oppositions, these alternatives can be grouped into a number of pairs, as follows:

Evolutionism *v.* synchronicism
Archaic–distinctive *v.* universal, general
Historic-documentary *v.* field-work-oriented
Cultural *v.* structural.

These are not all the possible binary options facing the subject, but they constitute, I think, a fairly fundamental set. Two very powerful but mutually opposed insights underlie each of the pairs of opposed alternatives or inspirations. Behind the evolutionist vision there is the strong and legitimate urge to know just *how we came to be here*. The crucial fact about humanity is that a species, which a few millennia ago consisted of small, powerless, and ignorant bands, is now unbelievably numerous, powerful and knowledgeable. This is *the* rags-to-riches story which, above all others, needs to be understood. And surely, if we do get this story right, it must also contain the clue to most other questions which intrigue mankind. The magic key which gave us such phenomenal success must also tell what we really are and where we should be going. These are the simple but enormously persuasive ideas which intoxicated so many thinkers during the nineteenth century, and which even or especially then had a particularly strong hold over the Russian mind.[3]

But the opposed idea is also very cogent. Sequences of events, as such, explain *nothing*. You have not really explained the movement of a ship or plane by plotting its course (though its course may indeed offer a clue to the nature of its propulsion). What goes for means of transport also goes for the development of human institutions. Their stability and their change alike are consequences, and not causes, of their inner structures. It is these which need to be identified if we are to have any genuine understanding.

It is a structure, in the sense of a system of synchronic interactions, which really explains either stability or growth. The present explains the present. Let the dead bury their dead. This forceful idea is behind the relative decline of evolutionism in the social sciences.

3 Cf. Alexander Vucinich, *Social Thought in Tsarist Russia* (Chicago, 1976).

The other binary options on our list may be less fundamental philosophically, but they are not unimportant. An anthropologist may be impelled by the pressing need to understand the vanishing primitive whilst there is still time; or alternatively he may spurn this as mere 'romantic anthropology' and insist firmly that the denizens of Neasden are as much a part of humanity as the most recently discovered tribe in New Guinea, and be just as revealing of the patterns of organization to which humanity is prone, and hence constitute just as legitimate an object of enquiry.

This does not exclude disagreements about the definition of the subject-matter of anthropology. This was particularly clear during the formative period of Soviet ethnography ... one tendency was to limit the tasks of ethnography to the study of archaic, 'survival' phenomena ... [this] tendency inevitably implies a conception of the subject-matter of ethnography [ethnology] as a kind of *peau de chagrin*, for what is characteristic of the present is the ever-increasing disappearance of archaisms from the life of nations.

In connection with the third dilemma, the anthropologist may make a virtue of the absence of written records, and discount the historian and the anthropologist for their reliance on them, and insist that only personal immersion in a concrete situation ever tells us what really happens – documents lie – and thus make of field work, of concrete contact, not so much a tool, as the very definition of his subject. 'Sometimes the distinctive trait of the ethnographic study of culture ... is seen in the method of direct observation ... It is difficult to agree with this ... ethnography is by no means restricted to this method in the study of contemporary nations.'

The difference between structure and culture is, roughly speaking, the difference between whom the bride married and what she wore. One may concentrate on the principles of organization, on the system of roles in a given society, and the manner in which it is sustained and in which people are recruited to positions within it, and consign the sartorial, ritual, gastronomic, etc., symbolism, in terms of which that system is expressed, to the folklorist or the novelist; or, conversely, one may consign organization to the political scientist or whoever, and concentrate on the unique texture of life of a given society, its 'culture'. This choice may well itself be influenced by the political background: Professor Ioan Lewis has recently argued[4] that the 'structural' bias of British anthropologists was linked to indirect rule in the erstwhile Empire, which made socio-political structures conspicuous, whereas the cultural orientation of the Americans and the French was related to

4 I. Lewis, *Social Anthropology in Perspective* (London, 1976).

greater political centralization, which left culture as the residual object of enquiry.

These four options, and the intuitions or values underlying them, are worth spelling out, for they enable us to draw a profile of any given anthropological tradition: by specifying its position on each of these issues, we can sense its general spirit.

The Malinowskian revolution in Britain, which still, in basic terms, sets the tone in this country (more so perhaps than those who take it for granted realize), took pretty definite stands on each of these four options. It was – *pace* Sir Edmund Leach[5] – synchronicist; it was oriented towards the simpler societies, and towards field work, and (under Radcliffe-Brown's influence perhaps) towards structure. Since the early days of this revolution, the profile has undergone marked change only with respect to the second choice: British-trained anthropologists are now found working all over the place, with only a small bias at most towards the 'simpler' societies. On the fourth fork, Lévi-Strauss's influence has been felt. It amounts, in a way, to the discovery that culture itself also has its own structure (in addition to the more patently 'organizational' aspects of society) and also to a somewhat slapdash method of identifying those structures-of-culture in myth, gastronomy, and so forth. However, Lévi-Strauss has come, but not conquered. History is more respectable again, but this is a matter of stress rather than of orientation.

The transformation of Soviet 'ethnography' under the leadership of Yulian Bromley has intriguing points both of similarity and of contrast with all this. The general approach to the study of 'ethnoses' is *relatively* synchronicist; it is markedly universalistic in its approach to man, rather than distinctively or preferentially archaism-oriented; its typical methods are either fieldwork or sociological, or what may generically be called contact methods, rather than historico-documentary; but its distinctive concern is culture rather than structure. Here, at the fourth option, we find a contrast, at least with British trends. All these judgements require very significant qualification – otherwise they are liable to be badly misleading. Nevertheless, as a first approximation, they do give one a certain profile of an academic community and its outlook.

One might say that, in Soviet thought, two transitions were conflated, which in British anthropology came successively and in different generations; the synchronicist vision (or, rather in the Soviet case, a relatively synchronicist or contemporary stress and orientation), replacing, or rather complementing, the partially exhausted evolutionist

5 Cf. *Current Anthropology*, vol. 7, 1966, pp. 560–76.

vision; and secondly the shift from a distinctive preoccupation with the archaic to a more general, undiscriminating concern with all humanity, however modern (or even a preference for the study of modern phenomena). Just as the rich have souls to be saved as much as the poor, so modern societies have structures and cultures to be explored, as much as the most backward and isolated of tribes. This shift of interest, in West or East, may be inspired by both positive and negative considerations. The negative one may be the increasing scarcity, not to say artificiality, of archaic phenomena: not merely tribes, but also archaic institutional survivals are becoming hard to come by. In the Soviet Union, it is institutional survivals within otherwise modernized cultures, rather than total isolated tribes, which are relevant. The positive consideration may be the desire of anthropologists to be of practical use, a praiseworthy humanitarian sentiment which can be further reinforced by the need to compete for scarce financial resources, whether in a Western University or in the Soviet Academy of Sciences. In the West, the desire to be of use has led to the vogue of applied anthropology, to the interest in economic development, and it is also one of the mainsprings of the recent revival of Western Marxist anthropology. In the Soviet Union, it seems to have led to a drive to make ethnography the specialized study of ethnic phenomena.

Now for the important qualifications. Soviet ethnography has been described as veering towards relatively synchronicist, universal (non-archaic), contact-research (rather than document-using), and cultural (rather than structural) visions of its own concerns. This is not, and cannot be, the whole and unqualified truth of the matter: that follows immediately from the fact that these are, after all, *Marxist* thinkers. Could Marxism be really synchronicist, i.e. devoid of concern with historical depth and change? (On the Left Bank in Paris this might well be possible, like virtually anything else, but then, we are not now dealing with the Left Bank.) Or again, could Marxism be preoccupied with culture to the detriment of social structure? In brief, in choosing a research strategy or *Problematik* which is relatively synchronistic and cultural, Russian anthropologists do not in any way reject or repudiate evolutionist[6] and structural vistas (for which in any case they use other

---

6 Russian anthropologists in any case repudiate the term 'evolutionist', but mainly, I think, because it suggests to them the doctrine of smooth continuous development, as opposed to dramatic revolutionary discontinuities. That issue is of course irrelevant here. I use 'evolutionism' to designate an approach concerned above all with the development *paths*, as opposed to a synchronicist concern with the balance of power at any one given time. In this usage, it covers any theoretical approach which concentrates on the evolutionary line, irrespective of whether the line is a smooth curve or a zig-zag with sharp corners.

terms); they merely push them away from the very centre of their own attention, no doubt in the confident expectation that other scholars, in neighbouring disciplines, will look after them. Historical depth, a keen sense of social change and of the transient, historical nature of social forms, and of the constraining, impersonal nature of social structures, can hardly be conjured away from Marxism, and there is not the least indication that Soviet anthropologists have either the slightest wish or indeed the opportunity to do so. Preoccupation with the overall historical trend is a Russian as well as a Marxist tradition.[7] It is merely that there is a partial tendency on the part of ethnos-specialists to leave these concerns to others. Which others?

Here we must look at the division of academic labour, both within Soviet ethnography and outside it. In as far as a major segment of Soviet ethnographers turns towards the study of contemporary ethnic pheno-mena – ethnic self-identification, inter-group relations, the cultural division of labour, and so forth, it follows that for them a concern with 'culture' is natural, if not mandatory. But contemporary society is already the concern of many other scholarly disciplines.

... there was a second [tendency], which conceived ethnography, or more correctly ethnology, as a kind of super-discipline, aspiring to investigate all elements of human activity ... this leads to insuperable difficulties in the delimitation of the scholarly tasks of ethnography and those of the numerous other scientific disciplines, investigating diverse aspects of the life of nations.

One can only lay claim to some single aspects of contemporary society, and cultural distinctiveness and identification (roughly: ethni-city) is important, becoming more so, is inadequately studied, is not pre-empted by any other school, and the ideas and tools suitable for investigating it fit in fairly well with the pre-existing conceptual and technical equipment of an anthropologist. (There is perhaps also the minor problem, within Marxism, of how to characterize the structures of post-capitalist societies. Marx's prediction of the structureless nature of communism is not now unduly prominent, and the organizational structure of socialism does present problems. Thus there may well be advantages in incorporating as much as possible within the notion of culture.) Moreover, under the name of the problem of nationalities, this issue has already a recognized place in the intellectual edifice; yet no one would claim, in the Soviet Union any more than in the West, that the problems arising in this sphere have been definitively solved. So, the anthropologist who turns towards the study of ethnoses, towards the nature of cultural distinctiveness, turns to a field which is relatively

7 Cf. Vucinich, *Social Thought in Tsarist Russia*.

untilled, which is conspicuously important, which is of practical use, constitutes a legitimate area of study, and is at least comparatively unperilous. Given all this, it is not at all puzzling that Soviet ethnographers should turn their attention in this direction. It would be more puzzling if they did *not* do so – though presumably the spark of leadership was also required. Yulian Bromley appears to be the man destined to lead the ethnographers towards the promised land of the ethnos.

The division of labour with other social and human disciplines follows a qualitative, rather than a territorial, boundary: ethnographers are to study one aspect of both modern and other societies, namely their ethnic aspect, whilst sociologists, political scientists, psychologists, linguists, etc., are to study other aspects of the social life of man. But there is also a division of labour *within* Soviet ethnography itself.

The outside observer of the Soviet ethnographic scene will discern roughly three loosely defined, overlapping, and neither exhaustive nor mutually exclusive groups or trends, which might be called the Ethnosists, the Primitivists, and the Ideologists. As stated, these groups may overlap, and some individuals may not be classifiable under any one of these three terms. Nevertheless, these seem to be the prominent clusters, both of people and of ideas. So far I have stressed the role of the ethnosists, who are the rising and already the dominant clan in the tribe; but they are certainly not the only one, and although they do now seem clearly to have attained leadership, there is nothing to indicate that they will now, or ever, obliterate, displace, or even ruthlessly dominate the other two. On the contrary, the relationship of these clans seems to be complementary and symbiotic rather than antagonistic. Though no doubt there is intellectual opposition between *some* members of these clans (or indeed within each), by and large each of them needs the other, even if it is now the study of ethnos, that sets the pace.

Something should be said of each of the other two clans. (The terminology is of course my own). The ideologists, in my sense, are those thinkers whose intellectual centre of gravity remains with that grand global story of human development, and whose concern with ethnographic detail is ultimately but a means towards the formulation of that total vision. The amazing story of humanity's progress, which so intoxicated so many nineteenth-century thinkers, but about which so many twentieth-century intellectuals have become rather blasé, still has a powerful hold on these scholars. It would be grossly unfair to them to say that they are not interested in detail, but it may well be true that the interest in detail is a function of the part it plays in the large vision. It may indeed be this background vision which makes some theoretical questions in Soviet anthropology sound more real and gripping, less strained, artificial, obscure than those of the recently fashionable timeless neo-idealisms of the West. The particular pattern which the ideologists discern is of course a Marxist one – but what distinguishes them from the other clans of Soviet ethnographers is not that the others fail to be Marxists, but rather that the others are not primarily or immediately concerned with the historic totality, but rather with specific issues within it.

Amongst such general thinkers, Yuri Semenov is perhaps the virtuoso. He is a meticulous and sympathetic student of Western anthropology, and his account of the emergence of economic anthropology in the West[8] is thorough, accurate, elegantly organized, perceptive, and free of prejudice. He is also deeply interested in substantive problems such as the nature of serfdom or slavery (whichever term may be more suitable) in ancient Asiatic societies. But for all this, his central intellectual concern is with the global Marxist vision of human history,[9] and in expounding this he displays a theologian's effortless mastery of those elusive key abstractions of Marxism – the Forces, Means and Relations of Production, that trinity of intertwined spirits which guide our destiny and whose subtle, intricate, elusive not to say Byzantine connections condemn all of us crude empiricists to Vulgar Marxism, if ever we have the temerity to articulate *the* Marxist position at all. This he fluently combines with a concrete sense of the pattern of history from its early Middle Eastern stirrings to the present day, and with a very sound philosophical appreciation of the problems which arise within it for Marxism, for instance from the non-synchronization of social stages in diverse civilizations, or from the overlay of endogenous and extraneous social causation, and so forth. Semenov's Marxism may be scholastic in the sense that it is abstract and that its ultimate loyalty is to a certain general vision, but it is not at all scholastic in as far as it is deeply internalized and its exposition is vibrant with life and feeling. At a conference in Austria in 1976 at which Soviet and Western anthropologists met, the senior Western anthropologist present, Professor Meyer Fortes of Cambridge, was so impressed by an impromptu exposition of Marxism by Semenov that he spontaneously declared it to be the highlight of the whole series of meetings.

Semenov and his approach do have their critics within the Soviet Union. In terms of my identification of the internal clans, these tend to come from within the ranks of the primitivists – though not of course from all of them, nor necessarily only from amongst them. Even his critics respect him as an outstanding intellectual representative of what

8 'Theoretical Problems of "Economic Anthropology"', cit. ch. 1, n. 6 above.
9 Semenov, *Kak vosniklo chelovechestvo* (*The Emergence of Mankind*), cit. ch. 1, n. 5; *Proiskhozhdenie braka i sem'i* (*The Origin of Marriage and the Family*) (Moscow, 1974).

might be called the deductive approach, one whose reasoning is sustained and attention to facts careful, but whose loyalty, in the end, is to the vision rather than to the problems which arise from the facts.

Who, generically speaking, are the primitivists? They are closer than either the ethnosists or the ideologists to the popular Western image of the anthropologist. They are interested in the more primitive peoples, or in the 'survivals' of primitive institutions amongst non-primitive ones. Here one must stress once again that 'primitive society' in Soviet terminology is not a loose general category. In the West, this phrase defines a broad area and perhaps indicates a set of problems, but it does so without containing within itself any very definite theory. Not so in Soviet Marxism. 'Primitive society' in Soviet Marxism is not merely a theory-laden term, it is loaded with a theory which is both precise and very central to the thought system of Soviet ethnographers. Primitive society is contrasted with class society. Class society is defined by the presence of antagonistic classes and of their inescapable correlate, the state. No classes, no state; no state, no classes. The transition from primitive society to class societies is a kind of expulsion from Eden (though a necessary one) and marks the beginning of exploitation. It is an endearing quality of Russian Marxists that they suppose that exploitation needed to be *invented*. Western man is inclined to think instead that there was no time when men did not take things from each other, but that if anything needed to be invented, it was *domination*. Much hinges perhaps on just how one sees the *Ur*-form of evil, but that is a big subject.

The people whom I call 'primitivists' in Soviet anthropology are those concerned with either primitive society proper or with the obviously very protracted, transitional stages between primitive and state-and-class society. Unambiguous class societies tend to be left to historians, orientalists, etc. In the West, one can distinguish historians from social scientists, roughly speaking, no longer by the societies they choose (document-endowed or devoid of documents is not a usable criterion), but rather by their style: by and large, historians still prefer narrative and sequence, and social scientists the specification of a structure. In the Soviet Union, this touchstone cannot be applied, for both historians and anthropologists, being Marxists, are concerned with structure (and its changes). Roughly, the line of demarcation between 'primitivists' and ordinary historians follows the level of development of societies.[10]

10 This point is illustrated by the fact that the most interesting discussion of typological problems in anthropology was in fact written by a historian, L. V. Danilova, in his 'Controversial Problems of the Theory of Precapitalist Societies', cit. ch. 1, n. 1 above. The theoretical problems are the same in historiography and anthropology, and a

So the primitivists are scholars who, on the basis of both archaeological and contemporary-ethnographic data, investigate pre-state societies, and the transitional periods on the way to this 'stage'.

To understand the 'ethnosist' revolution in Soviet ethnography, it is important to realize that there is no question of anything remotely resembling an elimination of either the ideologists or the primitivists. Both these clans are destined to survive and to be active; what is at issue is merely relative prominence. Each of these other clans are, in their own way, essential. The ideologists maintain the links with the wider orthodox vision and are its guardians. It is not so much that ethnic studies set out to be heterodox; but they operate in a relatively new and neutral field, and one perhaps inadequately explored by Marxism in the past.[11]

To claim to extend and complete Marxist theory on this point might be presumptuous; better by far to retain links with an area in which Marxism already possesses a clear and well-defined outline, ably looked after by the ideologists, and where it does not need to be worked out. Theory being so covered, one can get on with substance.

The relationship of the ethnosists to the primitivists is less immediately functional, in terms of intellectual complementarity. There is of course some overlap: men investigating one of the smaller Soviet ethnic groups from the viewpoint of cultural survivals may also have a contribution to make to the subject of cultural-ethnic distinctiveness under socialism. But this utilization of existing skills and expertise is not, I think, the main reason. The exclusion of a largish, active, and often distinguished group of scholars is hardly part of the present style and climate of opinion. Moreover, if the ideologists constitute a link with an established area of orthodoxy, and thus also a dispensation from the perilous need to formulate an orthodoxy in a new zone (such as faced sociologists), the primitivists in turn provide a kind of meaty filling, a substantive content, or an overall position which, on its own, could be rather abstract. Without these two complements, the study of ethnoses might well find itself a rather ballast-less condition in a choppy sea, and follow a rather uncertain and precarious course – such as seems to be the fate of newly revived sociology.[12]

---

historian feels no embarrassment and no ineptitude in telling anthropologists what they are about. This is hardly conceivable in the West. Cf. ch. 1.

11 Western Marxists overtly deplore the lack of a Marxist theory of nationalism or at any rate of a good one. Cf. Tom Nairn: 'The theory of nationalism represents Marxism's great historical failure . . . It is true that other traditions of Western thought have not done better.' In 'The Modern Janus', *New Left Review*, vol. 94, 1975, p. 3, and his *The Break-up of Britain, Crisis and Neo-Nationalism* (London, 1977).

12 Cf. Elisabeth Weinberg, *The Development of Sociology in the Soviet Union* (London, 1974).

In a way, *sociology* under communism is haunted by the very richness of the sociological ideas and suggestions already contained in Marxism: either it concentrates on the elaboration and exposition of these (and becomes a kind of theology), or it concentrates on relatively specific and technical issues in contemporary society, in which case it is in danger of becoming tediously narrow and untheoretical, a specimen of what C. Wright Mills in America called 'abstracted empiricism'. Moreover, in the Soviet Union as in the West, one must suppose that it is much harder to invent a new subject and to endow it with funds and an institutional basis, than it is to capture and redefine an old one. To create a Centre of Ethnic Studies would be difficult (as some have found in the West), however urgent the problem of ethnicity may be in the modern world; and even if it were successfully accomplished, one would then have to face the problem of elaborating a theory of the place of such studies within the existing and established scheme of things. To capture ethnography for ethnicity is, by comparison, an easier matter. The inherited older traditions within ethnography, apart from their intrinsic merits or importance, can in large measure take care of the problems of redefinition which would face an altogether new subject. So, all's for the best.

We have seen the methodological, so to speak, strategic-definitional aspect of Bromley's work: ethnography is defined as concerned primarily with the ethnos, with the ethnic aspect of social life, past and present. This provides an important contemporary research area, whilst retaining the setting of older anthropology. But what of his substantive doctrines concerning ethnicity? Leaving aside the form, what is the substance? Let us be Marxist enough to admit that form and substance interact, and that his substance is not independent of the formal traits already indicated. But just what is it?

I do not believe that his work, and that of his collaborators, has as yet reached its final form and completion, but certain aspects stand out: (*a*) a typology of ethnic phenomena, (*b*) certain generalizations articulated in terms of that typology, and (*c*) concrete empirical research strategies based on these.

The typology endeavours to do something which, to my knowledge, has not hitherto been attempted, unless one treats Anthony Smith's typology of nationalisms in *Theories of Nationalism*,[13] as an indirect typology of ethnic groups – a classification of the *kinds* of ethnic groupings. This is done in various ways: by listing the types of features which lead to the delimitation of groups as distinct, and which lead them to be seen as distinct, by themselves and others; and moreover by the

13 A. Smith, *Theories of Nationalism* (London, 1970).

cross-relating of ethnic groupings to two principles which cut across ethnicity (but which are mutually connected): one, the sociological categories of Marxism, and two, the presence or absence of political institutions. To illustrate this with Bromley's own example, the Ukrainians: they existed, he observes, as an ethnic unit under feudalism, capitalism, and socialism. Evidently ethnicity and social form are not identical, and ethnic continuity can straddle quite diverse social formations. Also, Ukrainians are found both in the Ukraine and in Canada. In one sense, they are all Ukrainians: but for any student of nationality, there is a crucial difference between the ethnic group, such as the Ukrainians of the Ukraine, which possesses its own socio-political institutions, and the Ukrainians in Canada, who do not.

The terminological distinctions elaborated by Bromley clearly endeavour to capture the distinction between ethnic groups which are merely 'tribal', those that possess political institutions (remember that within Marxism, tribalism and the state are mutually exclusive alternatives), those that possess pre-industrial class and state institutions, and finally industrial ethnic groups (capitalist and socialist). There is a further and separate distinction to be drawn between nationalities possessing full political institutions, and minoritarian or merely autonomous ones. There is presumably a difference between not possessing a state in a state-less era, and not possessing one when other ethnoses do have one.

Classifications on their own perhaps tell us little, though they may indicate a sensitivity to problems. In the case of Bromley's work, the sheer stress on the existence of ethnicity may well be as important as the distinctions drawn within it. A simplified Marxism, devoid of such a sensitivity, might well give the impression that all that matters is social formations: the cultural, 'ethnic' idiom in which they happen to be articulated is virtually epiphenomenal. There is little about the modern world which would encourage so complacent a view, and the merit of the taxonomical part of Bromley's work is that it gives one a language in which to speak about this.

The central problem considered by Western students of ethnicity is of course the issue of *nationalism*, the powerful (and not fully satisfiable) striving in the modern world to make ethnic and political boundaries congruent, the exacerbation of impatience with political units either too small or too large for the salient 'ethnic' boundaries, and the attempts to manipulate and change either ethnic or political boundaries (or both) so as to make them conform to each other. Soviet students of this problem may have some difficulty in considering this problem in any but a rather formal and abstract way. The issue of nationalism is inevitably the issue of irredentism, of the appeal and legitimacy of ethnic boundaries which contradict currently existing political boundaries, and of the question why this trend should be so very much stronger in the modern world than it had been previously. One has the impression that for a Soviet scholar to speculate and perform *Gedanken-experimente* concerning the redrawing of political frontiers, when applied to a country with which the USSR is on friendly terms, would be considered an undiplomatic and impermissible act. Will Ruritania survive, despite the tension between its diverse ethnic groups? One cannot quite see a Soviet scholar asking this, at a time when USSR–Ruritanian friendship is flourishing.

To ask such a question about internal arrangements might be even worse. This is reflected in the fact that the terminology overtly applies a different classification to ethnic groups which do and which do not possess their own political formation, even though otherwise they are at the same 'level of development'. This observation of course cries out for the articulation of certain questions concerning the general conditions under which ethnicity becomes a powerful political principle, whether in fact or in powerful aspiration. In brief, the language for posing this question is now available, but we may yet have to wait for a full utilization of it. The 'primitivists' amongst Soviet anthropologists in fact perform subtle and complex conceptual experimentation concerning the interplay of the class composition of societies and their political form;[14] but a similar exploration of the relationship between ethnic composition and politics may need to await a further relaxation in the intellectual climate.

But ethnicity and its politics is a topic as neglected in the West as in the Soviet Union, and in the West there is no excuse. There is no element in any of the prevailing Western belief systems which would inhibit the formulation of such questions, but, as far as I know, we are still not unduly rich in convincing explanations of a force which pervades our world. But those of us who have started work in this field will find some striking points of convergence, and perhaps also of contrast, in Bromley's work.

The key to this problem, in my view, is the quite different role played by *culture* in pre-industrial and industrial societies. Ethnicity (personal identification with one's culture) is quite a different thing on either side of this great divide, and the political shadow cast by ethnicity is correspondingly different. In this connection, Bromley makes a number of crucial observations. In simpler societies, culture is so to speak pervasive:

Seeing the ethnos through the prism of the fulfilling of ethnic functions enables us to indicate the central area of ethnographic (ethnological) enquiries. It is

14 Cf. e.g. Kubbel, *Songhai Empire*, and my discussion of it in ch. 4 above.

evident . . . that the heart of the subject will be constituted by culture in a broad
sense of the term . . . However, the role of everyday traditional culture is by no
means the same at diverse levels of social development . . . In pre-class and
early class societies, culture is almost coextensive with its traditional-archaic
level. This accounts for the well noted fact that when dealing with societies
which have remained pre-literate, ethnography studies their culture as a unity.

He refers to the 'syncretism of social life', the inseparability of
cultural religious and economic activities. In the West, the same idea is
often expressed by referring to the many-stranded, unspecialized nature
of relations in primitive society. In industrial societies, by contrast, the
earlier syncretism disappears or at least diminishes. The division of
labour becomes sharply accentuated, and the productive sphere
acquires a kind of autonomy. At the same time, mass media ensure a
certain homogenization and cultural interpretation, and at the same
time heighten cultural self-awareness in the population. Above all,
'professional intellectual activity plays an ever greater ethnic role in
highly developed countries.'

Compare this with an explanatory model which can be worked out in
the West for the rise of nationalism, or, in Soviet terms, for explaining
why ethnicity in developed societies (whether socialist or capitalist) is so
very different from its pre-industrial predecessors.[15]

The division of labour, occupational mobility, the importance of
education as a precondition of economic and political citizenship, the
pervasive influence of the mass media, all jointly help to ensure that the
linguistic and cultural medium becomes of supreme importance.
'Culture', i.e. the linguistic-cultural medium, becomes important
precisely because it is now detached from the archaic-folk aspects of life,
because it has become the *generic* precondition of highly specific
occupational roles, and because it is now tied to that 'professional
intellectual activity', which in turn pervades ever greater areas of life.
Both work and leisure are tied to it. An ever-increasing proportion of the
population is skilled, trained, literate, and dependent for both its
income and its dignity on these literacy-mediated skills. By contrast, in
pre-industrial societies, 'professional intellectual activity' was, if it
existed at all, in the hands of scribe strata, using a liturgical rather than
an ethnic language. In brief, post-industrial ethnicity is quite a new and
different animal, and, one may perhaps add, an incomparably more
important one. In a different idiom, an approach to a similar theory can
be discerned in Soviet work.

What concrete research strategies does this vision lead to in the

15 Cf. Smith, *Theories of Nationalism*, or my own *Thought and Change* ch. VI, or *Contemporary Thought and Politics*, ch. VI, or Nairn, *The Break-up of Britain*.

Soviet Union? This set of ideas has in fact led to a fascinating series of researches into various Soviet nationalities, which are of profound interest both to students of nationalism and of Soviet or communist society.[16] The questions which arise concern differential rates of social mobility in diverse ethnic groups, the relationship of ethnicity to professional specialization, the new cultural–national consciousness crystallizing, not so much amongst rural populations, but amongst literate urban ones, and the manner in which a new national culture is assembled from available elements by this stratum and so forth. A detailed examination of this work, which in any case is as yet uncompleted, would require a separate chapter.

The English volume which assembles Bromley's articles[17] also contains an extremely interesting transcription of an oral debate amongst Soviet scholars, and also enables one to reconstruct in some measure the history of the 'ethnos' development. The present debate seems to have started in 1969. In April of that year, Bromley delivered a paper on 'Ethnos and Endogamy' in Leningrad, and a paper of the same title, presumably identical with it, appeared in *Sov'etskaya Etnografiya* (Soviet Ethnography) in 1969. There are cross-references in earlier articles, published in 1967, by Cheboksarov and Gumilev.[18] A discussion of the article was held on 5 February 1970, and was published in *Sov'etskaya Etnografiya* of the same year,[19] and is now available in English, as part of *Soviet Ethnography: Main Trends*.[20] This will be of obvious interest to students of Soviet intellectual life. The spirit of the debate is perhaps best conveyed by excerpts from it:

It is pertinent to say that the discussion pertains to a phenomenon that falls within a scientific discipline which was regrettably undervalued in our country not so long ago. (Bromley)

16 Bromley, *Ethnos and Ethnography*: see ch. 1, n. 8 above; Yu. Arutunian (ed.), *Sotsial'noe i natsional'noe* (*Social and National*), Moscow 1973; Bromley (ed.), *Contemporary Ethnic Processes in the USSR*: see ch. 1, n. 8.

17 Bromley, 'Social Sciences Today', in *Soviet Ethnography: Main Trends* (Moscow 1976).

18 N. N. Cheboksarov, 'Problemy tipologii etnicheskikh obshchnostei v trudakh sovetskikh uchenykh' (Problems concerning the typology of ethnic communities in the works of Soviet scholars [my transl.], *Sov'etskaya etnografiya*, 4, 1967, p. 96. Translated in *Soviet Anthropology*, 2, 1970; L. N. Gumilev, O termine 'etnos', in *Doklady geograficheskogo obshchestva SSSR* (*Proceedings of the Geographical Society of the USSR*), 3, 1967. In fact, this whole issue of the geographers' journal is devoted to ethnicity, and also contains a further article by Gumilev on 'Ethnos as a phenomenon'. Gumilev wrote a further article in No. 15, 1970, of the same journal, entitled 'Ethnos and the category of time'. Gumilev has an intriguing personal background: he is the son of N. Akhmatova. I am indebted for this information to Professor T. Shanin of Manchester.

19 Also available in Yu V. Bromley, *Theoretical Ethnography* (Moscow, 1984).

20 See n. 17 above.

By reducing the essence of ethnos to 'physical or biological reality', Gumilev, in the final analysis, identifies it completely with a population. (Bromley)

Thus it is not the population that is the basis of an ethnos, but the social factors comprising the ethnos (ethnic self-identification being one of them) that transform it into a population. That is, the picture we see is precisely the opposite of what Gumilev presents. Inasmuch as the role of social phenomena ... is constantly increasing, social factors naturally begin to play a larger and larger role in the formation of populations. (Bromley)

... we are discussing a question of very great fundamental importance for our institute and for the direction in which research is developing in the Institute of Ethnography.

Under Bromley's concept the result is that, by means of endogamy, which creates an ethnic barrier, an ethnos preserved its distinctive characteristics both at the stage of primitive-communal society and that of the development of a nation. This follows from his entire concept. So what we get is direct line of maintenance of the specifics of an ethnos over the course of different stages in the development of human history in the periods of the existence of different socioeconomic systems. So interpreted, an ethnic unit acquires the character not of a sociohistoric phenomenon and category ... but of a biological category. And although Bromley says here that he opposed the idea of population proposed by Gumilev in essence he himself emerges as an advocate of that standpoint. (M. S. Ivanov)

It seems to me that Bromley does not substitute biological for social categories and that there is a fundamental difference between the positions taken by Gumilev and Bromley.

As for the fact that no reference is made to economic ties, we Marxists all know that economics is the determining phenomenon in the development of any socio-economic system. Therefore, if we sometimes eliminate the economic component from our focus of interest, this does not mean that we ignore it ... the criticisms ... are to a considerable degree based on a misunderstanding. (S. A. Arutiunov)

In Bromley's article we find a fundamentally new approach ... It opens a new stage in the study of ethnic history – a fundamentally new idea has been stated. What is of significance is the author's attempt to approach the ethnic unit as a system, a structural entity.

It seems to me that excessive attention is paid both in the article itself and in the discussion to the biological aspect ... Even if all mankind comprised an absolutely identical racial type, differing only in culture and language, the postulates of the article would have remained wholly valid. (S. A. Tokarev)

All of us, as Marxists, recognize the primacy of the social over the biological ... Any ethnic unit is not a biological, but a social, phenomenon ... However, each concrete ethnic unit is always characterized by the fact that most of its members' marriages are concluded within the group. This phenomenon, which is socially determined, has the result that the ethnic unit becomes relatively self-contained. (N. N. Cheboksarov)

Does ... the idea that population and ethnos are correlated represent a tendency to subject social phenomena to biological interpretation? I think that the statement and article under discussion provide no ground for any such fears. (I. A. Kryvelev)

The editors of *Sov'etskaya Etnografiya* concluded: 'As the discussion materials have demonstrated, virtually all the speakers supported the fundamental postulates of Bromley's article . . . while also expressing . . . thoughts which will promote further creative treatment . . .'

Victory in this debate seems to have ratified (or made possible) the movement towards the study of ethnicity which has been our theme. One must of course sympathize with Bromley's opposition to some kind of biologism, let alone racism. The issue of the relationship of the social to the biological is interesting, and parallel debates have occurred in the West. (Is kinship wholly social, or biological, or is it at the intersection of both?) For practical purposes, however, this seems somewhat of an irrelevance, though one which started very naturally because Bromley chose to open the debate through the topic of the role of in-marrying in the preservation of ethnic distinctiveness. In practice, however, there is no sign whatever that the direction initiated or led by Bromley leads to some kind of biologicization of anthropology. In fact, it is leading to a sustained study of the social aspects of ethnicity carried out in part with sociological methods, and with a stress on the contemporary world. Ethnicity is indeed a social phenomenon which frequently invokes real, imagined, created, or feigned biological phenomena (in other words, nationalists are often, though not always, racists); but by studying it and taking it seriously, one does not endorse nationalism's own view of itself (which in any case is highly variable). But all this no longer seems at issue. A *social* study of ethnicity is in progress.

Appendix 1

At the Wartenstein meeting of Soviet and Western anthropologists in 1976, the distinguished Soviet scholar Sergei Arutiunov schematized current Soviet anthropological terminology on the blackboard for the benefit of Western colleagues. Since then, he has, at my request, sent me a letter containing Table 6.1, summarizing Soviet usage. It must be stressed (and Dr Arutiunov would, I think, wish to see it so stressed) that

Table 6.1 Varieties of social formation

Formations	Super-ethnic units	Basic or main ethnic units proper	Sub-ethnic units
Socialist	ethnic and ethno-political com-munities (*obshchnosti*)	nations and asso-ciated nationali-ties	national groups, sub-ethnic groups, ethno-graphic groups
Capitalist	same as above	same as above	same as above
Feudal	ethnic communi-ties and groups (in some discus-sions – super-nationalities, pre-nations)	feudal nationality	local groups
Slave-owning	ethnic groups	slave-owning nationality	same as above
Early class (or Asiatic)	as above	nationality in process of forma-tion, tribal unions	tribes and local groups
Primitive	ethnolinguistic super-tribal com-munities	tribes, tribal federations, groups of related tribes	tribes (and for some, clan, *gens*)

this is merely his personal attempt to present contemporary Soviet terminology, offered simply in an attempt to be helpful to outside readers studying Soviet works. It does not commit any other scholars, has no formal standing so to speak, and presumably does not even necessarily commit Dr Arutiunov himself to any theories or views which may seem to be implicit in the terminology. It is simply a generous effort on his part to offer the best possible brief approximation to the current use of terms, without prejudice, either way, to the question whether a complete consensus exists on terminological or any other issues. I am reproducing the table in the spirit in which it has been provided.

In the interest of not distorting the original meaning by possible mistranslations, I here refer to Russian originals of the translation:

ethnic and ethnopolitical communities	*etnicheskie i etnopoliticheskie obshchnosti*
ethnic communities and groups	*etnicheskie obshchnosti i gruppy*
supernationalities, pre-nations	*nadnarodnosti, prednatsii*
ethnolinguistic super-tribal community	*etnolingvisticheskaya nadplemennaya obshchnost'*
nations and associated nationalities	*natsii i assotsiirovannye narodnosti*
feudal nationality	*feodal'naya narodnost'*
slave-owning nationality	*rabovladelcheskaya narodnost'*
nationality in process of formation, tribal union	*formiruyushchayasya narodnost', plemennoi soyuz*
tribe, tribes	*plemya, plemena*
tribal federation	*soplemennost'*
group of related tribes	*gruppa rodstvennykh plemen*
national groups	*natsional'nye gruppy*
sub-ethnic groups	*sub-etnicheskie gruppy*
ethnographic groups	*etnograficheskie gruppy*
local groups	*lokal'nye gruppy*
clan, *gens*	*rod*

Appendix 2

Since the previous part of the chapter was written, Yulian Bromley's ideas and, in effect, his efforts to redefine and redirect social anthropology, i.e. *etnografia*, in the context of Soviet thought and society, has become more accessible to English-speaking readers with a new publication in English.[21] The volume combines material drawn from two previous works of this author, and also republishes the 1970 debate, excerpts from which are already included in this chapter. The volume makes it possible to perceive the outline of the new form which the Director of the All-Union Institute of Ethnography endeavours to bestow on his discipline.

First of all, there is a moderate and qualified synchronicism: '. . . ethnography's primary object of research is modern peoples . . .' We shall note the qualifications in due course. The context of this partial synchronicism, the stress on contemporary culture, is quite different from the Malinowskian version. The latter was a charter of the intensive study of archaic societies, brutally shorn of speculation concerning their origin, or their place on some alleged evolutionary ladder. It emerged at a time

21 Yu. V. Bromley, *Theoretical Ethnography*, from which the rest of the quotations are taken.

when archaic societies were at their most accessible: incorporated in well pacified colonial empires, but not yet excessively disrupted by the modern world. By contrast, Bromley's stress is intimately linked to the awareness of the new and distinctive nature of the cultural situation *in* the modern, non-archaic world: 'a new socio-cultural and ethno-cultural situation had emerged, which required not only the study of problems new to ethnography, but also a review and refinement of the basic concepts of ethnography and of the boundaries of its subject-matter.'

Bromley tells us what this new situation is:

the Soviet Union entered, in the 1960s, a period of developed socialism . . . socio-economic development accelerated in conditions of the scientific and technological revolution, the broad masses had ever increasing access to cultural achievements under the influence of the country's ramified system of public education and that of the mass media.

In this new situation, *etnografia* seems to be making a bid to inherit the old nationalities problem, but to comprehend and handle it in its distinctive new setting, marked by the convergence of social structures and at the same time by a certain *intensification* of ethnic awareness, at a much higher level of literacy and professionalization. Bromley quotes Yuri Andropov: 'The success in settling the nationalities question by no means signifies that all the problems generated by the very fact of the life and work of numerous nations and nationalities in a single state have vanished.'

But they have, evidently, been transformed:

It is . . . necessary to take into account the enormous influence exerted by the scientific and technological revolution on ethnic processes . . . this influence is of a dual nature . . . it contributes to the evening out of the cultural level of ethnic entities . . . at the same time . . . stimulates the growth of ethnic self-awareness among the broadest masses of the population. This . . . exerts a reverse influence . . . imparting an ethnic significance to . . . components which previously lacked . . . it. . . . the specific ethnic features of modern peoples are gradually shifting from the sphere of material culture to that of non-material culture. The emergence of new traditions should also be borne in mind . . . professional, non-material culture is beginning to play an increasing ethnic role in industrially advanced countries. . . . basic ethnic functions are fulfilled not so much by archaic remnants as by new, comparatively stable components of non-material culture.

This view of the role of ethnicity in industrial society is of course strikingly convergent with the views of some of us in the West: the striking importance of ethnic identification in modern society is linked to the wide diffusion of a literate professional high culture, but *not* to any significant differences in material culture, and still less to any archaic survivals. The passage also makes plain that, although it is the distinctively Soviet situation which sets Bromley his local task, none the less the general problem with which he is coping is engendered by industrial society as such. This is also reflected in the terminological table: ethnic terms for capitalist and socialist societies are *identical*. So, as far as the problem of ethnicity at least is concerned, there seems to be a tacit acceptance of the convergence thesis:[22] '. . . the principal object of ethnographic science – ethnoses . . . become dynamic in present-day conditions. Accordingly, the study of the dynamics of modern ethnic systems . . . becomes a principal task facing ethnographic science.' The special dynamism of ethnicity under modern conditions is explicitly recognized.

Bromley notes 'the formation of the homogeneous social structure of a new historic community – the Soviet people.' But although he mentions the 'drawing together of the social structures of ethnic entities' in this new community as part of his subject, the implication would seem to be that the homogeneous *structure* as such is the concern of some other discipline. The specific concern of ethnography is the persisting, or even accentuated, new cultural–ethnic diversity within it.

One could say that Bromley and his followers are struggling for the recognition of ethnicity on two fronts, against two sets of opponents. On the one hand they defend the social nature and significance of ethnicity against those who try to uphold a biological definition of nationality. On the other hand, they endeavour to find a place for ethnicity among specifically *cultural* phenomena, as opposed to social structure, within which it may be both theoretically and practically difficult for them to accommodate the idea of the nation.

The qualification of Bromley's synchronicism, or concentration on contemporary process, arises because, whilst stressing contemporary ethnicity as the main problem area of ethnography, he none the less defines its domain as that of the *ethnos*, at any time. Hence past ethnoses also constitute legitimate objects of study for it. In practice, this seems to lead to a particular concern with early, 'primitive-communal' ethnoses. His recent volume does also contain a chapter devoted to the evaluation of recent ideas in this field. The Institute of Ethnography has indeed been very active in this area of late, producing a series of volumes intended to summarize the state of the art.[23] Nevertheless, the principle message seems to be: the proper concern of ethnography is modern ethnicity.

22 A table of ethnic terminology, specifying terms to be used for ethnic units in various historic stages, is also found in *Drevnie Kitaitsy* (*The Ancient Chinese*), ed. M. V. Kriukov et al. (Moscow, 1983). Here, too, the terminology for capitalism and socialism is identical, and convergence seems to be implied. This table makes no reference to Bromley and seems to be independent of it. The context of the argument is 'ethnogenesis', a speciality of Soviet anthropology which would deserve special treatment, and in particular, the distinctive form of 'nation-building' (as it would be put in the West) in a pre-modern situation, that of Chin and Han China.

23 See ch. 2, n. 6.

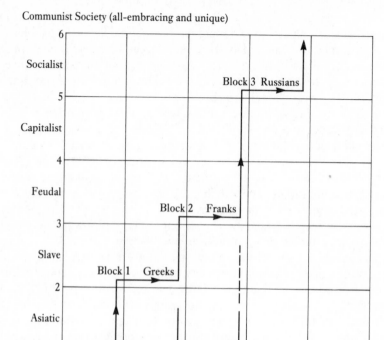

Figure 1 Schematic representation of Yu. Semenov's global neo-unilinealism

The horizontal strips represent evolutionary stages, 'social formations'. The vertical columns represent individual (unspecified) societies. The transactions are numbered, in historic sequence.

Transition 1 is symmetrical: all mankind starts from the same 'primordial communal' baseline. Quite a few societies have demonstrated their capacity to make this transition. Interaction *between* societies is not required to produce it, though given their large size, each 'Asiatic' society can be expected to absorb *many* primordial communities.

The final transition 6 is also symmetrical: the same terminus awaits all mankind. Laggards will be absorbed by the pioneers.

The three crucial transaitions 2, 3, and 5 however all presuppose the existence of a multiplicity of societies and presumably of nationalities, *and* the simultaneous presence of diverse levels of development. Each of them involves discontinuity and a shift in historical leadership. Greeks, Franks, and Russians are the new leaders in these three transitions.

Transition 4, from feudalism to capitalism, is curious and untypical and constitutes a problem for the scheme. It is fully endogenous, there is social continuity, *and* historical leadership is, roughly speaking, preserved.

Western social theory differs from Soviet Marxism above all at two points: it concentrates heavily on transition 4, which is so untypical and awkward for Semenov; and its preoccupation with transition 1 is, ironically, *more* materialist than is usual among Marxists, who stress social change (class formation) more than agriculture, which usually defines the first great jump for Western thought.

The continuous arrow indicates the path of the *leading* society or cluster of societies. Leadership is not merely a function of occupying a 'higher' position in the hierarchy of stages: it also depends on having the potential for bringing about the *next* stage. Hence, sometimes leadership can only be attributed with hindsight: the Owl of Minerva only flies at dusk.

7

One Highway or Many?

Yuri Semenov is a highly distinguished theoretician of Marxist and Soviet anthropology. His 'The theory of socio-economic formations and world history' is an elegant, coherent, beautifully argued and uncompromising defence of a unilineal interpretation of Marxism, and a defence of it as a valid account of human history.[1]

This in itself is a matter of considerable interest. Unilinealism has of late had a bad press, both inside and outside the Soviet Union, among Marxists and non-Marxists alike. No consensus exists on this question inside Soviet scholarship, or outside of course, and the authors with whom Semenov polemicizes include both scholars within his own country and Westerners, Marxists and non-Marxists. Though Semenov does not raise this explicitly in the main part of his argument, the question is of one is of very great political interest, and is not at all a simple technical issue of concern to historians only. The question whether human history is One or Many is obviously fundamental for any philosophy of history. It is also central to most debates about Marxism, and to problems in Marxist political strategy.

One of the commonest criticisms of Marxism hinges on unilinealism, and runs as follows: Why did the socialist revolution occur in backward and peripheral Russia? Ought it not, according to the theory of universal obligatory successive stages of human society (i.e. unilinealism), to have occurred in the highly developed capitalist countries, in which the anticipated contradictions of the capitalist mode of production were becoming most acute? Or again, there is the well-known dilemma facing Marxist revolutionaries in underdeveloped countries, endowed with peasantries and an emerging 'national bourgeoisie', but not yet with a numerous, powerful, or effective proletariat. Ought such revolutionaries,

---

1 Semenov's article is available in Gellner (ed.), *Soviet and Western Anthropology*. See ch. 2, n. 9 above.

in the light of unilinealism, to ally themselves with the national bourgeoisie and help further its ends in the patient expectation of a
subsequent more favourable situation, or ought they to fight the ultimate
enemy right now, and historic timetables be damned? (In Jewish
theology, there is a special name for the sin of endeavouring to
implement divine decrees prematurely, and the same might seem to
apply within Marxism.)

It is an interesting consequence of Semenov's formulation of Marxist
unilinealism, that if it is valid, these problems barely arise, or do not
arise at all. If his position is correct, the questions themselves were
profoundly misguided, and ought never to have been posed, at least in
those terms.

The manner in which Semenov demonstrates his conclusion, as well
as the conclusion itself, is of great interest. The argument is basically
philosophical rather than specific and historical. Historical data, and
those of a rather general kind, enter the argument only at relatively
marginal and tangential points. The burden of the proof hinges on
rather abstract and philosophical issues, and on two in particular – the
unity of human history, and the question of nominalism versus realism
(in the Platonic sense). These two issues turn out, once again, to be
related.

Consider the second of these, the problem of the relationship of
abstract concepts to reality. It may be as well to invoke a contemporary
authority, the American logician Quine, for a restatement of the
available alternatives:

The three main mediaeval points of view regarding universals are designated by
historians as *realism*, *conceptualism*, and *nominalism*. Essentially these same three
doctrines appear in twentieth-century surveys ... under the new names of
logicism, *intuitionism* and *formalism*.

Realism ... is the Platonic doctrine that universals or abstract entities have
being independently of mind ... *Conceptualism* holds that they are universal but
that they are mind-made. ... the *nominalists* of old, object[ed] to admitting
abstract entities at all.[2]

This was and evidently continues to be a central issue in philosophical thought, and in its time it could send those who were in error to their
death:

Then the Cardinal of Cambrai ... questioned Master Jan Hus if he regarded
universals as real apart from the thing itself. And he responded that he did,
since both St Anselm and others had so regarded them. Thereupon the cardinal
argued ... that ... it follows that with the cessation of the particular there also

2 Willard van Orman Quine, *From a Logical Point of View* (Cambridge, Mass., 1953),
pp. 14, 15.

ceased the universal substance of itself. Jan Hus replied that it ceased to exist in the substance of that particular bread . . . but despite that, in other particulars it remains the same.[3]

Within a month Jan Hus paid for his realist views at the stake. But the issue of realism/nominalism underlies not only the problem of transubstantiation, of the relationship of bread-in-general to the specific bread used in the Eucharist, but equally the relationship of socio-economic formations in general to specific, concrete societies.

Semenov clearly seems also to be a realist, and moreover he holds realism to be an essential prerequisite for the correct interpretation of Marxism. What is at issue now is the correct assessment of the ontological status, so to speak, of 'socio-economic formations'. Is there nothing in the world over and above concretely existing societies with which socio-economic formations must then be identified if the term is to refer to anything at all, or, on the other hand, are they merely logical artefacts of the mind, conceptual conveniences? These would seem to be the nominalist and conceptualist options, and they seem to be repudiated:

. . . a socio-economic formation in the pure sense . . . can only exist in theory, but not in historical reality. In history, it exists in distinct societies as their inner essence, their objective basis. A failure to see this can lead to theoretical errors. Thus, for instance, certain Soviet historians, having failed to locate within history pure, ideal socio-economic formations, reached the conclusion that formations do not exist in reality at all, that they represent only logical, theoretical constructions. The endeavour to avoid such a conclusion led several other scholars to the direct, immediate identification of socio-economic formations with actually existing social organisms, with distinct concrete societies . . . Either of these approaches is equally misguided. Either can lead to a repudiation of the materialist conception of history.[4]

Though socio-economic formations cannot exist independently of concrete individual societies, nevertheless they are not mere abstractions or conceptual conveniences. They exist as the inner essences of concrete societies, and determine their development. That inner essence is described, in so many words, as existing independently of the consciousness and will of men. Though this last remark seemed to be intended to apply above all to the minds and wills of participants in the historic process, it must presumably apply with even greater force to the

---

3 Report of the trial of Jan Hus in 1415 by Petr z Mladoňovic, quoted in C. M. D. Crowder (ed.), *Unity, Heresy and Reform, 1378–1460* (London, 1977), pp. 88–9.
4 Semenov, 'The theory of socio-economic formations and world history'. All subsequent quotations, not otherwise identified, are from this work.

historical observer. His mental acts do not make these systems of productive relations: they make him.

The question of the reality of abstractions may seem scholastic. Its relevance may however emerge more clearly if one looks at Semenov's other main consideration, namely the unity of human history and its implications for unilinealism and rival theories. What is unilinealism? It is the doctrine that, for the understanding of human history, we need to consider one and only one list of historic stages through which human society has passed (or is passing and will pass). Semenov quite cogently notes that the issue of unilinealism as such is quite independent of the subsidiary (though also important) question concerning just how many stages there are, or just what they are. (For example, are there just five of them, or is the Asiatic Mode of Production a distinctive stage, to be inserted between primitive communism and slave-owning society?)

Semenov's argument from the unity of human history runs as follows. To what could the *n* stages of human history (whatever the correct number may be) be meant to apply? There would seem to be two possibilities: First that they are meant to apply to the development of each and every society, taken individually. Secondly that they are meant to apply to the history of mankind at large (in some sense which is yet to emerge).

It is extremely interesting that Semenov concedes that the theory of socio-economic formations has generally been interpreted in the first sense. It wasn't even that the first interpretation was consciously preferred: it was unreflectively taken for granted:

The overwhelming majority of scholars, often without clearly realizing it themselves, in one way or another in the final analysis inclined towards the first solution. The treatment of the succession of social formations as successive changes of the type of individual social organism, corresponded all in all with the facts of European history, beginning with later feudalism ... This made it possible to treat the theory of socio-economic formations as the actualization of the development of each social organism taken on its own. The identification for practical purposes of the development of society as a whole, with the development of each society individually, was aided by the plurality of meanings of 'society' noted above.

The last sentence of the quotation refers to the ambiguity of 'society': it can mean a concrete society, with co-ordinates in time and space, a local habitation and a name, but it can also mean the generic thing, which is, for Semenov, both abstract and yet inherent, essential, explicative. The passage quoted highlights, amongst other things, the interdependence of the Platonic-realist and the historical-unity arguments. The unity applies to the generic essence, not to the individual society. But what is perhaps most interesting about it is the admission that the majority of scholars have in the past interpreted Marxism as requiring the unilineal succession to apply to individual societies – and this majority of course includes Marxists at least as much as the critics of Marxism. Hence Semenov's reformulation is a very significant advance within Marxism or, at the very least, the recovery and the making explicit of something which had long been lost and which, if originally present at all, had never been articulated with sufficient clarity or emphasis to make subsequent generations of scholars aware of the fact that they were contradicting it. Those who sinned against it generally did so, as Semenov stressed, without being aware of making any contentious assumption at all. 'This interpretation of the theory of socio-economic formations was presented as the only possible one and thus as identical with the theory itself.' If it was possible to do this, the correct interpretation could not have been very easily available, at least in explicit form.

Leaving aside the question of the originality of his formulation – is it *valid*? I find this central point in Semenov's argument entirely convincing. The idea that unilinealism requires every individual society to pass through every stage (a view which, like the rest of Semenov's silent majority, I had always taken for granted, without even being aware of it) only needs to be stated clearly to be seen to be absurd. Every society could only pass through every stage if societies were generally immortal, like Jonathan Swift's Struldbrugs, or alternatively if societies lived out their lives in isolation. But each of these assumptions is blatantly absurd. No contemporary northern-European society has a history going back beyond (at best) the Middle Ages. Through religion, modern Greece and Israel may perhaps claim some kind of rather dubious identity with ancient Byzantium and Israel respectively, though this identity immediately lapses if we insist on continuity of territorial occupation or of organization or of political sovereignty or anything of the kind.

It seems to follow that if, for instance, both slave-owning society and feudalism are such 'stages', then it is somewhat implausible to suppose that the same continuous society had at one period been slave-owning and at another, feudal. There was presumably never a time when slave-owners were required to hand in their deeds of ownership of slaves, and have them replaced by land-deeds to appropriate territory, carrying with them a given number of serfs, and corresponding military obligations to overlords, and so forth. It is a nice idea – one likes to think of queues of disgruntled slave-owners, waiting at the *municipium*, complaining to each other about the bad rate of exchange – 'ten erstwhile slaves for one acre with two serfs, now is that fair I ask you, the government is clearly making a packet out of this transition to feudalism, it's just one further hidden form of taxation' – and perhaps denouncing those who cheat – 'now

Lucanius over there, he hands in sick old slaves whom he had quickly bought up cheap when the change from slave-owning to feudalism was announced, but then he manages to collar the very best land with the youngest serfs! And I tell you another thing, this *ius primae noctis* which we are promised in the decree promulgating feudalism, it really isn't a patch on the fun we used to have with the Nubian slave-girls. If you ask me, it's a very retrogressive step, and it's always the middle classes who pay for it in the end . . .'

It is an attractive picture, but to the detriment of the continuity of history, it never happened that way. Semenov is so clearly right on this point that one is a bit puzzled that it had not been made with emphasis earlier. It is not plausible to expect every, or even any, concrete continuous society to pass through all stages. This being so, why had critics of Marxism and revisionists made so much fuss about the absence of some stages in some societies in particular? We shall have to return to this question.

If the succession of stages cannot plausibly be credited to single, continuous societies, which seems to be the case, a number of other questions arise which include: What is a single society? And in what sense can the series of stages be credited to human history or society as a whole? The former question is not answered in Semenov's article, but it is clearly highlighted by his whole approach. The second and crucial question is answered quite explicitly and very clearly. It is here that we shift from his negative position (stages may not be credited to the life stories of individual societies) to his positive doctrine (they must be credited to something else). But just what?

Though the history of mankind may be unitary, yet mankind, except perhaps in the very last stages of its history, does not form some kind of organic unity, recognizing itself as such and acting as one. For most of history so far, it is split into large number of units, often quite unaware of each other. In what sense then can such an history have 'stages'? Semenov quite explicitly, and plausibly, rejects any statistical answer to this. It would be quite pointless, for instance, to say that mankind at large is in the feudal stage at a time when the majority of societies is feudal. For one thing, how do you count feudal 'societies' – is there one per king, baron, or knight? Nor would it make sense to select a time when the majority of mankind lived under feudal regimes (if such a time existed, which is doubtful). What then?

Semenov's answer is profoundly Hegelian, and he does indeed invoke Hegel in his argument. The answer can best be summed up as the torch relay theory of history. The torch of leadership is passed on in the course of human history from one area to another and from one social system to another. Mankind as a whole is at a given stage, when the most advanced, and at the same time most influential area happens to be at the stage in question. The criterion for being the most influential seems to be in part that it exercises a great deal of influence on surrounding backward, peripheral areas; another criterion seems to be that it is also preparing the ground for the next stage. It would seem to follow that one can only identify the torch-carrying region with confidence after the event, when the next stage has arrived (provided it in turn can be identified), unless one can, which seems unlikely, do it with the help of a kind of sociological-genetic X-ray, identifying the seeds of the future before they have borne fruit. (But the owl of Minerva only flies at dusk.)

It also follows that parallel replication of the same stages in diverse societies is not merely no longer required by the theory, but becomes positively implausible, and would perhaps even contradict the theory. The powerful *rayonnement* of the torch-carrying zone, at any stage, changes the rules of the game so much that societies lagging behind will no longer pass through the same stages as the pioneers. The principle is in fact applied in another interesting work, L. E. Kubbel's *Songhai Empire*.[5] The author appears to share this view of Semenov's, and invokes it to explain why West African Sahelian societies did not move from the primitive-communal stage to a slave society, but to an early form of feudalism.

A number of things have happened in this reformulation. History acquires a strongly purposive, moralistic tinge. Though Semenov insists on the independence, from human consciousness and will, of the basic productive relations which determine all else, nevertheless the pattern which they generate can only be characterized in highly evaluative terms, and the story told seems dominated by a purpose which is both inexorable and which means well by mankind, in the end. But over and above this, it is diffusion which is heavily stressed, and which plays an absolutely indispensable part in this interpretation, in this reunification of human history, so to speak. Diffusion is indeed a very important process. In the nineteenth century, when anthropology was born, Europeans had the fact of diffusion under their very noses; they could see it happening all the time. The rival idea of evolution took a little more thought; one had to put together what the biologists were saying, with the history of one's own society, and then surmise that other societies moved along similar lines (only more slowly), and that the whole thing was similar to the biological story. The third idea, functionalism, starts from the observation that some societies do not change much, and the inference that this requires mechanisms for keeping them stable, and that it may be a bad thing to disturb those mechanisms. (This

5 See ch. 1, n. 4 above.

idea had long been available in conservative thought, it suited some
styles of colonial policy, and, contrary to the belief of some anthropologists, it was not invented within anthropology.) The question is,
which of these three ideas (if any) provides the clue to understanding
human society and history.

Marxism as conventionally interpreted (and in harmony, I think, with
the intentions of its founders) is basically evolutionist. I apologize for the
term, especially to Russian Marxists, for whom I think this immediately
conjures up the association of doctrines about evolutionary rather than
revolutionary development. The question about smooth continuity
versus occasional dramatic jumps is quite a separate one, not connected
with the present argument. The term 'evolutionism' is here used in a
generic manner, covering both these alternatives, and designating a stress
on endogenous development as the main and crucial process in human
history. The conventional interpretation repudiates the functionalist
stress on stability and functionality as spurious, as a case of taking the
façade for the reality: within the social sciences in the West, Marxists tend
to consider functionalists to be the main opposing trend. In Semenov's
reformulation, we shall see that the matter is more complex.

Now obviously Marxism never denied the fact of diffusion. It is
clearly implied in any unilineal version of Marxist philosophy of history
at two points at least: in as far as primitive-communal societies are small
and numerous, whereas asiatic or slave-owning ones are large, obviously
the relationship between the displacing and displaced social forms must
be of a few–many kind, if not actually of a one–many kind. Such
absorption by few or one or many is the extreme form of diffusion, of
course. Then again, with the coming of capitalism, its absorption of the
rest of the world is not merely implied, but explicitly commented on, by
Marx and Engels. In between these two transitions, the matter is not
clear. The progression Asiatic–slave-owning–feudal is not necessarily,
or at all, a progression in size, and thus does not require absorption of
new territory and/or population at each stage.

However, though Marxism, as conventionally interpreted, clearly
allows and requires diffusion at two points at least, and does not exclude
it elsewhere; nevertheless it stresses it much less than is the case in
Semenov's version, where diffusion features very conspicuously. Thus
Semenov stresses the impact of the torch-carrying centre on peripheral
regions, and on the continuous expansion of both centre and affected
periphery (as opposed to the backwoods which remain isolated). There
is a further extremely important point: on occasion, not only is the
centre an essential precondition of the attainment of the next stage, but
so is the periphery. The periphery becomes, at least on occasion, quite
indispensable.

This seems particularly true, according to Semenov, at the point of transition from Near-Eastern Asiatic society (ancient-oriental) to Mediterranean slave-owning society.

> ... it is possible to say a priori that the replacement of the Asiatic formation by another, more progressive one could not take place as the qualitative transformation of existing social organisms, which would have preserved themselves as such ... Nor did it take place simply in the form of the destruction or ruin of Asiatic social organisms and the emergence in their place of new, already slave-owning ones.
>
> The point is that social organisms of a new type did not emerge at all in that very same region ... but at one of the edges of the world system of Asiatic social organisms ...
>
> The replacement of the bronze age by the early iron age, which took place on the territory of Greece, made possible the transition to a new class-endowed socio-economic formation, and one more progressive than the Asiatic one which emerged in the copper and bronze age. But this possibility would never have become a reality had Greece not represented an admittedly marginal, but none the less inseparable part of the old centre ...

The influence of the old 'Asiatic' society was an essential precondition of this miracle. (There can be no doubt about Semenov's sympathy with it. One is reminded of what Hegel had said – in the ancient Orient, only *one* was free, but here *some* were free.) Moreover, the miracle apparently occurred once only – which, I suppose, justifies one in calling it a miracle (my term, not Semenov's). 'Slave-owning social organisms arose not throughout the territory of the old centre of global development but only at *one* of its distant limits' (italics mine). But this single *Wirtchafts-wunder* is the precondition of all the others in the Western historical sequence. The authority of Engels's *Anti-Dühring* is invoked for this: 'Without slavery, no Greek state, no Greek art and science; without slavery, no Roman Empire. But without Hellenism and the Roman Empire ... no modern Europe.'

Earlier, we are given an account of the ancient Near East which does indeed make it seem unlikely that the transition to a higher stage could have occurred internally, rather than at its limits:

> ... the ancient Orient, all of whose history offers a process of the successive emergence and disappearance of social organisms or conglomerates of such organisms ... It is possible to disagree about the nature of the socio-economic structure of the ancient Orient, but it seems unquestionable that the newly emerging social organisms belonged to the same type as those which perished.

Change of personnel, but not structure. Ibn Khaldun would endorse such a view. Semenov also puts forward an oscillation theory for this region and period of human history:

The most striking peculiarity of the development of class society of the ancient East is the perpetual transformation of the political map, the extinction of some and the emergence of other governmental formations. One of the main reasons for this is the alteration, characteristic of all countries of the ancient East, of periods of the existence of strong social organisms, and thereby also of strong centralized despotisms, with periods of their disintegration . . .

It is quite clear that the empires resulting from conquest could not be stable or lasting. With the weakening . . . at the core . . . the whole inevitably disintegrated . . . the parts into which it disintegrated found themselves under the power of a conqueror. Not infrequently these conquerors were the peoples of the periphery . . . the incursions of the peoples of the historic periphery into the region of the centre of historical development can under no circumstances be interpreted as deviations from normality. For the societies of the ancient east all this appears to be the norm or rule.

It is difficult to see how this could have normally led to any progress. If so many perished without ever producing the next stage, why should one of them some day creatively produce something new? This seed showed no sign of sprouting. But once only, in the far West of the ancient Eastern world, one of those incursions did eventually lead to an higher stage.

The unprogressive, stagnant nature of the Asiatic socio-economic formation, its low potential for self-propulsion to the next higher stage, is further visible from that second great incarnation of it, in the East proper (as opposed to the ancient Near East). In those regions, '. . . class society emerged sooner than in most of the regions of Europe . . .' but did not proceed to develop. Semenov does not altogether exclude the possibility that they might properly be characterized as feudal: 'The social structure found there during the periods which are frequently called feudal by scholars, differed substantially from European feudalism.' But this hardly matters; feudal or Asiatic, either way it was static: '. . . but [it] was very similar to that which was found there in antiquity.' Whatever it was, it was stagnant. The authority of Marx and Engels is invoked for this theory of Asiatic stagnation:

. . . the solution . . . was proposed by the very authors of the theory of socio-economic formations, Marx and Engels. It consisted of proposing that from the birth of class-endowed society right up to the eighteenth and even nineteenth centuries, the asiatic mode of production continued to exist in certain countries of the East. In other words, these countries remained in the stage of the first class-endowed socio-economic formation, just as all the original population of Australia remained up to the same period at the stage of primitive-communal structure. As is well known, Marx and Engels repeatedly wrote about the stagnant character of the evolution of the oriental countries.

As we have seen, Semenov overcomes the misguided interpretation of unilinealism by means of a judicious blend of diffusionism and what I have called the 'torch relay' view of history, and what may also be called the displacement effect, or the doctrine of the essential periphery. The historic periphery, one might say, is a subject, not an object, of history in Semenov's view: during various crucial transitions, i.e. the Asiatic–slave and the slave–feudal, it played a crucial rule in the attainment of the next historic step. (Though Semenov does not really spell this out, the same would now seem to be true for the capitalism–socialism transition.) The fact that historic leadership is displaced, that the torch is passed sideways, that its new erstwhile retarded recipients are also essential for further progress, dispenses both them and their predecessors from that irksome theoretical obligation to 'pass through all stages'. If the sideways displacement effect is essential not accidental, if the active participation and contribution of the periphery is a necessary precondition of further progress, it follows not merely that societies need not, but actually *cannot*, parallel each other's 'stages'. At the very least, the periphery (according to the hypothesis previously backward by 'stage' criteria) must leapfrog forward when it takes over leadership. If the participation of the periphery was essential for the attainment of the next stage, then parts of the old centre not affected by the agency of the newly active periphery are *ipso facto* debarred from being the originators of the next round, the next step up. Some transitions positively require a radical change of world leadership, it would appear.

As stated, this theoretical adjustment or reinterpretation of the theory contains a great amount of implicit diffusionism, of the invocation of the important process by which societies affect each other sideways, and have impact on each other, to the point of transforming each other. (This is in contrast with the 'evolutionist' model of an 'internal' or endogenous development.) This diffusionism is rather specific in the importance it attributes to what might otherwise be considered the passive, 'backward' or influence-receiving regions.

But functionalism is also present in this theory (and it has perhaps always been one of the constituents of Marxism). Evolutionists start from the fact of endogenous development (and the development of mankind as a whole must be endogenous, as Semenov might insist, if we exclude extra-terrestrial intrusions); diffusionists start from the equally conspicuous fact of lateral influence; and functionalists start from the sometimes most conspicuous fact of stability or stagnation. We have seen how much Semenov stresses the stagnation of the Orientals and the native Australians. 'The dragging of these countries into the zone of influence of the world capitalist system led to the overcoming of stagnation . . . Marx took this view.'

From all this it would seem to follow that functionalism – the doctrine that the main trait of societies is stability, self-perpetuation, and that consequently the job of the social analyst is to locate the mechanisms, the functions, which contribute to this end result – would seem a pretty good approximation to the truth, at any rate for the majority of societies, though not for all. Admittedly, this self-preserving equilibrium or stagnation of Oriental societies (though not of Australian aboriginal ones), is one of class-endowed, and hence antagonistic, structures, so that the stability is conflict-ridden rather than peaceful. Such a view however would in no way differentiate Semenov from many 'Western' functionalists, who often delight in finding conflict functional and seeing functions in conflict. The only difference would be that they would extend such a conflict-stressing account to primitive-communal societies as well, whether or not they possess 'classes'.

We now possess, I think, the outline skeleton of Semenov's position, sketched out as accurately and fairly as I am capable, though not at all times in his own words. Consider now the problems faced by this position.

First of all it is worth repeating that its central contention seems to me correct. If one considers the importance of diffusion in human history, and the ephemeral nature, on a historic time scale, of concrete societies, and the fact that 'stages' are inspired by historic epochs not by individual national histories, it does indeed follow that what Semenov rightly calls the customary interpretation of unilinealism is so implausible that it should never have been adopted, and that only certain idiosyncrasies of European history led to its implausibility remaining hidden. By abandoning that interpretation, socio-economic formations or stages are freed from the need to 'apply' to each and every society. *Ipso facto*, the critic of that theory finds himself deprived of a large part of his armoury, if not all of it. So is all well? Can the matter rest there?

There is in the West a well-known and influential theory of science, formulated by Sir Karl Popper, which runs roughly as follows: the merit of scientific theories lies in their exposure to risk. The more possible facts they deny, the more they are at risk, the greater their content and merit. So the misguided interpretation of unilinealism was clearly full of content, in so far as it denied all the facts assiduously assembled by its critics, concerning the failure of this or that society to pass through appropriate stages. Semenov's version is not vulnerable to these facts (or at any rate, not vulnerable to an important proportion of those facts). Does that mean that it is virtually without content, or at any rate that the substance of Marxism has been drastically impoverished?

Semenov's adjustment would seem to be *ad hoc* in the sense that it clearly appears to be provoked by those criticisms, and to be designed to render them harmless. But his reasoning is not merely in this sense *ad hoc*, it is also entirely cogent. The trouble with any uncritical or unselective repudiation of *ad hoc* adjustments is that arguments may be both *ad hoc* and good. Popperians may be in danger of forgetting that such theories, like all others, must benefit from the principle that the origin of a theory is unconnected with its merit. Being *ad hoc* is a kind of origin. Such bastardy should not disqualify a candidate of merit.

The truth of the matter would seem to be that although Semenov's reformulation withdraws unilinealism from the reach of some objections, it does not withdraw it from the reach of all of them. Moreover, not only does it not lose all the empirical content and testability exposure of the old formulation, it actually highlights some new and interesting problems, which, by the criteria of the philosophy of science mentioned above, is a hallmark of a good and fertile theory. Both the retained-old and the newly acquired problems deserve discussion.

First of all, whilst the reformulation frees society from the obligation to pass through all stages, it surely cannot give them *carte blanche* to do entirely as they please. They were exempted from the old obligation in virtue of the importance of diffusion, of the lateral influence of world leaders, in the sociological sense. Hence they can only claim their exemption from the old obligatory stages when such lateral influence does operate. It can only permit them to evade the proper sequence under the influence of a world centre which drags them into another 'stage'. But if insulated (and does insulation never occur?) they must either follow the proper order of stages, or perhaps be stagnant. Otherwise, they continue to pose a problem for unilinealism, Semenov's reformulation notwithstanding.

Take a concrete example. In the West, scholars concerned with the phenomenon of slavery disagree about the exact number of societies actually based on the institution of slavery, but they seem to be agreed that the Caribbean and the southern states of the USA, in the appropriate parts of the eighteenth and nineteenth centuries, fall into this category. This retrogression, from late feudalism or early capitalism, without the benefit of the influence of any global centre of slave-owning (which in any case would not be a torch-carrying world leader, but itself a case of retrogression), must continue to pose a problem for unilinealism.

Or take the problem of stagnation – in other words, the fact that 'static' functionalism does seem true for such a large proportion of human societies. Although Semenov's reformulation rightly allows the phenomenon of primitive-communal societies being dragged from their periphery into 'higher' world systems, it must presumably still be true that had this not occurred, those laggards would eventually propel themselves upwards by their own inner resources. I suppose we can now never know whether indeed they would have done so. For my own part, I would quite gladly accept a modified quasi-evolutionist version of the transition from primitive-communal to Asiatic, which might be called the frequency or statistical theory, and which would run as follows: not every primitive-communal society contains adequate or sufficient seeds of change. The conditions of upward development are more complex, and require additional propitious circumstances (say, an alluvial river valley suitable for intensive irrigation agriculture – a theory which admittedly looks plausible only for the 'old world', but I am using it only for the sake of argument). The theory would only require that this combination of circumstances is sufficiently probable to ensure that it should occur sooner or later. Once it occurred, the processes of torch-of-leadership assumption and of diffusion, so much stressed (in other terms) by Semenov, would ensure the perpetuation of the new stage. It would constitute no objection to such a theory that the initial endogenous transformation would only occur in a minority of primitive-communal societies.

Semenov does not actually elaborate such a theory, but it seems to me consistent with his position, and in its spirit, and moreover to be intrinsically plausible and attractive. What the theory really requires is that the spontaneous, endogenous primitive–Asiatic transition should have occurred at least often enough for us to be able, so to speak, to rely on it. This seems to be the case, and Semenov also holds it to be so:

A first class-endowed society formed itself fully only in two delimited areas, the Nile valley and the area between the rivers Tigris and Euphrates ... The subsequent development of mankind followed, on the one hand, the line of the emergence of new independent regional centres of historic development (the valleys of the Indus and the Hwang Ho).

The only class formation which can arise exclusively on the basis of the disintegration of primitive society alone appears to be the asiatic one ... Asiatic societies can emerge as islands, to a considerable extent isolated from each other in a sea of peoples remaining in the pre-class stage ... All class societies, emerging in areas which at the time were outside the influence of previously formed centres of civilization, inevitably had to be Asiatic rather than slave-owning or feudal. The data available ... [from] pre-Colomban America, Oceania, and sub-Saharan Africa fully confirm this.

Given the multiplicity of these independent, isolated 'Asiatic islands', in four or five continents, we seem to be safe. If by some accident of geography, the Nile flowed into the Indian Ocean and the Sahara stretched to Suez, there would have been no Pharaonic Egypt, but the transition from Primitive to Asiatic would have been safe. The Chinese or the Hawaians, the Aztecs and the Incas would still have been there. History might have been delayed a bit, but its basic law would have remained unaltered. Only the timetable would have been amended.

But what does make one feel rather nervous is when one sees the torch of progress in one pair of hands only. If those feet had stumbled, if that leader had faltered, if those hands had failed, what then? It makes one scared even to think of it.

For just this seems to have been the situation, on at least one crucial occasion: 'the limitation in space and time of the emergence of slave-owning society . . . slave-owning social organisms arose not throughout the territory of the old centre . . . but only at one of its distant edges . . .' Semenov does not discuss the question of the existence of other slave-owning societies, but as far as the successors to the old Near-Eastern world system are concerned, the ancient Mediterranean seems to have been an unique case. This is curious, in as far as the three pre-conditions he specifies – iron, pre-existing Asiatic society, and early-class invaders – must often have come together. For one thing, why did the new formation not spread with Alexander? And after Alexander, there have been many invaders of Asiatic societies, endowed both with an early class structure presumably comparable to that of the Dorians, and with iron, and yet Asiatic society stubbornly remained stagnant, and it took the brutal prince of capitalism to rouse that sleeping beauty from her slumber.

Here we come to a profound methodological problem which faces Semenov's reinterpretation. The endogenous, acorn-to-oak-tree vision of human history seems essential to Marxism and to evolutionist theories generally; in fact, it defines evolutionism. But how do we know that acorns generate oak trees? The answer is that we have numerous examples of this particular development. No oak tree is known to have sprung from something other than an acorn. But the matter becomes more difficult if we possess one instance only of a particular transition. Too many factors are present for us to be able to single out the crucial ones. It may be different in modern genetics. It may be that microscopic investigation of the genetic equipment enables the geneticist to identify its growth potential a priori. But in history and the social sciences, we simply cannot read the genetic code – whether because our theories are not good and precise enough, or because social structures are not as tightly organized and uniquely determined in their effects as biological ones, or both. If there is only one specimen of slave-owning society, at any rate within the mainstream of history, and that one is in turn the precondition of all subsequent progress, then we are methodologically in a very difficult situation. One of Semenov's opponents on this issue within the Soviet Union, whom he very fairly quotes, does indeed single out this problem as absolutely central: 'there turned out to be more deviations and exceptions than cases falling under the rule [of unilinealism], and secondly – and this is the main point – the regularities operating here showed themselves to be so specific, that they could not be explained simply by the influence of historic environment alone.'[6]

This may indeed be the main point. If one specific conjuncture of circumstances produced an unique event – the emergence of slave-owning society – which, however, also turns out to be an essential link in the chain leading to the present, what happens to the necessity of historical development? Semenov does not abjure historical necessity. He asserts it in the abstract:

The theory of every distinct social formation reflects the objective necessity of the development of *all* social organisms, which have at their base the corresponding system of productive relations.

The characteristic trait of a world system of social organisms of a given type appears to be the fact that their development *inevitably* prepares the appearance of a new, more progressive world system, so that its existence appears to be a *necessary* link in the history of mankind. (Italics mine)

He is also willing to implement this abstract historical determinism by specific historically guaranteed predictions: 'The world-socialist system appears as the only one which can be and necessarily will become global. And in the more distant future, with the transition to communism, human society will inevitably transform itself into a single social organism.'

This final prediction is interesting. By what criterion will the global communist society be one organism? Presumably not by political criteria, in as far as there can be no room for state authorities in a classless society. The other plausible criterion would be a shared culture, which is indeed in our age the most important criterion of 'nationality'. But why should we expect mankind in the communist stage to become culturally homogeneous? Many people would find such a prospect depressing. But what is interesting about the prediction is the implied suggestion – it is no more – that lateral boundaries (between 'social organisms', or 'nations') also express antagonisms. What else, other than the absence of antagonisms, would account for the inevitable erosion of lateral boundaries? If this is so, one could indeed expect lateral boundaries to go by the board, if one anticipates a stage of human history which will be free of social antagonisms. The idea that lateral inter-organism relations, or at least some of them, are also antagonistic, is indeed implied in Semenov's scheme. It would seem to follow from the importance given within it to the relation between the periphery and the centre. Certain crucial transitions can only take place through the

6 Danilova, 'Controversial problems in the theory of pre-capitalist societies', also quoted in Semenov's article. See ch. 1, n. 1 above.

interaction between centre and periphery. The relationship between the two is not immediately a relation between the classes, but it is a relationship between organisms at different stages, and hence containing diverse classes at their helm. In this sense, it is also a kind of class antagonism. The stress on centre–periphery relations and the attempt to extend the notion of class relation to it is of course shared by Soviet and Western Marxists, and is prominent in the recent work of influential Western Marxists such as Wallerstein.[7] The whole notion of 'periphery', as recently used, is, I suppose, an attempt to turn 'underdevelopment' into a timeless and generic notion, available for use retrospectively on the historic past.

However these are tangential issues. The one central methodological issue facing the Semenov reinterpretation arises from the essential and yet more or less unique character of at least one stage, namely Mediterranean slave-owning society. The obverse of this uniqueness (which Semenov does not assert in so many words) is the fact that we cannot rely on this formation to arise on the foundation of its predecessor, Asiatic society, in the Orient. (This failure Semenov stresses explicitly.) Slave-owning society, if not unique, at least is not a reliable consequence of its historic antecedents, unlike Asiatic society itself, which appears to be a hardy plant flowering irrepressibly in many parts of the globe.

The most influential single sociologist in the West is, I suppose, Max Weber. It would be bizarre to reduce his disagreement with Marx to the issue of idealism–materialism. The real difference is something else: it is the issue between the acorn–oaktree model and the gatekeeper models of human progress. In the Hegelian–Marxist tradition, the seeds of progress are there and will come to fruition one way or another. On the gatekeeper model, the way forward is barred, but one gate happened, fortuitously, to be open. The former model naturally leads to a sense of the unity of mankind and its history (a sense which Semenov shares so strongly), because it is as it were guaranteed by the potency of those shared seeds, whereas the latter vision implies the opposite. Weber was indeed obsessed by the distinctiveness of Western history, its non-universality. It is significant that the real international popularity of Weber's thought came at a period obsessed with the failure of non-Western acorns to grow easily and quickly into Western oak trees, i.e. at the time of preoccupation with the difficulties of 'economic development' (and/or its desired political accompaniments.) This is the heart of the matter. The one crucial opening in the gate was for him a consequence of an accidental combination of circumstances. (Like

7 I. Wallerstein, *The Modern World System* (New York, 1974).

Semenov, he thought he could nevertheless give a causal account of it, despite its uniqueness.) He was only an idealist in the thin sense that one element in the set of circumstances was an ideological one. The other elements were not, and for most societies and situations, he could be as materialist as they come.

Semenov's nearly unique gate or opening is located much further back than Weber's. It is, as we saw, located at the emergence of slave-owning in the Balkans and Italy, over 2,000 years prior to the passage of Weber's special gateway. But this does not affect the logical aspect of the problem. What happens to historical inevitability, to the generation of one stage by another, if one of the stages is quasi-unique or in any case simply cannot be relied upon to emerge from its predecessor? This is one of the problems Semenov's reformulation will have to face.

Whilst Semenov successfully demonstrates that individual societies do not need to pass through each and every stage, and that they may skip stages when they come under the influence of more advanced, torch-carrying centres, nevertheless certain possibilities presumably must still remain excluded; there is still a certain overlap in requirements between Semenov's unitary-history unilinealism, and the old parallel-unilinealism. Societies must not jump stages when not impelled to do so by any outside advanced centre, for instance. Semenov does not discuss the case of Japan, the one society which, though Asiatic in a geographic sense, is widely held to have had a genuine feudalism. If slave society was absent in the East, but is held to be a precondition of the emergence of feudalism, how was this possible? Societies must not go into reverse gear and regress into 'earlier' stages, with or without the impulsion of some more powerful centre. Can there be centres of retardation too which also exercise an influence? In brief, the unity of world history, the stress on diffusion of more advanced modes of production from centres of excellence, does not remove all the problems facing unilinealism. The reinterpretation does not give unilinealism a completely clean bill of health, it merely removes some of its difficulties.

But let us leave these problems, and consider some of the new tasks which the interpretation suggests. Semenov's insistence on the importance of the periphery and of the sideways passing of the torch is reminiscent of a certain familiar philosophy of history, which has often been formulated: civilizations or nations or societies must, like three-quarters in rugby football, pass the ball sideways if they are to advance. There is a poetic formulation of this idea by the Austrian poet and playwright Grillparzer, for instance:

Denn alle Völker dieser weiten Erde,
Sie treten auf den Schauplatz nach und nach,
Die an dem Po und bei den Alpen wohnen,
Dann zu den Pyranäen kehrt die Macht.
Die aus der Seine trinken und der Rhone,
Schauspieler stets, sie spielen drauf den Herrn.
Der Brite spannt das Netz von seiner Insel,
Und treibt die Fische in sein goldnes Garn.
Ja, selbst die Menschen jenseits eurer Berge,
Das blaugeaugte Volk voll roher Kraft,
Das nur im Fortschritt kaum bewahrt die Stärke
Blind, wenn es handelt, thatlos, wenn es denkt,
Auch sie bestrahlt der Weltensonne Schimmer,
Und Erbe aller Frühern glänzt ihr Stern.
Dann kommt's auf euch, an euch und eure Brüder,
Der letzte Aufschwung ist's der matten Welt.
Die lang gedient, sie werden enlich herrschen,
Zwar breit und weit, allein nicht hoch, noch tief;
Die Kraft, entfernt von ihrem ersten Ursprung,
Wird schwächer, ist nur noch erborgte Kraft.
Doch werdet herrschen ihr und euren Namen
Als Siegel drücken auf der kunftgen Zeit.

(Grillparzer, *Libussa*, Act V)

Thus spoke Libuše, while presiding over the transition from matriarchy to early state formation and urbanization among the Western Slavs; the occasion of the prophecy was the foundation of the city of Prague. My translation follows:

Thus all the peoples on the expanse of earth
The worldly stage ascend, each turn by turn,
Those living by the Po and in the Alps,
Then to the Pyrenees the power shifts.
Those who drink from the Seine and from the Rhone,
Were actors ever, then they played the lords.
The Briton spreads a net from his fair isle,
And drives the fish into his golden thread.
Yea, even the men who live beyond your hills,
The blue-eyed nation full of uncouth strength,
A folk which barely keeps its force in progress,
Blind when it acts, and deedless when it thinks;
They too will feel the rays of the world's sun,
Their star will shine, succeeding all the rest.
Your turn will come, for you and for your brethren,
The final upsurge of a weary earth.
Those who have served so long will rule at last,

Though far and wide, yet without height or depth;
The strength, so far now from its primal spring,
Grows weaker, being now but borrowed force.
Yet you will rule, and press your name as seal
On time to come, time which is yet to be.

But there is a certain asymmetry in Semenov's version. The torch
needs to be advanced sideways on numerous occasions, but not always.
In the first transition (primitive–Asiatic), the question of it being
passed from a more advanced centre to a retarded periphery simply did
not arise, as there weren't any advanced centres. If you break up
'primitive society' into a number of substages, as is done by the Soviet
scholar Maretin, this point then applies once again to the first of these
substages.[8] Thus, in the first transition, everyone is equally retarded, or
if you like, no one is retarded, and without any centre, there can be no
periphery. At the next transition (Asiatic–slave) the sidestep was
essential: the Asiatic heartlands do not seem to have the potential for
endogenous growth, but sank into canonically documented stagnation. The same is repeated next time: the slave–feudal transition
once again takes place at the edge of the old centre. But the feudal-
capitalist transition is exceptional: it is, so to speak, a centre-preserving
transition, and this is quite idiosyncratic, if one spells out Semenov's
schema in detail. Is this connected with the fact that it is the one
transition to which Western historical sociology is really sensitive? If
there is at present any kind of philosophy of history at all in the West, it
is an unsystematized one, which concentrates on the big social transformation wrought by industrialization. It perceives two historical
transformations – the neolithic and the industrial revolutions. In
between, there are conquests rather than inwardly destined and deep
metamorphoses. No one has yet articulated this vision with philosophic
depth. The philosophy of 'industrial society' has not yet found its
Hegel. But if the feudal–capitalist tradition is so unusual, how is it to
be explained? Why is one particular transition centre-preserving,
whereas all others (except the first, which had no option) are centre-
shifting? The last transition, which is yet to come, will also be unique, in
that it will be neither centre-preserving nor centre-displacing, but
centre-dissolving.

Strictly speaking, not one, but two contrasts are involved here. Some
transitions preserve leadership, and some can only be accomplished by
means of the displacement of the advanced centre. But furthermore
there is also the contrast between society-preserving and society-
destroying transitions (irrespective of the question of national leadership). The two distinctions are not identical and cut across each other.

8 Maretin, 'The Community and its types in Indonesia', cit. ch. 1, n. 4 above.

As far as the very first epochal transition is concerned, the issue of society-preservation does already arise (whereas the issue of the preservation of leadership could not yet arise, there not having been any prior leaders). Semenov explicitly says that the first class-endowed societies emerge not through a metamorphosis of primitive ones, but through their destruction, and on their ruins. Both questions arise in the second and third transitions, to slavery and to feudalism, which exemplify both 'displacement of leadership' and 'discontinuity of societies' transitions. The next transition, to capitalism, is doubly contrasted with them: leadership stays put, and societies preserve themselves. The transition from capitalism to socialism is the most interesting one, from this viewpoint: leadership does shift sideways, but at the same time societies are preserved. The last transition, Semenov predicts, will dissolve the previously existing distinct societies, and we can on general Marxist grounds assume that leadership will move only in the sense of dissolving altogether. It will move, but not to anyone. It will just move away.

This second contrast between society-preserving transitions and others, obviously crucial and central for any further development of this philosophy of history, in effect brings to the fore the whole question of why there are, and also why sometimes there are not, continuous societies, nations, cultures, or whatever. Traditional Marxism can be accused, at best, of not highlighting the question, and at worst of treating it as something epiphenomenal and of no great interest. A dismissive attitude to this question simply is not possible within Semenov's schema. The diversity and plurality of nations and cultures is not a contingent accident, a by-product of the isolation and hence of the linguistic and other idiosyncrasies of primitive communities, but an essential fact, without which the whole process of world history could not work. This seems to follow, if from nothing else, from the crucial role played by peripheral nations on those three supremely important occasions in world history, the arrival of slavery, of feudalism and of socialism. If a backward and distinct periphery is essential for some steps forward, there could be no progress in a world with one nation only.

The schema highlights a point which others have reached by different paths: that ethnicity seems to have a different role in the later stages of history, and in the course of the later transitions, from the one it had during earlier epochs. In connection, for instance, with the Asiatic mode of production and its epoch, Semenov notes the non-congruence between political organization and 'social organism'. Though he does not say so, the same is also conspicuously true of slave-owning society, whose political units varied from small city states to the ecumenical Roman empire, without apparently any corresponding radical change in the underlying relations of production. (The same appears to be true in Mongolia and central Asia, according to the material of a Soviet scholar,

S. I. Vainstein. In her introduction to his study of the Tuvinians, *Nomads of South Siberia*,[9] Caroline Humphrey writes, 'Vainstein's material adds up to the following conclusion: there are no transformations in the technology of herding, nor of agriculture, nor of craft or commodity production, which "account for" the rise and fall of the steppe empires.' Non-congruence between ethnicity and polity also seems hardly disputable for the feudal age, with its shadowy larger units and its fragmented political micro-units. It is during the subsequent two stages that two of the things occur which may well be connected: societies acquire a kind of persistence, become continuous and 'pass through' the transitions, and ethnicity becomes an important (though not the exclusive) principle of political-unit delimitation. One can add to this the idiosyncratic fact that no sideways passing of the torch occurs during the first of the two great modern transitions, which at the same time looks like being the big and crucial transition for bourgeois sociologists: the emergence of 'rational' production.

One can of course think of good *ad hoc* reasons why the transition from feudalism to capitalism had to be endogenous and society-preserving. It was a transition in which commercial and production-oriented strata took over from a predatory or display-oriented military nobility – a contrast which of course greatly struck the early European sociologists. This being so, it could hardly be a transition in which the historical midwife would be a war of conquest and domination. It was the un-martial ones – at least in their outward aspect – who were the victors then. It was the warriors who were the vanquished. They could hardly be defeated at their own game and in their own field by upstarts ill suited for it. The victory had to be effected by internal mechanisms inside a society. If it was decided by war at all, it was civil war, which preserved the continuity of state and society even if it changed the identity of rulers within it. One can also put the case negatively: is it conceivable that the emergence of bourgeois society out of a feudal one would have been the work of peripheral – bluntly: barbarian – invaders? There is something bizarre about the idea of such tribal invaders demolishing the baron's castle and then settling down in its ruins as burghers, traders, financiers, and entrepreneurs.

No, this transition for once had to be endogenous, and hence both society- and national-leadership-preserving. But I must confess that I find the *ad hoc* reasons which I have sketched out above, in order to explain the idiosyncrasy, rather inelegant precisely because of their *ad*

9 See ch. 5, n. 23 above.

hoc quality. They are plausible as far as they go, but if history is such a unity – if transitions generally involve a side-step, but not on this one occasion – I'd like to see some good general reason for this asymmetry. What I have described as the implicit, unformulated Western philosophy of history, does seem to have the advantage here: by treating the transition to industrialism as in any case quite unique, it is not embarrassed by then finding further unique traits in it. Semenov's version of the Hegelo–Marxist vision transforms it from an essentially Eurocentric self-congratulatory one – which it had been normally – into an encouraging pat on the back for late developers. But in doing this, it finds one particular transition, the feudalism–capitalism one, embarrassingly idiosyncratic.

Let us return however to the overall conceptual strategy of Semenov's work and its place in the intellectual world of Soviet scholarship. He has saved unilinealism from at any rate some of the historical objections to it by means of his strong stress on the unity of history, on the inequality between centre and periphery which nevertheless are parts of one single process, on the diffusion from centre to periphery, which is however accompanied by the essential role of periphery in the course of crucial transitions; in brief he adopts what may be called the relay torch pattern of historical leadership, which stresses the importance of leadership and emulation. The last shall be first. This was always a Marxist view, but Semenov's schema gives it an ethnic twist in addition to its old class meaning. The consequence of all this has been a schema which highlights not only the highly problematical nature of the historical continuity of societies or nations, but also certain specific and intriguing oddities in this field – that the patterns of social continuity and of global leadership by societies are rather different at different stages and in the course of diverse traditions. Once noted and stressed, these questions can hardly be ignored.

But the suggestiveness of Semenov's ideas in this direction is not, so to speak, simply an irrelevant price or by-product of the main objective, namely the defence of unilinealism. Though the relevance is not spelt out, let alone underscored by him, it is there: the most conspicuous research innovation within Soviet anthropology recently has been a concern with ethnicity, with the ethnos, and moreover a concern with it in the modern, non-archaic period, which is marked by the idiosyncratic persistence of ethnoses. In other words, there is a sense in which the world-historical theoretical formulation proposed by Semenov, and the concrete research into ethnicity led by Bromley, dovetail very neatly.

The argument would not merely explain why the existence of distinctive ethnic groups is essential to world history, it would also, and in intimate connection with the previous point, help explain the persistence and historic importance of real war, as opposed to the metaphorical class war. In a remarkable book, W. B. Gallie argues:

This problem arises . . . from the fact that the existence of war . . . cannot be considered or dealt with or controlled, simply as one facet or by-product of mankind's great constructive task of achieving a just and satisfying economic order. Or to speak more simply, from its first beginnings Marxist overall social theory was defective, through its failure to place and explain the different possible roles of war in human history. [10]

Whatever other functions warfare may have – and Semenov no doubt would not disagree with Marx's account of its essential role in ancient slave-owning society – during the crucial side-stepping movements it would be an inevitable agent of the diffusion or even the very establishment of the new social order. Gallie quotes that devastatingly accurate prediction by Engels of the nature of the First World War, published as early as 1888; but goes on to add that Engels misunderstood the practical implications of his theoretical insight, whilst Lenin understood the practical implications without necessarily appreciating the theoretical point. War was essential to the emergence of a new order on the periphery. As Gallie puts it:

For, contrary to Marx and Engels, who had maintained that Tsarism would fall only to a revolution from within, Lenin was persuaded that it would fall only as the result of an utterly disastrous war – and that meant as long a war, and as generalized a global war, as possible . . . In sum, Lenin's stance in 1914 was not simply good Marxism, a faithful adherence to its classic doctrines . . . it was also a necessity of his particular task as leader of the Russian Marxist Socialists . . . Lenin was committed, in fact if not in word, to international socialism *for the sake of one country*, from 1911 onwards, if not from the outset of his revolutionary career. [11]

Semenov's schema is also suggestive or expressive in other intriguing ways. These additional ideas or suggestions are implicit in the arrangement of the material and not articulated by Semenov himself, who consequently cannot in fairness be held in any way responsible for them, one way or the other. They are in the eye of this beholder or interpreter, who must consequently assume complete responsibility for them.

A striking trait of the schema is its strong sense, not of world-historical individuals (none are mentioned, and there is conspicuous absence of any cult personality in this philosophy of history), but of, so to speak, *welthistorische Voelker*. (Bryce Gallie, for instance, said about Lenin that 'he was to become the one unquestionably "world-historical

10 W. B. Gallie, *Philosophers of Peace and War* (Cambridge, 1978), p. 99.
11 Ibid., p. 98.

individual" of our century.' But no world-historical individuals appear on Semenov's tableau. His heroes are nations or collectivities.) They are the nations who assume leadership, and the criteria of leadership are ultimately moral – a contribution towards the fulfilment of the ultimate destiny of mankind as a whole, a destiny whose culmination, both in a chronological and an evaluative sense, is known. The West has lost all such confidence, and despises its Victorian predecessors for having had it. A Western anthropologist who dared speak, without irony, of the *mission civilisatrice* or of the 'white man's burden', would be more or less ostracized by his professional community. Semenov had no hesitation in using the notion of differences or level of development and referring to the obligations of global leadership which this carries with it.

The major mechanism of progress in the past has been the leadership and influence exercised by an advanced centre over the retarded periphery. This influence defined leadership and the location of leadership in turn defined the world-historical epoch. Secondly, Semenov tells us that the most advanced world-system in existence now is the socialist one. The joint implication of these two assertions is not spelt out, but it is obvious. The moral obligations of leadership which this imposes on that system and on its centre are clear. If such leadership is exercised in the course of aiding nations which had been for too long committed to stagnation, it may well fail to be properly appreciated. It may be no accident that it is precisely the previously most stagnant society which is also now the most recalcitrant in accepting guidance from the leading centre.

But that is not all. Russia was once expected to be the third Rome. This did not come to be – at least not literally. However, three times in our single and united pan-human history did mankind advance only by taking a step sideways; thrice was the torch of progress handed over to a nation on the periphery, advance being blocked by the centre. Three times did the marginals at the edge of the historic world take over leadership and open up the future. Once the torch was passed to the Dorians when they established a slave-owning society at the far West of the ancient Orient; once it was handed over to the Franks when they built the centre of feudalism in the outlying marchlands of declining slave society. More recently the banner of leadership was transmitted for the third time. The backwardness of Russia at the time of the Revolution used to be a problem for Marxist theory: in Semenov's version, it becomes its confirmation.

8

Explanation and Materialism

Estonia is one of the smallest, but also one of the intellectually most active and most prosperous, republics of the Soviet Union. The contribution of its ancient university of Tartu (founded by Gustavus Adolphus shortly before he fell on the field of Luetzen) to the development of Russian literary structuralism is fairly well known. Less well known is an active group of philosophers, who apparently play a major part in the cultural life of their country, and receive regular allocations of time in the mass media. One can only speculate about the contribution made to this situation by the proximity, a few hours' sail across the water and within range of television broadcasting, of the sister nation of Finland, with a mutually comprehensible language, and with its world-class philosophers such as G. H. von Wright and Jaako Hintikka.

Eero Loone is one of these Estonian philosophers. A historian by training (and ancestry), he has turned to the philosophy of history which he practises in what can only be described as an impeccably analytic style. His sense of the distinction between conceptual and factual issues, between descriptive and evaluative ones, between substantive, theoretical and meta-theoretical ones, certainly could not be improved or sharpened, were he a product of one of those anglophone institutions, either side of the Atlantic, which pride themselves on their fastidiousness in these matters. His talk of clarifying 'families of concepts' sounds as if he were a *habitué* of the Aristotelian Society. In fact, were he a product of one of those establishments, one might approach his book *Contemporary Philosophy of History*[1] with a touch of apprehension: will this machine be fed with any interesting substance? But Loone is not a product of one of those establishments, and his deployment of razor-

---

1 E. Loone, *Sovremennaya filosofiya istorii* (*Contemporary Philosophy of History*) (Tallin, 1984). A useful general study of Soviet philosophy is now available: James P. Scanlon, *Marxism in the USSR* (Ithaca, NY, 1985). See also Loren R. Graham, *Science, Philosophy and Human Behaviour in the Soviet Union*, (New York, 1987).

sharp analysis is not simply the display of a locally routinized skill. On the contrary, it constitutes evidence of great intellectual independence, and of the capacity to master a style of thought not endowed with immediately obvious local bases. I am not saying that this book should be judged by relaxed standards because of its provenance: it would be an outstanding book by any standards. I am saying that the formal skills it displays deserve special note. The substance on which they are deployed is the Marxist theory of history.

The book consists of four parts. The first three in effect introduce the Russian reader to philosophy of history in its Western modal sense, and he can learn from them about the ideas of Collingwood (soon to be available in Russian), Walsh, Popper, Danto, Mandelbaum, G. H. Nadel, Hempel, Gardiner, Dray, Frankel, Passmore, M. White, W. B. Gallie, A. Naess, M. Bunge, M. Hollis, Kuhn, Momigliano, Plumb, and others. A lucid introduction to this tradition or traditions must obviously be of great interest to the Soviet reader, whereas the part which would really teach something new to the Western reader is the fourth one, in which Loone turns his analytical powers on to Marxism itself.

One occasionally hears a debate in the West, as to whether there is anyone left in Eastern Europe and the USSR who still believes in Marxism. I am inclined to consider the reports of the death of Marxist faith to be somewhat exaggerated, at least as far as the Soviet Union is concerned, but the interest of Loone's work is really quite independent of the truth of the matter. Whether or not people positively believe in the Marxist scheme, no coherent, well-articulated rival pattern has emerged, West or East; and as people must needs think against some kind of grid, even (or perhaps especially) those who do not accept the Marxist theory of history tend to lean upon its ideas when they wish to say what they do positively believe.

Loone rightly singles out the theory of socio-economic formations as central to Marxism. As he puts it, it is its paradigmatic precondition. What is at issue here is a typology of societies, and one which contains, or helps articulate, the Marxist theory of history.

Soviet Marxism, as it crystallized during the Stalin period, had a clear and sharp outline, with its theory of a single dominant historical highway, leading from primitive communism via slave society, feudalism, and capitalism, to the final terminus of communism. This celebrated unilinealism is easy to attack (as a Soviet critic pointed out in a book published in 1968, the exceptions to the theory would seem to be more numerous than its positive exemplifications), and it has been widely though not universally disavowed.

The abandonment of unilinealism raises problems which are very deep. If it is disavowed and not replaced by anything, one may well ask whether one is left with any theory at all, or merely with the debris of a theory. Marxism is supposed to be a theory of historical change, providing a key to its motive force and, presumably, its overall pattern. If any kind of society can follow any other kind, without any constraints, if societies may stagnate for ever, what kind of meaning can be attached to the attribution of primacy to the forces of production, or indeed to anything else? If there are no constraints on the possible patterns of change, what point is there in seeking the underlying mechanism or the secret of constraint, when no constraint exists to be explained? If anything is possible, what could a theory explain, and what theory could be true? Those Western Marxists who blithely disavow unilinealism, as a kind of irritating and unnecessary encumbrance, without even trying to replace it with something else, do not seem to realize that all they are left with is a label, but no theory. Though unilinealism is indeed false, its unqualified abandonment leaves Marxism vacuous.

It is this situation which in effect provides Loone with his problem, and with his implicit (and to a large extent explicit) terms of reference. He is eager to reformulate a Marxism which is not merely free from the shackles of Stalinism (that goes without saying, or with a quiet reference to the unfortunate intrusion of extra-scientific considerations into the scholarship of that period): but a Marxism which also incorporates the historiographical and social science advances of our time, including quantitative and logical techniques, but which above all is formulated in a way which satisfies modern analytic criteria of theory-formation and of explanation. It is this last aspiration that is perhaps strongest in him. In some ways, his work is comparable to that of G. A. Cohen of All Souls College, Oxford, or Jon Elster of Olso. The last part of the book might as well have been called 'Der logische Aufbau des Marxismus'. It owes as much to Hempel as it does to the Founding Fathers of Marxism.

Yet Loone is in no way a scholastic. His eagerness to formalize the conceptual structure of Marxism is conspicuously and pervasively inspired by a most praiseworthy aim: to make clear what the theory does and does not explain, what historical facts it can and cannot accom-modate – in brief, to avoid that vacuity and untestability which accompany sloppy formulation. Loone has a virtually Oxbridge sense of logical propriety, of the distinction between factual and conceptual issues. He deals with the latter, and goes out of his way to make clear that he is not prejudging any of the facts – please historians, do come in and settle this, once I've explained to you what the issue is, and what you are to settle. He really has the manners of an impassive civil servant, explaining technical alternatives, without allowing himself any overt opinion on matters of substantive decision.

In his endeavour (NB, without prejudice to any facts) to endow Marxism with a clear logical structure *and* to save it from the vacuity which threatens its over-liberal versions, one of the first issues he turns to is the stratified or layered conception of social structure, which is inherent in Marxism: the breaking up of social life into productive, administrative, and cultural activity. (I translate *dukhovnaya* as 'cultural' rather than the more literal 'spiritual', which has too many misleading associations.)

Loone notes appositely that there exists no terminology for classifying administrative and cultural forms, corresponding to the classification of 'modes of production'. This is highly significant: the failure to possess such a terminology or typology is a sign of the absence of attempts to define species of polity and culture *independently* of the economic base which they serve. Unless they are so defined, he notes, what content can be given to the thesis that the economic or productive base determines the superstructural layers of social life? If it were the case that any old administrative and religious–cultural system could serve, say, the feudal mode of production, the whole contention to the effect that the base determines the other layers would become uninformative and empty. The correlation of elements from two domains (productive and super-structural), which is an essential element in 'historical materialism', only has a determinate meaning if the elements in the two domains are independently defined. If one set of elements is not defined at all (let alone defined in a way that ensures independence), something has gone seriously wrong with the formulation of the theory. Fashionable Western forms of Marxism do exist, and are common in France, as Loone notes, which actually incorporate superstructural elements such as politics or religion *in* the economic base. That would certainly seem to ensure that the thesis of the primacy of the base will not be challenged by any facts.

Thus, as we shall see, though Loone's Marxism is pliable at some interesting points, it makes no concessions to vacuity here and it does not approach tautology. On the contrary, at its core there is a strong, testable thesis. It can perhaps best be conveyed by the diagram below (which he himself does not use).

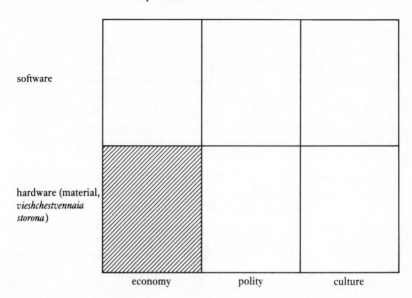

I am not absolutely sure whether the modern notion of 'hardware', material equipment, and 'software', its specific deployment, corresponds fully to the distinction between material activity and productive relations: it may be that the 'material side' includes equipment *and* its use, but just how much is not clear to me. Note that the word Loone uses, *vieshchestvennaia*, could be rendered in English as 'thing-y'. What the worker does with the tool is perhaps material activity, but the fact that he does so under a foreman, is part of the 'relations'. Can the two be separated?

The thesis of historical materialism can be interpreted as saying either that the hardware, of *all* the columns jointly, determines the higher level of software as a whole; or, that the economic column, hardware and software together, determines the other two columns. Loone, if I understand him correctly, espouses the strongest possible version of Marxism, the logical *product* of the two positions – in other words, the claim that the material, technical part of the economic column (shaded in diagram 1) determines both the upper part of its own column *and* the totality of the other two columns. (Western tautological Marxism, on the other hand, consists of the logical *sum* of the two doctrines, in other words the claim that *all* aspects of *all* activities, taken jointly, determine the condition of a society. No doubt.)

That is Loone's strong, uncompromising side. But he insists on pliable, flexible interpretation, when it comes to the demands of synchronization between conditions and changes at the various distinct levels of social life. Here he offers an interestingly and refreshingly precise account of how two elements in Marxism, not immediately compatible can after all be harmonized. Marxism is markedly 'functionalist' in that it refuses to see society as a thing of shreds and patches: political and cultural institutions are there to serve the system. But it also insists on conflict and disharmony (above all between the forces and the relations of production, the hardware and the software) as the prime agent of inevitable change. Just how do these two doctrines dovetail?

Loone's version requires co-ordination of appropriate elements at each level (production, polity, culture) by and large, but not at all times: moreover *any* level can, quite independently, get out of step with the other two. What he insists on, however (thereby avoiding vacuity), is that *if* the form of organization at any level gets out of step with the other two, then either the other two follow suit before too long, or the dissident layer reverts to its previous condition, or the society in question disintegrates and ceases to exist. This formula on its own treats the three levels as of equal importance; but Loone goes on to add that changes of the non-dominant (i.e. other than economic) layer can never be the *full* cause of the transition of a society from one type of social formation to another.

This looks as if the materialism were being watered down, but, as we shall see, that is not so. The refinement does, however, have an important consequence. It makes sense of politically initiated transformations, such as the October Revolution, or the many socialist revolutions in underdeveloped countries since, in which a seemingly unripe country is propelled to a higher stage by its political rulers, rather than by changes internal to the productive layer. It makes an honest woman of such revolutions. The economy is deprived of its privilege of *initium*. The theory merely requires that the other layers follow the political initiative, which of course presupposes that they have at least reached a level where they are capable of doing so, or that the revolution fail and the polity revert to an appropriate earlier type, or that the society fall apart.

The main part of Loone's argument, however, concerns, in effect, the replacement of unilinealism by something more elastic, but not infinitely and vacuously so, and the specification of the underlying core mechanism, the deep structure, which would explain the new, non-unilineal pattern. In the interests of brevity, it will be best to begin with the deep, and follow on with the surface, though Loone, like a good novelist, maintains tension by doing it the other way round. It is at the deep level that one also sees that Loone's materialism is unalloyed and uncorrupted.

The deep motor of historical change lies in the intertwined relationship of two lines on a graph, one straight and one oscillating (rather like

the snake and the staff of Aesculapius). The straight line represents the
ever-growing *forces* of production: the snake the *relations* of production.
The relations of production aid the forces (when the gradient of the
snake is steeper than that of the line), or hamper them (when the snake is
less steep than the line). The forces grow steadily; the relations oscillate.

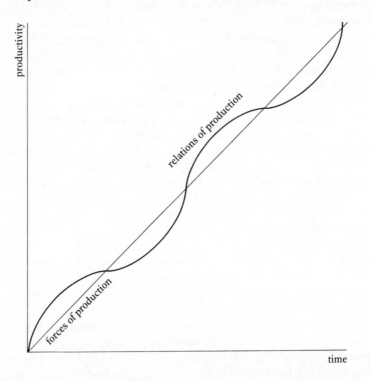

Strictly speaking, the 'relations of production' curve represents actual
productivity, as it is under the joint impact of both the forces of
production and the relations of production. The straight line gives us
what Loone himself calls the 'normal' effectiveness of productive forces
(he himself uses the inverted commas). This presumably can only be
worked out as some kind of average productivity of given technical
equipment, over all the social relations with which it is compatible at all.
(Tools on their own, unaccompanied by any 'social relations', cannot
produce anything.) Loone is not unaware of the enormous difficulties
which would be involved in operationalizing such computations. It all
assumes that there can be a measure of productivity of tool-systems
independent of any one social form. He notes that in exceptional
circumstances, the curved line can actually dip downwards (which
means an actual decline in productivity), indicating a profound crisis in

the mode of production within which this occurs. He does not say whether this is more liable to happen in the death agonies of an old mode, or in the birth pangs of a new one. Loone is familiar with the work of Marshall Sahlins, and must have reflected on the fact that, if Sahlin's view of hunter–gatherer economies as 'the first affluent society' is correct, then the whole of human history between the Neolithic Revolution and the Industrial Revolution is marked by an enormous trough on the curve, a kind of gigantic crater, indicating a global decline in productivity *per caput* between roughly the eighth millennium BC and the eighteenth century AD.

The basic text of Marx's here is of course his celebrated remark in the Preface to the *Contribution to the Critique of Political Economy*, and the underlying theory is: man's technological powers are perpetually growing. The social arrangements accompanying our technology sometimes further, and sometimes diminish, the fruitfulness of our technology. These are the basic premises. And now comes the heart of the Marxist theory, as seen by Loone.

Social arrangements are lumpy, they come in package deals, they cannot really be presented along a single continuous line on a graph. In fact, on earlier graphs, Loone represents them by discontinuous and distant dots. (The graph suggests, on the other hand, that technological progress can be plotted by a single continuous line, and a straight one at that: but I do not suppose that Loone would wish to be held to this implication of what is, after all, only a simplifying expository device.) Anyway, whether or not the progress of technology is smooth, that of social forms is not. They come in distinct kinds, such as 'feudalism' and 'capitalism'. These are radically distinct from each other. Now the really important law is this: each of these social forms is allocated a part, and part only, of the line charting the growth of human technology. Feudalism, for instance, is not possible before a certain technical level, and ceases to be feasible again after a certain other and higher level. The area between these extreme points is, if you like, the zone within which, and within which only, feudalism is possible,

In its Loonean version, the theory further requires, I think, that the zones of diverse social forms should never be identical. But they not only may, but *must* overlap at least a bit. Were this not so, progress would cease to be possible. If the highest level of which feudalism is capable were lower than the lowest level at which capitalism can begin, then even the most advanced feudal society would be incapable of initiating capitalism, and mankind would have had to make do with feudalism for ever. Happily this does not seem to be the case, and overlaps seem to have been common enough to allow a good deal of historical change.

Here Loone can make plain what the truth about various social forms would have been like, had unilinealism been true. It would have meant that the zones of the possible social forms would have been such that the highest part of the first zone overlapped, at least a little, with the lowest zone of the second one, and so on, till the final stage. There would, however, be no other and multiple overlaps. But unilinealism evidently is not true (though in his analytical exposition, Loone does not choose to prejudge any factual issues); so the zones of diverse social forms, along the single line of technical progress, were not so neatly distributed. And here Loone works out the kind of zone distribution which must go with multilineal succession of social forms, and also works out the kinds of multilineality that are possible, without contradicting the basic deep structure of history (the doctrine about the interaction of forces and relations of production), and without degenerating into a formless, chaotic, untestable pseudo-theory, in which Marxist phraseology can coexist with virtually any historical facts.

His argument here is intricate and complex and cannot be reproduced briefly. One can only hope that at least this quarter of his book (the reconstruction of Marxism) will be made available in English. But it is worth commenting on some of his specific points. He notes, correctly in my view, that the theory simply cannot accommodate cases of permanent stagnation. Marxists used to sneer at functionalists – yah, you cannot account for social change. The time has come to return the compliment and point out that Marxism cannot live with well-documented stagnation. Loone sees this clearly, but in discussing the matter in detail, seems to me to commit the one case of contradiction that I have spotted in his work.

Strangely enough, this contradiction occurs in the course of two discussions of historical dead ends, of stagnation, which are very close to each other in the book. In one of his discussions of concrete historical cases, Loone raises the possibility (invoking the Soviet classicists, Shtaerman and Trofimova) that in slave society, internal brakes on development become so strong that they altogether arrest the growth of productive forces. He adds that further progress out of slavery might depend on whether the transition *to* slavery had taken place early or late (presumably, in the development of the preceding formation). If slavery inherits, as it were, weakly developed productive forces from its predecessor, and its own sclerosis sets in on those weak forces, no point of possible transition to the next stage is ever reached. If, on the other hand, the previous runner in this relay hands over the torch to slave-owners late, the slave-owners, it would seem, can hand on adequately rich technical inheritance to the feudals, and hardly need to bother to move on themselves. It would all seem to make slave-owning a redundant stage, and in any case, what happens to the law of constant growth of productive forces? And if it is the non-economic layers of social life which contain those brakes, what happens to historical materialism?

A little later, however, discussing the problem of stagnation in the abstract, Loone gives quite a different account of social stagnation. He remarks that dead ends (the expressive Russian word is *tupik*) are incompatible with Marxism, because they would require that the dead-end social formation, never due for replacement, should be allocated an infinitely large zone along the line of the development of productive forces. In other words, the dead end would display perpetual economic growth, and eternal social stability. (It sounds more like the dream of liberal affluence than the familiar culs-de-sac of history.) This is concretely implausible, but certainly follows from his premisses, and does indeed constitute, given the premisses, a convincing *reductio ad absurdum* of dead ends. But the fact that the theory only allows dead ends of this kind would seem to cast some doubt on the plausibility of the theory itself. The theory seems to make social stagnation a consequence of endless economic growth, and not of economic deadlock! This has some affinity with the 'One-dimensional Man' thesis, but Loone uses this idea as a *reductio ad absurdum*, rather than as a diagnosis of any contemporary society.

Loone makes some entirely convincing observations about other aspects of the theory. Marxism contains no a priori delimitation of the number of possible formations, but it does require that their number be finite. (Otherwise, the Marxist promise of salvation would go by the board, though he does not make this point. Equally, it is necessary that there be no circular developments, but this is already excluded by his premisses.) There must be some limits on the length of time of various historical stages, though this has not yet been properly explored: but filibusters in history must not be allowed. He explores the possibility of very rapid transitions, masquerading as stage-jumping. (The fact that stages may be missing as a consequence of external interference was never in dispute.)

Loone notes that both the elasticity of the theory, and historical fact, favour the admission of mixed social formations, though again, only within limits which he tries to specify. He notes (with a touch of amused malice?) that Marxist historians will have to pay their price in hard work for the abandonment of unilinealism: as long as unilinealism was assumed, any transitional society could be described rather mechanically on an allocation-of-shares principle – such and such a proportion to the preceding social form, such and such a proportion to the following one, and Bob's your uncle. But once you no longer know for sure just which pure forms this particular society is *between*, you will have to put a bit more work into finding out what it is really like. The answer will only come out at the end, and not at the beginning.

A very interesting notion Loone introduces is that of metaformation (*nadformatsiya*). Over and above relatively concrete social forms (such as feudalism or capitalism), one can also classify human societies at one more abstract level, in terms of two criteria – presence or absence of a surplus, and presence or absence of exploitation. Primitive communism had neither; all class-endowed formations had both; communism-to-come will have the one without the other.

This three-stage philosophy of history is interesting a number of times over. At this level, fruitful confrontation is possible with what is now the tacit but prevalent philosophy of history in the West, which also sees social development in terms of three stages – hunting–gathering, agrarian, and industrial. The curious thing is that the Western theory is materialist whilst the Marxist one is social: the Western one unambiguously sees the three great distinct ball-games in terms of their productive base. Of course, the Western theory can afford to be insouciantly materialist, precisely because it is also non-deterministic. It allows, and indeed expects, a diversity of social forms at each of the three great stages, whereas Marxism tended to see at least the first and the third as obligatorily homogeneous, whilst the diversity within the second stage was committed to a more or less fixed sequence. So Western materialism is taxonomic only, and contains little if any theoretical load. The material base sets us our problem: it does not uniquely determine our solutions.

But the supposition that each of the three big stages, each of the two big jumps, eventually entails irreversible changes in social organization, is convincing, and can perhaps be usefully contrasted with the three-stage theory which Loone (and not only he) has also extracted from Marxism. On the other hand, the idea of a series of irreversible steps within agrarian society each with its own distinctive level of productive effectiveness, even if ingeniously combined with a multi-path theory, will find little echo in Western historiography or sociology. It is interesting to note that theoretical attempts to lump all societies between primitive communism and capitalism together as one stage, the age of non-economic constraint or of slave-feudal society, have occurred within the Soviet Union. Loone rejects this, and polemicizes with one theoretician, V. P. Ilyushechkin, who proposed this in 1970.

Marxism is curiously un-materialist, in that its conception of the two most important cut-off points in human history is defined not in economic or technological terms, but in social, organizational ones. It is the emergence of private property, classes, and the state which mark the first transition, and their disappearance marks the second. The theory maintains in its abstract formulations that these transitions reflect changes in the 'productive forces', but it will have some difficulty in demonstrating this empirically. The trouble is that Marxism crystallized prior to the diffusion of the notion of the 'Neolithic Revolution'. Once one shifts to the truly materialist viewpoint of seeing the birth of agrarian society, and of industrial–scientific society, as the two crucial watersheds, one is faced with the obvious problem that organizational changes in general are *not* neatly correlated with those two tremendous transformations of the economic base in the way Marxism requires.

Also the Western view tends to see the two great changes as inherently lumpy and discontinuous, while being prepared to allow some continuities in the social organization which might even span these economic chasms. For instance, James Woodburn's plausible theory suggests that some hunters acquired the social preconditions of agriculture (expectations of delayed return, long-term mutual obligations, with all the organizational implications this has) while still hunters, and that this is the key to the emergence of agriculture.[2] Theories explaining the emergence of industrialism in terms of the accidental acquisition, by some agrarian societies, of the ethos and/or organization appropriate to industrialism, are of course highly fashionable in the West. By contrast, Marxism (especially in Loone's version) seems to see technological change as fairly continuous and perpetual, while socio-organizational change is expected to be discontinuous. Revolution is not merely the carnival of the oppressed, it is the historic celebration of a switch to a new package deal, permitting greater economic effectiveness. It is almost as if the engine of technological progress were moving forward steadily, but dragged behind itself an awkward misshapen lump called social organization, which ends up acting as a brake, until at last the taut wire connecting it to the onward-moving tractor jerks it on brutally, so as to bring it alongside once again.

Though this of course is not part of Loone's argument, Karl Marx was, far more so than Adam Smith or Samuel Smiles or Benjamin Franklin, the supreme expression of the bourgeois spirit. He saw humanity at large as ever engaged in augmenting its wealth and productivity. The essence of man was work for its own sake, whilst work-as-a-means was a sign of corruption and of fall from grace, and due for eventual elimination. Social relations were a bit of a nuisance, liable to hamper and obstruct productive activities, and were consequently destined for brutal, ruthless, and traumatic reorganization

---

2 Woodburn, 'Hunters and Gatherers today and reconstruction of the past', cit. ch. 5, n. 16 above.

from time to time (rather like a man who changes house and spouse each time the old ones can no longer keep up with his new work level and start to impede his effectiveness). In the end, social relations were destined to become entirely loose, in the interest of permitting maximum fulfilment through self-chosen work. The delay-producing nuisance-power of politics and ideology notwithstanding, it was productive rather than coercive activities which dominated and determined the course of history. The idea that all this should be so would seem to be the day-dream of bourgeois producers, with their distaste for lazy, economically static, parasitic predators, whose bluster, according to this wish-fulfilment theory, is empty, and whose power is in the end illusory. Marxism taught that this middle-class fantasy of the *Allmacht der Erzeugung* contained the hidden deep truth of history. Adam Smith knew that burgher merchants made better developers of rural property than landed gentry who were born to it, but he also knew that power passed to the former only in special and favourable circumstances. According to Marxism, at a deeper level, power is *always* located in the productive activities. But if it is this doctrine which is the real delusion, it is a perilous one: some predators may now devour us, whilst invoking the theory, reassuring for their victims and accomplices, that predation *is* and ought to be the slave of production, and hence that we have nothing to fear. But here I go far beyond Loone's book.

Loone also notes that the homogeneity of 'primitive society' has not been seriously questioned (by Soviet Marxists), though some attempts to locate sequences within it do exist. This assumption of a homogeneous primordial community certainly pervades at least the speech habits of Soviet anthropologists. At the moment, a major project, involving a considerable number of people, is afoot in Soviet anthropology, dedicated to a thorough re-examination of this notion, and should come out with its results in a year or so.[3] But Loone himself clearly has doubts about this assumption, and points out that one must not infer from the homogeneity of the meta-formation (which follows from its very definition), to the homogeneity or uniqueness of social forms within it. They may differ a good deal within the limits set by the definition of the meta-formation. Loone does not also explicitly make the same point about the final meta-formation, communism. But the point would be exactly parallel. It would have the same force, and if he did intend it, it would not be the first time that a Soviet thinker had used an observation about the past to say something about contemporary problems.

But it must be stressed once again that in this book, Loone presents

3 See *History of Primitive Society: The Epoch of Kin Community*, cit. ch. 5, n. 24 above.

himself as a formal, analytical thinker, a veritable under-labourer, whose task is to clear the decks for those who will finish the job. (No matter, says he, whether they are called philosophers or historians.) The ground which this astonishing Estonian journeyman has prepared is so neat, so clear and well marked out, that it makes Wembley look like a potato field. To play in such conditions would be a pleasure and refereeing ought to be (almost) easy. On such a pitch, I feel my team would win, but let us not be too complacent. The really interesting question is whether the game will ever be played.

Postface

Marxism is the major sociological theory to have emerged in the nineteenth century. Its standing is confirmed by the fact that such a large proportion of non-Marxist social thinkers continue to define their positions by reference to it. But it is of course far more than merely a sociological theory. It is also an ethic and political philosophy, a promise of the collective salvation of mankind, of its deliverance from exploitation and oppression. Furthermore, it has in the twentieth century become the official doctrine of a number of important states, in the first instance the Soviet Union.

All this means that, in the intellectual life of the USSR, Marxism functions under a triple set of constraints. Its contentions, or those of them that have a concrete social and historical reference, must relate to the available data in the ordinary way. But at the same time, the promise of collective human salvation must be maintained: at the very least, the deliverance from exploitation and oppression must be possible. Naturally, a stronger, and much preferred, version of Marxism maintains the view that this deliverance is not merely possible, but inevitable. Moreover, a society which employs Marxism for the legitimation of its own organization and policies must also claim that what it itself does, is an integral part fulfilment of the historic plan.

It may be useful to list the minimal set of propositions which need to be true if Marxism is indeed to map out the path to our collective salvation.

1 *Human essence* (*Gattungswesen*). It is important that there be a way of identifying and validating the desirable and fulfilling social condition, and of damning those alternatives which are to be damned. Basically, Marxism does this by postulating a generic human essence which finds proper fulfilment in the approved social formation, but which is thwarted, 'alienated', in all others.

2 *The Instability Postulate*. All exploitative social systems are, appearances notwithstanding, deeply unstable in the long run, and eventually destroy themselves. Their ideological superstructure serves them well, by presenting them as eternal, or absolute, and based on supposedly inherent human attributes. All this is however unavailing in the end. This postulate must exclude not merely stagnation, but also cyclical, and hence repetitive, social change. In the long run, there are no stalemates in history.

3 *The Limited Social Variety Postulate*. This postulate is not normally affirmed, but it is absolutely essential. If there were an infinity of exploitative social forms, the inherent and ultimately irremediable instability of all of them taken individually, would still fail to guarantee the liberation of mankind in the end. Each single exploitative form might ineluctably blow itself up in the end, and none the less, mankind might haplessly wander from one such form to another. These forms must be limited in number, if we are to be able to reply on the promise of deliverance.

4 *The Derivativeness of Coercion*. Though violence does have its place in history as the authorized midwife of new social forms, it cannot either initiate change nor arrest it. The materialist conception of history was originally born of a reaction to the Hegelian view that concepts, abstractions, are the hidden force behind historic change. The rival view, claiming that concrete men and the concrete activities of men, not abstractions, are what really determine the course of history, has at least the appearance of great plausibility, almost of self-evidence. It was this movement of thought which really gave birth to Marxism.

In due course, however, the Founding Fathers moved from this position to another and more contentious one, namely: *within* the class of concrete activities, productive ones are more fundamental and decisive than coercive ones. The switch from a seemingly self-evident proposition, to the manifestly contentious one, was not a simple sleight of hand; it was defended by sustained argument, to the effect that coercion could only operate within the context of a given system of production. It could not set up such a system on its own.

There is little doubt in my mind but that the intuitive appeal and force, which does attach to the idea of historical materialism, springs from the simpler and more general interpretation – from the denial of the historical agency of abstractions. The more specific doctrine, concerning the primacy of production over coercion, though interesting and deserving of investigation, has no such overwhelmingly persuasive quality. It has benefited from being conflated with, or not being clearly distinguished from, the more and perhaps self-justifying general doctrine.

	A Abstract ideas govern history	B Concrete men and activities determine history
I Production		////////
II Coercion		

The move from A to B (from invoking the agency of abstractions, to invoking concrete human activity), can be presented as virtually self-evident – as a mere demystification rather than a genuine discovery. It is in this context that historical materialism makes its appearance in *The German Ideology*. The shift from a stress on coercion and politics to the ultimate dominance of relations of production is incomparably more contentious. The trouble is that expositions of Marxism have not distinguished clearly enough between these two transitions, and underplayed their distinctiveness – even if the latter claim was independently defended by appeals to the argument that coercion cannot occur outside a social context. In fact, the second and highly contentious move in no way follows from the first and relatively uncontentious one. The fairly trivial form of 'historical materialism' merely asserts that B and not A is true; the wholly distinct and highly contentious version claims that I not II is crucial; and the strongest version affirms that I/B is the only area which really matters.

5 The historical irrelevance of human groups other than classes, where classes are defined in terms of the relation to the means of production. For instance – nations are historically inessential?

These are the theoretical issues facing Marxism as a belief system: the minimal set of propositions which are essential for it, if it is to offer a message of hope to humanity. It is natural that, as long as the system retains any vitality, these contentions should be scrutinized and re-examined, and confront whatever new evidence has come to light.

But there is also a set of problems facing the Soviet Union, as a concrete society with a distinctive history and environment. The problems which the Soviet Union has faced, or is facing, do not necessarily constitute a tidy and well-ordered list. No doubt diverse commentators would identify different problems. But it is well worth while attempting to list them, even if any list must inevitably be in some measure arbitrary.

A The problem of open and violent internal conflict and of internal enemies during the early years of Soviet power, in particular amongst the minority nationalities of the Soviet Union. (By contrast, conflict with the politically absolutist and economically capitalist Tsarist regime, or its non-Bolshevik successor, hardly calls for much explanation.)

B The rather different problem of ethnic plurality at a later and predominantly non-violent stage, which nevertheless calls for theoretical and practical interpretation and which may yet come to constitute a serious problem.

C The relationship of economic and coercive institutions, not only in human history in general, but in a 'mature' socialist society in particular. I suspect that this constitutes by far the gravest problem, theoretically and practically, that Marxism faces.

D The relationship of the Soviet Union to other socialist societies and to the developing world, for whom it provides, or aspires to provide, leadership. In this area, the conflict with China is presumably the most serious and most troubling issue.

E The relationship and rivalry with the non-socialist developed world, and in particular to post-Marxist Western thought.

The official doctrine of the state and society must obviously have something to say about these issues, if it is to play any role in the intellectual life of the country, and not degenerate into a mere liturgy. This does seem to be its fate in some of the socialist countries of Eastern Europe, where real political legitimation of the regime has come to rely on a mixture of paternalism, populism, opportunism ('lest worse befall'), appeal to relative prosperity, 'realism' (the acceptance of what is unavoidable), and nationalism. Though these elements may not be wholly absent in the Soviet Union either, it would be incorrect to say that Soviet Marxism has atrophied to such an extent.

Soviet intellectuals are assumed to be Marxists, unless formally enlisted in religious organizations. Hence Marxism constitutes a kind of automatically presumed baseline of expectation, and a shared idiom. A vigorous intellectual life does exist within the USSR. The material assembled in this volume endeavours to analyse specimens of it. But in as far as it is public, it does observe the recognized conventions. It is hard for an outsider, and perhaps for anyone, to estimate to what extent this idiom is used because it is the only available one, and to what extent it springs from conviction. The boundary between these two elements is in any case not a sharp one. Marxism is a language as well as a doctrine, and even an agnostic can use the language, whether or not he embraces all its elements. One uses the language of one's milieu. Where is the line between idiom of convenience and doctrinal commitment? Some categories and assumptions of Marxism in any case overlap with ideas current amongst non-Marxists. But it would be wrong to assume that conviction is always absent.

In addition to the set of theoretical issues facing Marxism as a doctrine, and the set of practical problems facing the Soviet Union as an actual society, there is also what might be called the stratigraphical strain within Marxism. The doctrine was formulated by its Founding Fathers during the half-century following the 1840s. This was of course one of the most active and turbulent periods in the history of European ideas. Some of the sea changes which took place during this period are familiar and well explored. Roughly speaking, the period witnessed a shift from Hegelianism to positivism and scientism, a change to which the Founding Fathers of Marxism were not insensitive, and which left its mark on their own style and thought. The consequence is the well-known debate between the partisans of early and of late Marxism (and those who maintain that the two remained identical). Early Marxism is generally held to have a great moral and critical suggestiveness, whilst the later version seems to contain a greater recognition of the brutal constraints of history, and of the claims of hard science.

Related to this rather well-explored issue, there are at least two other major shifts which took place during the same period, and which have perhaps been less thoroughly explored. One is the marked diminution of Eurocentrism. In the 1840s, it was on the whole assumed that history is about Europe. During the later decades of the century, the idea that not only the marchlands of Europe, but even the extra-European world, might be of some importance for the revolutionary and other potential of human society, became prominent. It was in this period that the discipline of social anthropology assumed its modern form.

One could also say that in this period man ceased to be merely a part of history, and also became truly a part of nature. Darwin had published, and ethnographic evidence concerning simpler societies became more plentifully available. It fed the now inescapable interest in the early, prehistoric development of humanity. The commencement of human history was no longer located in some Middle Eastern despotism, but rather in a primordial community. The switch in vision is aptly symbolized by the pregnant little change which Engels saw fit to introduce in the Communist Manifesto. He modified the famous generalization about the ubiquity of class struggle: the newly introduced clause recognized that recorded history did not cover everything, by adding the observation that it applies only to 'all written history'. From now on, there was also non-recorded history, and what it had to say was significant and modified the picture. So Ethnography shows us another significant aspect of the world.

One might sum this up by saying that Marxist materialism switched from being an inversion of Hegel, to becoming an extrapolation of Morgan. Any attempt at a content analysis of the preoccupations of Soviet thinkers ought really to include this: is the argument also concerned with what one might call the Hegel-to-Morgan shift? Here we are dealing with only two alternatives – either the writer in question is, or is not, concerned with this issue. So we may symbolize the presence of this preoccupation by H–M, and the absence of this preoccupation by the absence of this sign.

If we identify each of the chapters with the topic which is its main theme, we are left with a table of Soviet intellectual preoccupations.

1	The Soviet and the Savage	2, 3, 4	C, E	
2	The Human Essence	1, 4	C	H–M
3	The Asiatic Trauma	2, 3, 4	C, D	H–M
4	The Nomadism Debate	2, 3, 4	A, C	
5	Feudalism in Africa	2, 3, 4	D, E	
6	Modern Ethnicity	5	B, E	
7	One Highway or Many?	2, 3, 4, 5	A, C, D, E	
8	Explanation and Materialism	2, 3, 4, 5	C, D, E	

The scheme is of course only a rough approximation, and hinges on how we interpret the various thinkers. The issues are all deeply interrelated. It would be easy to argue that all the writers under discussion have something to say which is relevant to *all* the problems. None the less, it is useful to have this more restrictive and rough guide to their more visible and conspicuous preoccupations.

The schema as such cannot of course claim to be any kind of accurate survey of the concerns of Soviet intellectuals in general. The writers chosen were simply those whose work I found interesting and meritorious, with no conscious search for any theme. The sample is in no way random. It is heavily biased towards anthropologists, though at least one historian and one philosopher are included. A number of the writers however straddle disciplinary boundaries, being both historians and anthropologists, or both anthropologists and philosophers. But though it is in no statistical sense representative, the sample does, I like to think, provide insight into the preoccupations and problem situation of Soviet intellectuals. The fact that theme 4 and theme C, the autonomy of derivativeness of power in general, and its role under conditions of contemporary socialism, are most pervasive, is suggestive. It may just reflect my interests, or it may be a clue to the deepest Soviet problem.

Bibliography of Ernest Gellner's Soviet and East European Writings,
by I. C. Jarvie

The numbering–dating system is that of the complete bibliography of Gellner which has appeared in four parts in *The Devil in Modern Philosophy* (London, 1974), *Spectacles and Predicaments* (Cambridge, 1980), *Relativism and the Social Sciences* (Cambridge, 1986), and *Culture, Identity, and Politics* (Cambridge, 1987).

† indicates items included in this volume.

1956*e* Review of Margaret Hasluck, *The Unwritten Law in Albania*, British *Journal of Sociology*, vol. 7, pp. 280–1

1971*g* 'The Anti-Levellers of Prague', *New Society*, vol. 18, 5 August, pp. 232–4

1971*i* 'Stratification With a Human Face', *Times Literary Supplement*, no. 3633, 15 November, pp. 1275–6

1971*j* 'The Pluralist Anti-Levellers of Prague', *European Journal of Sociology*, vol. 12, 312–25; *Dissent*, Summer 1972, pp. 471–82; *Government and Opposition*, vol. 7, no. 1, Winter 1972

1972*d* Review of Vladimir Kusín, *The Intellectual Origins of the Prague Spring*, *British Journal of Sociology*, vol. 23, pp. 258–60

1973*j* Review of Yu. V. Maretin and D. A. Olderogge, eds, *Strany i narody vostoka* (*Countries and Peoples of the East*), *Man*, vol. 8, p. 505

1973*k* Review of G. V. Osipov, ed., *Town, Country and People*, *Man*, vol. 8, pp. 506–8

1973*l* 'Primitive Communism', review article on *Okhotniki, sobirateli, rybolovy* (*Hunters, Gatherers, Fishermen*), *Man*, vol. 8, pp. 536–42

1974*i* Trs. of Yu. I. Semenov, 'Theoretical Problems of "Economic Anthropology"', *Philosophy of the Social Sciences*, vol. 4, pp. 201–31

1974*j* 'The Soviet and the Savage', *Times Literary Supplement*, no. 3789, 18 October, pp. 1166–8†

1976g 'From the Revolution to Liberalization', *Government and Opposition*, vol. 11, pp. 257–72

1977d 'Gone and Gone Forever', review of H. Gordon Skilling, *Czechoslovakia's Interrupted Revolution*, *Government and Opposition*, vol. 12, pp. 371–8
1977h 'Premisses for Dissidence', review of Valentin Turchin, *Inertsiya Strakha (The Inertia of Fear)*, *Times Literary Supplement*, no. 3948, 25 November, p. 1369
1977m 'Ethnicity and Anthropology in the Soviet Union', *European Journal of Sociology*, vol. 18, pp. 201–20†
1977n 'State Before Class, the Soviet Treatment of African Feudalism', *European Journal of Sociology*, vol. 18, pp. 299–32; also in Percy Cohen and William A. Shack, eds, *Politics in Leadership: A Comparative Perspective* (Oxford, 1979), pp. 193–220†

1978j 'Getting Along in Czechoslovakia' (unsigned) *New York Review of Books*, vol. 25, no. 17, 9 November, pp. 30, 35–8

1979c Review of Alexander Vucinich, *Social Thought in Tsarist Russia*, *Philosophy of the Social Sciences*, vol. 9, pp. 121–2
1979f Review of Mervyn Matthews, *Soviet Sociology, 1964—75*, *Slavonic and East European Review*, vol. 57, pp. 473–4
1979m 'Viewpoint: "A Blobologist in Vodkobuzia"' *Times Literary Supplement*, no. 4001, 23 November, p. 23

1980f Edited *Soviet and Western Anthropology* (London, Duckworth)
1980g Preface to 1980f
1980h Trs. of Yu. I. Semenov, 'Theory of Socio-Economic Formations and World History', in 1980f, pp. 29–58
1980i 'A Russian Marxist Philosophy of History', in 1980f, pp. 59–82; also in *Theory and Society*, vol. 9, pp. 757–77†
1980m Review of Terence Cox, *Rural Society in the Soviet Union*, *Journal of Peasant Studies*, vol. 8, pp. 116–18
1980o Letter, 'Soviet Anthropology', *RAIN*, 41, December, p. 12
1980p 'Ethnicity Between Culture, Class and Power' in Peter F. Sugar (ed.), *Ethnic Diversity and Conflict in Eastern Europe*, pp. 237–77

1981a 'How Socialism Has Made Czechoslovakia the Captive Hamlet of Europe', *Times Higher Education Supplement*, no. 433, 20 February, pp. 10–11
1981b 'Anomalies of no Fixed Abode', review of Sevyan Vainstein, *Nomads of South Siberia*, *Times Literary Supplement*, no. 4067, 13 March, p. 273

1984*a* 'Along the Historical Highway', review of Eero Loone, *Sovremennaya filosofiya istorii* (*Contemporary Philosophy of History*), *Times Literary Supplement*, no. 4224, 16 March, pp. 279–80†

1984*f* Introduction to A. M. Khazanov, *Nomads and the Outside World*, Cambridge, pp. ix–xxv†

1984*h* 'Soviets Against Wittfogel, or the Anthropological Preconditions of Marxism', in Jean-Claude Galey (ed.), *Différences, valeurs, hiérarchie: textes offerts à Louis Dumont* (Paris), pp. 183–211; also in John A. Hall (ed.), *States in History* (Oxford, 1986), pp. 78–108; also in *Theory and Society*, vol. 16, no. 5, September 1987†

1984*j* 'Foreword' to Eva Schmidt-Hartmann, *Thomas G. Masaryk's Realism: Origins of a Czech Political Concept* (Munich), pp. 7–8

1984*k* 'The State of Poland' (under the pseudonym 'Philip Peters'), *Times Literary Supplement*, no. 4246, 17 August, p. 916

1985*a* Review of *The Engineer of Human Souls*, by Josef Škvorecký, *Times Literary Supplement*, no. 4275, 8 March, p. 256

1986*l* 'Between Loyalty and Truth', review of Václav Havel et al., *The Power of the Powerless*, Introduction by Steven Lukes; ed. John Keane, *Times Literary Supplement*, no. 4357, 3 October, p. 1090

1987*d* Review of V. N. Basilov, *Izbranniki dukhov* (*Chosen by spirits*), in *Man*, vol. 22, no. 1, March, p. 188

1987*e* 'Buddha and Marx', review of Caroline Humphrey, *Karl Marx Collective: Economy, Society and Religion in a Siberian Collective Farm*, in *Comparative Studies in Society and History*, vol. 29, no. 2, April, pp. 381–4

1987*h* 'Zeno of Cracow', in *Culture, Identity, and Politics* (Cambridge University Press, 1987); also in *Malinowski Between Two Worlds*, edited by R. Ellen (Cambridge University Press, forthcoming)

1987*i* 'How Did Mankind Acquire its Essence?', in Outhwaite, William and Mulkay, Michael, eds., *Social Theory and Social Criticism: Essays for Tom Bottomore* (Blackwells, 1987)

1987*l* 'Advice Unheeded', review of Andrey Snesarev, *Avganistan*, in *The Time Literary Supplement*, 25 September–1 October, no. 4, 408, p. 1046

1987*m* Review of Yu. V. Bromley, *Theoretical Ethnography*, in *Man*, vol. 22, no. 3, September, p. 576

1987*p* 'The Economic Interpretation of History', in *The New Palgrave: A Dictionary of Economics*, edited by John Eatwell, Murray Milgate and Peter Newman (Macmillan 1987)

Name Index

by I. C. Jarvie

Following a page number, *n* signifies that the reference is in a note, *q* that the person is quoted, and *t* that a term is discussed.

Subject Index

by I. C. Jarvie